Scotland's
Life and Work

Frontispiece: 'I wager this new-fangled nonsense will not catch on!'

Scotland's
Life and Work

A Scottish view of God's world through *Life and Work*: 1879-1979

R D Kernohan

THE SAINT ANDREW PRESS
EDINBURGH

First published in Great Britain by
The Saint Andrew Press, Edinburgh, 1979.

Copyright© R D Kernohan, 1979

ISBN 0 7152 0421 1

Printed in Scotland by McCorquodale (Scotland) Ltd. Glasgow

Dedication

For all the saints, who from their labours rest—and especially to the editors among them; and most especially to the founder of *Life and Work*

Archibald Hamilton Charteris (1835-1908)
a great Victorian but an even greater Christian.

Contents

LIST OF ILLUSTRATIONS

Frontispiece: 'I wager this new-fangled nonsense will not catch on!'

Acknowledgments

Far too many people have helped with this book for me to mention them by name. A few I have thanked in person or by letter as the work went along, the others I thank now. They range from two of the most eminent of our Church historians—one in a university, the other in a country parish—and from former Moderators to colleagues in Church Publicity and Publications and people in various parts of the Kirk (many of them encountered by chance or providence) whose recollections and keepsakes have been of immense value.

Obviously I owe a special debt to my predecessors, since I have fearlessly plundered their work and commented on it when they are in no position to answer back. I can only hope that some day some distant successor will be as cavalier in his treatment of me and those who follow immediately after.

I am particularly grateful to those who helped in the preparation of the book, doing their best after I had done my share, especially to Miss Ellen McGillivray for typing her way successfully through a maze of rough typescript and manuscript additions.

Introduction:
a view from Scotland

This is a book which marks the centenary of a magazine which has always been Christian, presbyterian, and Scottish without being unco guid or even wholly holy. It is a story which mixes social history and church life and discovers some of the achievements and limitations of Scottish Christians, especially those of the Church of Scotland, first in the Auld Kirk and then in the reunited national church which includes the vast majority of Presbyterians and most of Scotland's protestant Christians.

It is about passing fashions as well as the truth which, though revealed, has to be rediscovered by every pilgrim in his own progress through a changing landscape. But the last river has still to be crossed; and the pilgrims who go that way still discover that if Vanity Fair is little changed the Delectable Mountains are quite unspoiled. And the City across the river still beckons.

A hundred years ago, as Glasgow spread along the Great Western Road, *Life and Work* began publication, though it was only later that it acquired a sub-title resembling the present one of 'The Record of the Church of Scotland'.

It was later still that it became the official magazine of the Church of Scotland that we know today for, in the heyday of Victorianism when *Life and Work* was launched, the 'established' or 'national' church (the Auld Kirk) which had kept the title of Church of Scotland was only one of three major divisions of Scottish presbyterianism, the others being the Free Church and the United Presbyterians.

But in publishing, continuity and character go together. *Life and Work* is now the magazine of a much changed Church of Scotland in a very different setting; though one with the same Lord, the same creed, the same sense of continuity as a church of the Reformation and of a true apostolic succession linking it with the early Church and the other provinces of the Universal Church.

Its centenary, however, is an event for the whole national Church to celebrate. The vision and skill of *Life and Work*'s founders, and especially of that eminent and efficient Victorian, Dr Charteris, gave something to all their successors: something to sustain and adapt in changing conditions. Those who inherit it have to make it as effective in their own times, remembering that no publication of character can stand still. Character in a periodical is an evolving, changing thing. Not to change is to die.

But *Life and Work*, through its purpose and ownership, is not like any other periodical. It responds to a changing world and reflects it. This book largely reflects the place of the magazine in a changing church, a changing Scotland, a changing world. But Jesus Christ, the only Head of the Church, is the same, yesterday, today, forever. God is from everlasting to everlasting. In the beginning was the Word.

This is the story of some words in the service of that Word—of a publication belonging to people who belong to God. It tries to avoid the pitfalls of official history and commemorative celebration. And because the book tries to avoid that commemorative approach that too often leads to a Slough of Literary Despond it is much less a history of how the church ran *Life and Work* than of how the changing things and the changeless things have been mingled in a century of Scottish life. To some extent it shows how the Kirk saw itself as well as how it changed itself. But it also shows the life of Scottish church and Scottish people in changing contexts: of self-confident conviction in the power and possibilities of progress; of imperial expansion which stimulated the missionary expansion which proved in most places more enduring than empire; of war, depression, war again, and the period of the unending adjustment and never-distant perils which have marked the second half of the century.

The main source of material has, of course, been *Life and Work* itself, together with the other magazines which have joined with it—especially the UF *Record*, whose partnership is affirmed in the fact that the full title of the magazine is still *Life and Work: the Record of the Church of Scotland*.

I have had access to the minutes of the Church of Scotland's relevant committees and sub-committees and to those of the UF Church, and I am grateful. They have been useful, and at times frustrating. Good writers of minutes record decisions rather than the discussion by which the decisions were arrived at. They also sometimes conceal the real substance of a discussion. When an especially tantalising issue is referred to (usually a complaint from a minister or member with a real or imagined grievance against committee or editor), the fact of the complaint rather than its nature is usually stated. There is also a strong flavour of bromide about the way some arguments within the committee have been recorded—and, of course, those involved are generally beyond our reach, except for recent years.

But this is not an account of committee policy but of the printed word and an image of Scotland: a view of Scotland, a view from Scotland.

1. Charteris: 'The Young Professor'

Chapter 1
A Presbyterian in print

'It is difficult for anyone who has not read these English popular periodicals from a purely Scottish point of view to understand either how unintelligible they are, and how unsuitable for wide circulation on this side of the Tweed, or how necessary it is that we in Scotland should have a distinctively Scottish magazine.'

It may come as a surprise that the first paragraphs of *Life and Work*, which appeared in January 1879, should read like an elegant and slightly ornate manifesto for the milder forms of Scottish nationalism. They were not so intended. They are words that need to be set in their time and place—like the now archaic but proud description of his nationality chosen by their author, the founder and first editor of *Life and Work*, Archibald Hamilton Charteris. 'What', he wrote, 'can an ordinary Scotchman make of allusions to Epiphany and Advent, commendations of a child who has learned the collect of the day, casual mention of the chancel, the offertory, the surplice, of even the litany? All such terms, familiar to every English reader, are Hebrew and Greek to many of our countrymen; and even to those who do understand them, they speak of the "Life and Work" of another country, and not that of our own.'

It was ministers who had tried anglican magazines, and found them wanting, Charteris claimed, who had pressed the Kirk to 'speak with a Scottish tongue to their countrymen'. That Scottish tongue—admittedly using the elegant words of Victorians reared on the classics—was to be heard in the new magazine of the Kirk.

Yet this was not the the Scotland of the Darien scheme nor of our recent age of introspection following the imperial sunset. It was Charteris, a great Victorian, writing almost at the zenith of the British Empire.

It was 1879 when these words appeared, twenty years since the appearance of Darwin's *Origin of Species*. The ageing Disraeli, disguised as Lord Beaconsfield, was Queen Victoria's Prime Minister. The year was to bring the Zulu War and, before it was out, Gladstone had begun his Midlothian campaign. Lord Roberts was about to march to Kandahar. Rider Haggard had run up the Union Flag in Pretoria and the Transvaal had been annexed to the

1

British Crown. Livingstone was dead but Livingstonia and Blantyre had been founded in what would become Nyasaland.

The peace of Europe, despite the decay of the Ottoman Empire and the excitement it stirred in Gladstone, had been preserved by the Congress of Berlin.

But at home there were hard times. The failure of the City of Glasgow Bank had shocked Scotland so much that even Edinburgh congregations were dipping deep and generously into their pockets for the relief of the victims of the crash. When Marshall Lang of the Barony (father of a Moderator and of Archbishop Cosmo Gordon Lang) led a mission in Glasgow he found on the opening day that attention was absorbed in the trial of the Bank's directors. It is estimated that the unemployment rate rose from 4.7% in 1877 to 11.4% in 1879. British agriculture had entered an age of depression. Ireland, suffering hardship that brought back memories of the Great Famine, was beginning the bitter time of the 'Land War'.

Yet hard times and economic cycles of boom and recession scarcely shook the Victorian idea of progress.

2. The Charteris Memorial

Dundee had a fine new railway bridge across the Tay. There was progress in health, in housing, above all in education. The tax on knowledge had gone. English education was trying to catch up with Scotland; Lord Northcliffe and television lay in the future. Education was valued and increasingly available. It was the age of the penny savings bank, the penny magazine, the penny paper, and soon enough the penny dreadful.

'The Press has made a revolution in every family in the land', wrote Charteris. 'It is for good or ill reaching every responsible member of the community every day.'

Where there is no vision the people perish. While Charteris was around visions were not likely to be allowed to slip away. In him there was more than a normal quota of Victorian practical piety. His achievement was so varied that the designer of the memorial in what today is Kirk o' Field parish church in Edinburgh (originally the Charteris Memorial) omitted *Life and Work* from the graven record—or so it seemed to the present editor when he admired it. Later the leading contemporary layman of the Kirk, Lord Balfour of Burleigh, summed up his character and the achievement which makes him a founding father not only of *Life and Work* but of the Woman's Guild and the Order of Deaconesses of the Kirk: 'The true notes of the Christian character are loyalty and love of service. When to these are added practical ability, enthusiasm and that subtle influence which is called power of successful organisation we have a rare combination of qualities.'

Others remembered the way he was loved and admired in no ordinary degree, and how his manifest holiness went with a fearless zeal for new effort. Later, inevitably, he was Moderator of the General Assembly and from 1868 to 1898 (ten years before his death) he was Professor of Biblical Criticism at Edinburgh, a moderate conservative in theological matters as in political ones.

Charteris was one of nature's bishops (the best kind) but he was a Presbyterian through and through. He was, he said, a Calvinist who found the Confession too harsh on predestination. He could thunder in the correspondence colums of *The Times* against episcopalian attempts to 'make Scotland reverse the teaching of her history' and told the famous Bishop Charles Wordsworth, nephew of the poet, first warden of Glenalmond, and bearer of an olive-branch from the anglican side: 'There is no hope of any such reunion as you advocate until Episcopalians admit the full validity of Presbyterian orders.'

This was no Scot with an inferiority complex. He knew Europe, urging his students to learn German and visit the universities of Germany as he himself had done, even if he disliked some of the theology taught there. He cared

3

passionately about the Italian Protestants. He got on well with Queen Victoria, one of whose chaplains he was. 'Did you like the theology you saw in Bonn?' the Queen once asked him. 'I did ma'am for it is evangelical and liberal.' She replied, 'I agree with you, that is the best kind.' Sensible and godly woman, as well as gracious Queen!

Charteris does not seem now to historians to be a scholar and theologian of the first rank, though he did not deserve the harsh words he drew from the great controversial scholar of the Free Kirk, Robertson Smith. Stung by a harsh review in 1876 Smith called him 'a raw preacher thrust for party ends into a professor's chair.' By 1879—though *Life and Work* avoided the subject—Smith was approaching the climax of the case in which his views on Biblical history were alleged to be heresy.

But if Charteris was only a good scholar he was a great man of action. To call him an ecclesiastical politician would convey the wrong shade of meaning, and to call him a statesman of the church sounds altogether too pompous. Although he could push his causes hard enough to cause irritation—foreign missions, for example—he was a leader with political gifts, both in controversy and gentle manipulation, not merely in lobbying the great but in getting ordinary people to move. It is said, for example, that he discovered the power of the questionnaire. Ask ministers to send returns about whether their congregations were engaged in this or that good work and they might take the local lead in seeing that things were done.

From the Committee on Christian Life and Work, which he inspired and led—not a magazine committee mainly but a powerhouse for evangelical and social work initiative—came not only the institutions that look to Charteris as founder, and the title for the new magazine it sponsored, but such practical and continuing notions as disjunction certificates, the Kirk Yearbook, and quinquennial visitations. He was in a way a Renaissance man in his versatility, as well as a man of the considerable renaissance which followed once the Auld Kirk, the Church of Scotland by law established, had recovered from the great, sad day in 1843. On that day, a third of its ministers, and many of the best of its elders and people, opted out at the Disruption to form their own Church of Scotland, free and protesting—the original Free Kirk. Reunion with the successors of these Free Churchmen (and indeed with the United Presbyterians deriving from earlier secessions) was one of Charteris' causes, and one of the few he was not to see make much headway in his lifetime.

The majority of the descendants of the Disruption were indeed to unite with the UPs, but before then, and before presbyterian reunion was to become really practical politics, there was to be a time when relations between Auld

Kirk and Free Kirk were to be strained by the controversy over disestablishment. It was a controversy in which Charteris was to take a leading part and make full use of the magazine he launched in 1879. (See below, p. 45.)

Life and Work, however, was not closed to Free Churchmen, provided they expounded the reformed doctrine the two kirks held in common and not the politics of ecclesiastical estrangement. As early as 1879 Dr Hugh Macmillan, a leading Free Kirk divine, was declaring the difference between 'the fruitful tree and the useless chaff'.

Charteris was, in the idiom of the day, a Scottish churchman. That meant that he was a middle-of-the-road man. He believed in the maintenance of a national, established church, though one free to order its own affairs as distinct from one run on the lines of an English free or Scottish 'voluntary' church. He was a Presbyterian who resisted the anglicising and anglicanising influence which then (and even now) could weaken the character of the Scottish upper classes, whether defined by accident of birth or quality of education. For this man, the Christian faith was at the centre of all things. Christan life and work meant applying the gospel to all of life; taking up the promise of eternal life.

He was a man of action as well as faith, for he never separated the two. As he once told students:

> Your hold of Christ's hand will make you follow whither He draws, where ignorance has to be taught and pain has to be soothed and sorrow brightened. Would you like to learn how little you know? Try and teach a Sunday class. Would you like to be sure of your grip of the truth? Visit that artisan who doubts it. Would you like to follow Christ more closely? Then you must go where he still goes, as in Palestine—to the needy, the suffering and the poor.

There was much need, suffering, and poverty in the Scotland of 1879. Some of it was to be brilliantly recorded in the early years of *Life and Work*. But there was also confidence, conviction, faith, missionary spirit, zeal for both self-betterment and doing good. Charteris was a great do-gooder, following the greatest Good-doer. His creation of *Life and Work* followed from that conception of the full humanity which Jesus Christ integrated with divinity. It began not as the record of the institutional church but as a sharing in print of all Christian life and work, rooted in grace, faith, and obedience.

As it happened, the Auld Kirk had a magazine—*The Mission Record*—

which was not absorbed into *Life and Work* till 1900. It was literally what its title suggested, a record of what the mission committees of the Kirk were doing, and how and why. Founded in 1838 and published monthly, it read like an annual report on the instalment pattern, and it was heavily weighed down with such basic information as the record of small donations to great causes. To open its bound volumes today at certain pages is fascinating, but it is often the fascination of looking up an old railway timetable or accounts book. And of course, the record of committee work and achievement left little opportunity for editorial initiative of distinctive character. That, of course, is probably how some committees liked things then, and how doubtless some would like things now.

Life and Work had both character and initiative from the start, for it had Charteris not only as founder but as first editor. He had vision and marked literary and journalistic skills, the two going together in his age in a way which was rarely possible after the revolution which Lord Northcliffe inflicted on the British press a generation later, starting the process which produced in turn the *Mail*, *Express*, *Mirror*, and *Sun*.

Literacy was valued. Literacy was growing. The new barbarism, the schools that tolerate or even cultivate illiteracy, lay far in the future. *Life and Work* set out to be popular. If it had any direct inspiration it may have been the independent *Good Words* which Norman Macleod of the Barony had edited. But that had been sixpence-worth. *Life and Work* was to be a penny, though some parishes seem to have added an optional halfpenny for the local supplement.

Charteris was well aware that the established church had been left behind by the vigour, evangelism and skills mobilised by the other parts of the national presbyterian tradition. In the cause that led to the Disruption, for example, there was a notable contribution by a lay journalist, the brilliant but unstable Hugh Miller of Cromarty, editor of *The Witness* and stonemason turned geologist; a writer whose unfinished work *The Testimony of the Rocks* brought out only too well the mid-Victorian tension between religion and science, a tension one could encounter in Charteris's age too.

In 1879 there were vigorous Free Kirk and UP publications; and there was a flourishing denominational press in England, even if it never quite achieved the influence and diversity of its American counterpart, Indeed Charteris's attack on the 'unsuitability' of English penny magazines may have concealed a problem which, as a believer in presbyterian reunion, he played down: the most suitable London magazines which might have appealed to a Scots presbyterian readership would have fitted in better with a church run on the

3. Hugh Miller of Cromarty

'voluntary principle'.

That is what the Free Kirk was becoming despite the establishment principles of Chalmers and the men of 1843.

It was what the United Presbyterians, inheriting Relief and secessionist traditions, were almost bound to be. The *Christian's Penny Magazine*, for example, a lively production which scarified sin and roasted Rome, can be found bound together with reports of the Free Kirk's General Assembly. The Auld Kirk needed something that was not only Scottish but committed to establishment—though of the national free church in a free state which Charteris wanted. In London establishment was linked to those unfamiliar and unwelcome surplices, chancels, and litanies.

But if Charteris was conscious of a denominational need, he cared even more for an evangelical one: 'The Christian Church has probably never yet made full use of the mighty powers of the Press; certainly the Church of Scotland never has', he wrote. But he thought the process was beginning: 'Reports of congregational work and pastoral letters by ministers are becoming more common every year', he claimed. But he wanted a 'wider use of this great power' with the one aim 'to promote pure and undefiled religion in our beloved land.'

He was conscious, as every one of his successors had to be, of the diversity even within Scotland, even within his section of presbyterianism. In his introductory notice for the new magazine he wrote:

> In subsequent numbers we hope to have sketches of the lives of great missonaries; notices of famous workers at home and abroad; descriptions of country life which may be news to dwellers in the heart of great cities; and facts in city life which may wake sympathy in those who live far from the smoke and hurry of the town.

'Our main thrust', he said, 'is the personal efforts of ministers through their parochial organisations.' His successors have had to echo that, too. But he invited landowners, farmers, owners of factories, and other employers of labour, 'and all who are interested in the welfare of their neighbours', to help. He had got orders for twenty-five thousand copies before printing; he needed thirty-five thousand to break even. In the rather dated words of his biographer, Arthur Gordon, 'This ecclesiastical "Pink Un" soon distanced all expectations; 76,000 copies of the first number were distributed and by its third year had built up to a circulation of 85,000.'

But these are the things that were reported to committees and General Assemblies. There is more reality to the history which rediscovers what people thought, did, and read.

It is worth looking at what Dr Charteris, the editor-professor, offered—not least to discover that the Victorians were not nearly so dull as they have been painted. It was a good pennyworth, especially if, as Charteris wanted, the new *Life and Work* was closely linked to parish supplements. From its first days in 1879 *Life and Work*, far from being in competition with local church newsletters and magazines, has done best where they have been strongest. Indeed the national *Life and Work* called itself 'a parish magazine'—a magazine, that is, for the parishes.

4. Editor McMurtrie

Take for example Edinburgh's St Bernard's parish magazine. The minister there since 1866, John McMurtrie, was to succeed Charteris, his intimate friend, as editor of *Life and Work*. Like sensible ministers since, McMurtrie, an Ayr man, pushed *Life and Work* hard; echoing Charteris's words about the power of the press, he claimed that the apostles themselves would have used it 'had they lived in these days'.

Here, in the parish pages, *Life and Work* is seen in its context. Every Tuesday night there is a sewing class for girls in the mission hall; every Saturday night in the same hall three of the eighteen penny savings bank managers are in attendance. There are five hundred accounts, most of them fairly healthy, though they dip a bit on the Saturday before Martinmas, when the rents are due.

But man does not live by banks alone. There is a new prayer meeting in the mission hall every second Wednesday. New fangled communion cards are replacing metal tokens, though the more traditionalist members prefer the old two communions a year to the new quarterly ones. There are record numbers in the two-shift Sunday school and one hundred and forty-three adults in the minister's Bible classes. Sunday begins with a young men's fellowship meeting at 9.45 am, and ends with the provision of a 'library of Sunday reading' after the evening service. There has also been a social meeting for university students connected with the church; at least twenty-five proved to be regular church attenders.

Among people of such diligence, providence, and enthusiasm for education and improvement, *Life and Work* was founded; and this people, whose powers of reading had been developed by reading the scriptures in the Authorised Version, opened up what is said to have been a pink cover bearing a symbolic plough and anchor. Alas, this pink skin to their pennyworth has vanished from the bound volumes, for the binder probably thought it beneath the dignity of the contents. These bound volumes also lack the information that the magazine was published by David Douglas under the 'supervision of a committee of the General Assembly' and printed—as it was until the 1930's—by R & R Clark of Edinburgh, who acted as 'agents' from 1884.

Dignity the contents had, for Charteris's *apologia* was followed by an article, in rather sermonical style, from Principal Tulloch of St Mary's College, St Andrews, on 'the higher life'. Its theme was that without the resurrection of Jesus there can be no higher life, for he is the source of all awakening to higher thoughts and a better life. Tulloch's appearance perhaps testifies that Charteris did what his successors were wise to do: give scope to a wide range of theological opinion. For Tulloch was enough of a liberal to seem an odd man out in the Kirk of his day—a historian of religious ideas whose temperament and enthusiasms had something in common with the Cambridge Platonists. But the Kirk was broad-minded enough to make him Moderator in 1878.

And what next? Charteris had a good stock of material as he addressed himself to his page-plans and make-up: Bible thoughts; a prayer; a children's page to bring up the rear; plenty of fillers; a long poem on that most moving theme to which Victorian attitudes and bitter experience gave a special emphasis, as any Dickens reader knows—the mystery of child-death:

> Lost only as the stars are lost in blaze of glorious day . . .
> Lost not to tenant unfamiliar lands
> But in a second home and rendezvous
> To live for endless years.

There was also 'a country minister' whose anonymity could alone have protected him from the gratitude of the insurance industry, whose benefits, he claimed, were 'not sufficiently understood by the working classes'. He had the happy thought that where information was needed it might be 'obtained by anyone from his minister, who ought to be interested in all that concerns the welfare of the people'.

Regular savings, friendly society, and building societies won equal approval and his provident advice (with free advertising for the Oddfellows and Foresters) also extended to avoiding early marriages. Young men and women should 'tarry a little to collect their means as well as their wits'.

But Charteris did not follow his own keynote article on Christian teaching with this mixture of piety and earthly providence. Pride of place after Tulloch went to the first instalment of a serial story by one of the most popular fiction writers of the day: R M Ballantyne, nephew of Sir Walter Scott's printer and still at the height of his fame twenty years after *Coral Island*. Ostensibly, Ballantyne wrote mainly for boys; but boys of all ages and beribboned tomboys could share the excitement, punctuated by impromptu hornpipes, Irish howls, and 'rousing British cheers', which he brought to the Victorian Sunday. He was to reappear regularly in *Life and Work* till his death in 1894.

Our hero is 'Philosopher Jack', who gave the serial its title, a student who by force of circumstances and the end of the first instalment has taken ship for the Antipodes. But as the good ship passed from the shores of Britain, till her sails quivered like a petrel's wings on the horizon, we are about to be introduced to another intrepid but stowaway hero, 'a bright little fellow of fourteen', among the pork-barrels, tar-cakes, oil-cans, and coils of rope deep in the hull 'where he would have looked like a doubled-up overgrown hedgehog if there had been light enough to reveal him'. As late as 1910 the philosopher was still remembered. A note then from a country minister, who got a deserved place of honour in the magazine for canvassing his parish for new subscribers—he got a thirty per cent increase—quoted a farm-servant:

> Who minds fine when it came oot. That was lang before he drove horse, when he was a callant. 'Was not yon a grand story in it, Philosopher Jack?'

And *Life and Work*, too, was under full sail. In the century since it has run on a few reefs and occasionally into the doldrums. Now and again it has had to weather a storm. But on the whole it has been a prosperous voyage.

5. 'Philosopher Jack'. He was shipwrecked but helped launch the magazine.

Chapter 2
The condition of Scotland

'The object of our visit to Glasgow Green was to learn what the intelligent portion of the working classes who have only a slender or no connection with our churches were thinking and talking about; and we were surprised at the range of subjects, their depth and accuracy of comprehension, and their powers of debate and exposition. Social, philosophical, and religious questions were sometimes handled in a really able manner and seemed in their discussion to be popular themes for the listening crowds.'

(From 'A Sunday Hour on Glasgow Green' by the Rev Thomas Young, *Life and Work* September 1882.)

Time goes on. Philosopher Jack, whose wanderings took him to the 'California gold-diggings' as well as the South Seas, has married the captain's daughter and the stowaway has found a new home.

Life and Work has found a new serial in Mrs Oliphant's *Wallyford*. It is set 'in the long lull that followed the great Peninsular wars' at a time when there is nothing much in the newspapers, for people are beginning to think 'that war would never be known on the earth again'. As Mrs Oliphant wisely remarks, 'They were mistaken, as we all know.' She also lectures her readers a little about her characters nonchalantly walking home—'the most natural way'— from Edinburgh out in the Musselburgh direction. 'It would not seem so natural now when there is a railway and many omnibuses.'

But the railway to Dundee has to go the long way round. For the fine new railway bridge collapsed on the last Sunday of 1879. Perhaps a few zealots thought it was a judgment on that doomed trainload of Sunday travellers, not merely the disastrous result of an error in construction.

A H Charteris, who has so much to get on with, has decided to hand over the editorship to John McMurtrie of St Bernard's, and the committee duly appointed him editor from the start of 1880 (though for nearly thirty years Charteris will remain incomparably the most powerful contributor the magazine can call on). He can, to borrow a phrase, look on his work and see that it is good. In less than a year regular circulation has built up to 76,000 and supplements to *Life and Work* are giving the Auld Kirk, perhaps for the first time, a power of communication to match that of the other Scots Presbyterians and the highly articulate English denominations.

There is a Gaelic supplement—as there still is today, though the most devoted of its readers insist that the English-language magazine is really the supplement: they pay for the Gaelic and get a lovely magazine in English thrown in free. So it has been since at least January 1880.

As the magazine moves into the 1880's there are upwards of seventy local 'supplements' which are parish and congregational, or even presbytery, magazines. There has even been a special supplement for congregations in Ceylon, the first of several overseas magazines linked to *Life and Work* or drawing inspiration from Charteris's Scottish concept.

There are also plans for a Forces Supplement from the middle of 1880— yet another tradition maintained today; chaplains are taking note of the magazine itself and contributing. From the North-West Frontier of India the Rev G W Manson marched with Roberts to Kabul and though much of his concern was with the sick and wounded he found time to note the effect of the pipes and drums on the 'Cabuli crowds, indifferent to our fine brass bands'. He also recorded that he could distribute in hospital 'any number of the current parts of *Life and Work*: the men like it.' Writing home to Charteris for publication he assumed the temporary rank of recruiting sergeant: 'Do not be led away by the silly idea that to be connected with the Army is a misfortune and a disgrace', he wrote. 'There are many of you who would do well to enlist.'

He also became a minor prophet when he told young men at home how the discipline and education gained in foreign service could not only 'make better men of you: Nay more, the road to a high career is open.' But there was tragedy in the prophecy. After mentioning a Lieutenant Greer of the 72nd (the Seaforths) who had been commissioned from the ranks he gave another example, 'that of Col-Sergt Hector McDonald, 92nd, twice mentioned in despatches, for whom I am confident a similar reward is in store.'

It was indeed. This must have been among the first mentions (in June 1880) in the British press of 'Fighting Mac' of the Gordon Highlanders—Major-General Sir Hector Macdonald, the Ross-shire boy who became a Scottish hero as well as notable general in the Omdurman campaign and Boer War before a personal scandal in Ceylon and a pistol shot in Paris ended his career, though legends lingered.

Inevitably in the 1880's the magazine's concern with the condition of

Scotland as well as the condition of man broadened naturally into a worldwide concern. Editor McMurtrie, not Moderator McMurtrie till 1904, was one of the greatest enthusiasts in the Kirk's history for the support of foreign missions. He had scarcely taken over from Charteris (another enthusiast from the time when as a small boy he walked seven miles to hear Alexander Duff speak about his work in Calcutta) before he commenced slipping in answers to those who doubted the value of missions abroad. The Scot in those days was often a traveller and might be an emigrant, even when he didn't choose to see the world as a soldier or missionary.

The earliest 'advertising sheet' with *Life and Work* to be traced includes some very Victorian praise of cod liver oil emulsion, with the usual caution against 'a host of imitations'; of quinine wine, 'the best tonic yet introduced'; and of a Yorkshire relish, so deliciously famous that 'unprincipled makers of sauce are filling our old bottles with their worthless preparations'. Immediately after the bottles come the ships of the Anchor Line offering steerage tickets to New York for six guineas and a saloon cabin passage to India for fifty.

Not everyone in the Kirk, then or now, finds it easy to enthuse all the time for a good cause. Charteris and his committee had their detractors, some of whom didn't care for the new magazine. To read the emphatic and perhaps too-much-protesting assurances that *Life and Work* was not in competition with the twopenny *Mission Record* rouses the suspicion that some people thought it was, or at least hoped it was, and that this might get Charteris and his committee into trouble.

In the 1881 General Assembly great hilarity was produced when some of the suspicions, usually decently concealed, came to the surface of what, for those days, was a light-hearted speech by Principal Cunningham, behind whose jibe, later wrote the great Judge and Kirk layman Lord Sands, 'lay the distrust or contemptuous dislike with which in these days the whole Christian Life and Work movement was regarded by a section of churchmen whose sympathies were a curious blend of new liberalism with old moderatism. The *bêtes noires* of this school were Charteris and *Life and Work*, and Scott and the Baird Trust.'

Said Cunningham, Suppose I were to contribute a little luminous matter to that somewhat nebulous body which has recently risen above the horizons of the Church and always makes me think of these lines

Twinkle, twinkle little star
How I wonder what you are!

15

ST. GEORGE'S HALL PREPARATORY CLASSES FOR LADIES
FOR THE
EDINBURGH UNIVERSITY LOCAL EXAMINATIONS
OR FOR HELP IN PRIVATE STUDY.

These Classes will Re-open in ST. GEORGE'S HALL, Randolph Place, on November 1st.

SUBJECTS.

Preliminary Subjects, Latin, English Literature, Logic, Mathematics, Geology, French, German, and Harmony.

Instruction by Correspondence will be carried on in connection with the above.

Correspondence Classes for Boys will also be opened.

Parents who wish to direct the Home Education of their Children, and those who wish for guidance in systematic study, are recommended to try the Correspondence System of teaching.

BURSARIES & PRIZES.

Bursaries for St. George's Hall Students.
For Girls, £20 ; for Boys, £20.—For either, Two Prizes of £5 ; Six of £3 ; and Three of £2.

Open to all Candidates for Examination.
For Boys or Girls, One Bursary of £20 ; for Girls only, Three Bursaries of £10 and One of £15.—For either, £5.

Special Prize of £5 for Competition among Girls entering the M.D. College.

TERMS—AVERAGE FEE, 10s. 6d. PER QUARTER.

Prospectuses may be obtained from Messrs. Douglas & Foulis, Castle Street, or Mr. Thin, South Bridge, Edinburgh.

A TRIUMPH OF PHARMACY.

COD-LIVER OIL RENDERED AGREEABLE AND DOUBLY EFFICACIOUS BY

MACKENZIE'S COMPOUND COD-LIVER OIL EMULSION.

Composed of Select Cod-Liver Oil, Pepsine, and Hypophosphite of Lime.

THESE valuable therapeutic agents are combined in a most agreeable form, easily taken by adults and children, and retained by the weakest stomach. This Emulsion is extensively prescribed by leading physicians throughout the kingdom, and has received their *highest approval.* As a remedy for wasting diseases, bronchitis, and affections of the chest generally, and for imparting muscular strength, with a healthy appearance, it is unsurpassed—the great objection to the use of Cod-Liver Oil in such cases being entirely overcome. *In Bottles at 2s., 3s. 6d., and 6s. each.* To be had of all Chemists. Prepared only by MACKENZIE AND CO., OPERATIVE CHEMISTS, *45 Forrest Road and 11 Shandwick Place, Edinburgh,* who originally introduced this preparation. *Its success has been followed by a host of imitations, against which the public are cautioned.*

SEVEN PRIZE MEDALS AWARDED.

GOODALL'S YORKSHIRE RELISH
Bottles, 6d., 1s., and 2s. each.

THE MOST DELICIOUS SAUCE IN THE WORLD.

GOODALL'S BAKING POWDER
1d. Packets ; 6d., 1s., 2s., and 5s. Tins.

THE BEST IN THE WORLD.

GOODALL'S QUININE WINE
Bottles, 1s., 1s. 1½d., 2s., and 2s. 3d. each.

THE BEST TONIC YET INTRODUCED.

GOODALL'S CUSTARD POWDER
In Boxes, 6d. and 1s. each.

MAKES DELICIOUS CUSTARDS WITHOUT EGGS, AND AT HALF THE PRICE.

CAUTION.—Some unprincipled makers of Sauce are filling our old bottles with their worthless preparations, and using a colourable imitation of our " Yorkshire Relish " Label ; we therefore beg to caution the public that none is genuine unless a label be over the stopper of each bottle, with our Trade Mark, " Willow Pattern Plate," and name, " Goodall, Backhouse, & Co."

Sold by Grocers, Chemists, Patent Medicine Dealers, and Oilmen, &c.

Shippers and the Trade supplied by the sole Proprietors, GOODALL, BACKHOUSE, & Co., LEEDS.

ANCHOR LINE
AMERICAN MAIL STEAMSHIPS.

The Large and Powerful Steamers of this Line are despatched as follows :—

GLASGOW to NEW YORK,
Every THURSDAY (calling at Moville).

INDIAN SERVICE.
GLASGOW and LIVERPOOL to BOMBAY,
Every Three Weeks.

LONDON to NEW YORK,
Every SATURDAY.

MEDITERRANEAN SERVICE.
GLASGOW to LISBON, GIBRALTAR, GENOA, LEGHORN, NAPLES, MESSINA, & PALERMO, every Fortnight.

FARES.—GLASGOW to NEW YORK : Saloon Cabin, 12, 14, and 16 Guineas ; Second Cabin (including bedding, &c.), 8 Guineas ; Steerage, 6 Guineas. RETURN RATES : Saloon, 21, 23, and 25 Guineas.—LONDON to NEW YORK : Saloon Cabin, 12 to 15 Guineas ; Steerage, 6 Guineas. Passengers Booked to all parts of the UNITED STATES and CANADA.—LIVERPOOL to BOMBAY : Saloon Cabin, 50 Guineas.—GLASGOW to LISBON, £6 : 6s.; Gibraltar, £8 : 8s.; Genoa, £12 : 12s.; Leghorn, £13 : 13s.; Naples, £14 : 14s.; Messina or Paiermo, £16 : 16s. Round Voyage, Glasgow to Mediterranean Ports and Back to Liverpool, 35 Guineas. Apply to HENDERSON BROTHERS, 19 Leadenhall Street, London ; 17 Water Street, Liverpool ; 1 Panmure Street, Dundee ; or to

HENDERSON BROTHERS, 47 Union Street, Glasgow.

6. An early advertising sheet

'Great laughter', said the report in *The Scotsman*. 'I refer to the magazine *Life and Work*', said Cunningham (renewed laughter), getting another laugh apparently when he made his point that if the editor asked 'such a man as me' to contribute he could not be held responsible for the other writers.

If the editor did rush to ask Cunningham to contribute he drew a blank, to judge from the index. But perhaps he didn't rush. Perhaps he was, in the sedate Victorian way, having to avoid being knocked down in the rush of volunteers. Then, as now, *Life and Work* was a magazine written by its readers—and indeed by its local correspondents and sales representatives! Charteris, though a Wamphray schoolmaster's son, had a good many aristocratic contacts, and titled ladies began to appear. Ministers, then as now, were a literary lot, often married to literary ladies. There are signs that as early as Charteris's day editors had to make a conscious effort to ensure that a decent proportion of material came from the vast majority of the Kirk which is neither in the ordained ministry nor married to it: one sign of the effort is a 'layman's sermon' on mortality and 'vanity of vanities' which shows considerable literary powers and a power of personality which those close to him might have found awe-inspiring or even oppressive: it was signed only by initials but written by Thomas Stevenson, father of Robert Louis. Apart from Mrs Oliphant and Ballantyne there were 'big names' like Mrs Craik, who wrote as 'The Author of John Halifax, Gentleman'. Among them might be ranked the hymn-writer George Matheson (who succeeded McMurtrie at St Bernard's in 1886), remembered when the statesmen of the Kirk are forgotten. Not all those who love his hymns may take at first to his prose meditations. They probably need to be read and re-read. A writer—best described, perhaps, as an 'essayist'— who had clearly an immense appeal in his day was Dr Andrew Kennedy Hutchison Boyd, one of the inspirers of the first Church Hymnary. The name is worth giving in full as he wrote as 'AKHB'. For a long time he was what today we would call a popular columnist, though with a very Victorian consciousness of style. He was also Moderator in 1890.

From time to time there also appear some of the names which figure in histories of the church where the emphasis is on theological and doctrinal development. The Auld Kirk had its controversy (it still has) over the place of the Westminister Confession of Faith as well as over the effect of critical scholarship on traditional understanding of the Bible. But it was spared the kind of confrontation which arose in the Free Church at the time of the Robertson Smith affair.

In 1882, however, Charteris's Edinburgh colleague, Robert Flint, Professor of Divinity, wrote a sermon which touched on some of the themes he developed when he defended his subscription to the Confession and asserted his right to interpret it in ways which today we tend to regard as an inheritance from the Free Church under Principal Rainy and the United Presbyterians. Flint warned that the reasonable and salutary doctrine stated in the Confession about the perseverance of saints could be perverted and abused, adding: 'No man has a right to conclude that he has been certainly elected and effectually called of God unless he is giving all diligence to make his calling and election sure; no man can be aware that his conversion was a genuine one apart from the continuance and increase of the spiritual life which he then supposed to have begun within him.'

Serious theological teaching was common even in a magazine meant for the common man and woman; but it usually avoided current controversy and came from those who sought a middle way in it.

The big names were even more evident in the illustration—a major part of the appeal of a magazine in days before picture-papers, far less television. Until well into the twentieth century, editors regarded the magazine's drawings as both prestige symbols and selling points. Sir George Reid, who was a notable portrait painter and president of the Royal Scottish Academy, became 'adviser and helper in all that relates to the arts'. He presented a great deal of his own work (largely of Scottish churches) for reproduction and ensured a supply of material from other artists, some of whose work may not be to modern taste but who ranked high in their time. Some, like McTaggart, MacWhirter and Lavery, rank high today too.

But what really records the condition of Scotland is a mixture of commissioned series and unsolicited articles from authors whose names mean nothing today, even where (like Dr John Gray of Auchterless) they became popular in their time. Gray, who wrote as 'An Old Farm Servant' enjoyed a vogue for many years and turned his work into a book with a ready sale. But others who testified to the condition of Scotland and their efforts to improve it—usually economically and socially, as well as spiritually—were anonymous then and virtually untraceable now. There are writers as well as soldiers 'known only to God'.

They had a ready readership. McMurtrie had a knack of pleasing his readers and built up the circulation to 100,000 by 1885 (and to 108,000 when he retired as editor in 1898). He was an evangelical of his time—though one who kept a large collection of German theology in the corner of his study which he called 'my wicked library'. When the jubilee of *Life and Work* was celebrated, on the eve of the great reunion of the kirks in 1929, the editor of the day even claimed that under McMurtrie it had improved in quality and grown

"HERE WE ARE AGAIN!!!"

7. *Punch's view of Gladstone on the eve of the Home Rule crisis.*

in influence. Influence, perhaps, especially when Charteris was to use it to campaign against Gladstone's inclination to tinker with disestablishment in Scotland. But quality? Perhaps the very qualities—some of them growing in the neighbourhood of the literary kailyard—which won a popular following at the time are those which look less well from the perspective of a century afterwards. For today's taste from its own time and place, looks *gey dreich* But the very drabness and dullness—which have to be compared with the horrors of, say, *Punch* at the same time—make it easier to see the colour that Charteris brought to the early magazine and the qualities of the best of the material in the rest of the nineteenth century. Its popularity also reflected the Kirk's affinity at the time with what a modern minister-critic, Campbell Maclean, called a 'picture of couthy Scotland wrapped up in fanciful whimsy and impeccable genteelism'.

To read the magazine is often to enter another world. It was by no means a world in which everyone went to kirk every Sunday: far from it, although the established Kirk had half a million communicants and, to quote Charteris in one of his exhortations for Christian giving for mission at home and abroad, 'four-fifths of our parish churches do not require giving for self-support as dissenting churches do'. Even though the other presbyterian churches approached the Kirk in membership and perhaps together surpassed it in active and committed members (the exact meaning of religious statistics has always been a matter of hot dispute), there were large numbers of Scots, quite apart from the mainly Irish-descended Roman Catholics, who were beyond the reach of either 'national church' or national presbyterian tradition.

It is, of course, the accepted tradition of modern times that the church lost touch with many industrial workers, even if too much can be made of this. The point was often admitted at the time, as in Mr Young's 'Sunday Hour on Glasgow Green' quoted at the start of this chapter. But although the established Churches of Scotland and England, and the Free Kirk, often did lose touch, the gap they left was sometimes filled by other protestant denominations. For example, the church on the eastern outskirts of Glasgow in which the present editor of *Life and Work* grew up (by that time a charge of the national Kirk) had virtually been a 'parish church' serving its community in the nineteenth century, although it had been 'Relief' and became United Presbyterian. If a social historian were to seek evidence there of the alienation of the industrial workers, he might not find it till the twentieth century, or he might find it in the effect of shades and nuances of division within what a Marxist would call the proletariat. He might also find that the middle-class members of today's Kirk are often the children and grandchildren of the supposedly alienated workers.

20

8. An early illustration: children at play

Would he also find that some of the alienation took place before the workers moved into the cities? Some of the most eloquent testimony of the social history which *Life and Work* so abundantly provides is of an evangelical concern for the conversion of the people of the Scottish countryside. For example, the efforts which the magazine made which promised 'to lessen intemperance' were not only directed to those who had a pub on either side of the close-mouth but to a rural population much larger then than now and perhaps as remote in working conditions from modern farms as a modern factory is from Blake's dark satanic mills. Perhaps *Life and Work* drew too much on Aberdeenshire for its examples and exhortations. Until it developed widespread use of letters to the editor (a fairly modern innovation) it is difficult to get from its pages an indication of how readers reacted. Correspondence, for example, arising out of the long-running contributions of Gray of Auchterless might have been fascinating—especially as he devoted a good deal of pointed if not too specific attention to sexual mores as well as drinking habits and social customs. But his world is not unlike that of Lewis

21

Grassic Gibbon despite the very different point of view from which it is seen and the response of readers and book-buyers makes clear that much of what came forth from the pen of the Old Farm Servant and his kindred spirit (or was it his *alter ego*?), an Aberdeenshire Minister, was of fairly wide application in rural Scotland.

The world they described, already changing under the impact of industrialisation, emigration, and agricultural depression, was one of hard work, early rising, and low—sometimes lowered—wages. Old Farm Servant would not have gone down well with that section of the modern church which enthusiastically backs union attitudes, for part of his advice was that there were times when at the six-monthly feeing market farm workers might have to accept lower wages rather than say: 'I'll not come down to bide', which he thoughtfully rendered into standard English as 'I'll not stay in my present place for less wages than I now have.'

Gray exhorted with all the passion of someone who had been through it himself: 'one of yourselves only somewhat better schooled and able to spell and write somewhat better than most of you and so able to talk with you through the pages of his magazine'. He also lambasted grieves, foremen, and second horsemen who cursed, swore, and used obscene language, and pled with his readers to put most of their wages in the bank, not just for old age and sickness but 'for the glorious privilege of being independent'. He thought a man could manage £20 a year and a woman £8, on average wages. (Elsewhere he suggests saving £12 out of £24 a year!)

Sometimes his vision of farm vice is a little weak for his strong words—as in Sabbath-breaking: 'lolling and dozing in bed, in reading the *People's Journal*'. Sometimes his virtue must have been a little hard to take—as when he waxed about the bad old days (or were they the good old days?) of working from four am to seven at night at turnip-time. He calculated, 'you have two days a week all to yourself', (a five-day-week reckoning composed of the Lord's Day plus six times four hours when workers were neither labouring nor sleeping). But he wanted this leisure time devoted to education in mutual improvement associations, just as he wanted a change in feeing-market customs. 'Don't seek that hateful poisonous whisky', he advised, 'but call for a refreshing cup of good tea or coffee with a fine mutton chop or a nice bit of cold beef.' And if farm workers were still offered whisky he advised a fine rhetorical reply: 'The curse of God and the shame and misery of our country are upon that loathsome, accursed whisky of yours. Not a farthing of my money shall be wasted upon it, not a drop of it shall poison and degrade my body and soul.'

Strong words for strong drink. But he didn't want wages to go to the

22

9. Sunday in the Highlands

drink-sellers as soon as paid; and he wanted to curb the 'animal lust' which he listed among other problems at the feeing-market.

The Victorians were not as prudish as they are often painted, not in *Life and Work* at any rate. 'Fallen women' are not to be denounced but to be redeemed; they depended, of course, on ready-to-fall gentlemen who were by no means all outside the pastoral care of the Kirk. Some circumstances are also accepted as providing special, and even all but unavoidable, temptations. In February 1884, for example, the 'Aberdeenshire Minister' is frank about a farm environment in which after supper the foreman and cattlemen retire to their own houses, leaving the unmarried second and third horsemen, a loon or two, and two women-servants in the 'farm-kitchen'. 'Then those five or six young me and women from 14 to 20 years of age are left in that kitchen to conduct themselves pretty much as they choose.' What, he asked, can we expect 'but just the dire results that make other parts of the country point the finger of scorn at us?' He wanted a separate sitting-room for the unmarried men, though he added with a touch of italicised realism: 'I don't say that even this would cure the evil I allude to; but it would give the female servants a *chance* of protecting their virtue, which under this system they hardly have.'

Perhaps there was nothing about the poorer parts of the cities that was quite so good of its kind, or at least quite so authentically coming from the people whose problems it described. To say that is not to underrate Charteris's passion for social improvement. It is simply that the journalism about the urban poor is not as vivid as the passion of the ploughboy-turned-minister.

There was a significant phrase in the moderatorial address of Dr John Rankine in 1883 on practicable church reforms, facing up to the 'undetermined but very large' proportion of the population outside every form of the Christian Church. Speaking of working men he said: 'The minister and they are strangers. Their ways of thought are unknown or only theoretically guessed at.' That sometimes shows through. 'The parish church is nothing to them but a building where others worship', said Rankine, who attacked seat-rents as an anomaly—though they survived after a fashion till the 1940's even in ex-UP churches, and perhaps are not yet extinct—and complained that in villages and small towns people couldn't be accommodated in church if they chose to come. 'These can be accommodated in our churches only by the permission or the courtesy of the persons to whom the sittings have already been allocated.' He went on to make if clear that in 1883 the unchristian words 'Excuse me, you're sitting in my seat' were only too familiar, and had the force of law and custom behind them, even where kirk sessions 'suggested the propriety of accommodating others'.

There is a graphic picture in an account of the 'dangerous temptations' of the pawnshop which tells a story. Indeed, point is given to the story by the editor's decision 'for the benefit of readers happily ignorant' that he had better explain how a pawnshop works.

The anonymous writer is rattling through a sequence of customers: wives with their husbands' Sunday suit; a bride with her wedding dress; a removal man brought low by 'an ill-timed glass of whisky for helping to carry a piano into a Christian lady's drawing room'; an old woman with the clothes she got the day before from the kirk's clothing store; a miner who overstayed a Saturday trip to town; and now a girl:

> She looked round her house for something she could put in pawn to raise the money. The large Bible was never used, she could send that. But the pawnbroker would not take it in. He was overstocked with Bibles. They were never redeemed and at the end of the legal year they would not sell. The young wife took back the Bible with a curse and sent her Sunday bonnet.

The evil of drink, the abuse of which is still a curse of Scotland, was a more frequent theme. The General Assembly's temperance convener, the Rev George Wilson, claimed that seventy-five per cent of paupers were on the Poor Roll because of drunkenness and that drink created the majority both of lunatics and criminals. He had political skills and a turn of phrase which enabled him to handle the awkward fact—awkward then and now—that the Kirk included ardent total abstainers and those for whom temperance meant something different, sometimes something very different. But Wilson offered an interesting bit of social analysis after a skilful phrase about 'the immense advantage of being without the daily use of alcoholic stimulants': 'Drunkenness is now considered a disgrace among the educated classes and the upper half of the working classes.'

But what of the lower half of the working classes, especially if we note the very proper use of the plural—classes, not class? For different trades, traditions, customs and environment make it difficult to be too sweeping about how Scotland lived then or what its attitude was to religion.

Some modern critics would argue that the Auld Kirk was closer to many of these groups than the politically more liberal and even radical Presbyterians of the Free Church and the United Presbyterians. It had, for example, the notable evangelical and social ministry of Norman Macleod of the Barony in Glasgow, though that was past when Charteris reached his zenith. It had another notable Macleod ministry (not the last) in Govan from John Macleod who also taught solid doctrine in *Life and Work*. How many social gospellers now would use their access to the printed word to explain the deep mystery of the Trinity, and insist that we must use the terms which the experience of more than eighteen centuries has proved necessary? At first they create confusion, he says, but they come gradually to yield up an ever-deepening meaning. But the Auld Kirk's best men did not claim to meet all the people's needs.

Charteris's passion for the social work of the church was trying to extend this range of ministry. He and his colleagues knew that they had much still to do and that others might even be doing God's work better. Charteris was at his best in reviewing William Booth's *In Darkest England* in 1890, at a time when the established churches were not as Christian in all their dealings with The Salvation Army as conscience (and good example) later taught them to be.

What attracted him was not only Booth's evangelical zeal and integrity: it was the scale on which he thought, lived and worked, with the aim of overcoming poverty as well as paganism.

Seven years earlier, however, editor McMurtrie printed what he obviously regarded as a none too sound article about The Salvation Army's campaigning in a dark enough bit of Edinburgh (off the Grassmarket) because he wanted the churches to consider 'why they are making so little impression on the classes from which The Salvation Army draws its converts'. The article, which ended with a sonnet, was from one of the most colourful, notable, and versatile classical scholars of the time, Professor J Stuart Blackie, whose interests ranged from the ancient world to modern celtic languages. He had also won himself a niche in history by his declaration in 1839, when nominated to the Humanity Chair in Marischal College, that he had signed the required adherence to the Westminster Confession as 'a professional duty', and not as his private Christian confession of faith.

The sonnet of 1883 itself bears reprinting, for it has some fine lines and no more archaically poetic diction than much that is far better known:

Strange world in sooth! wild whirl of joy and sadness!
Unseasoned medley of things good and bad,
Things basely sober, and things crudely mad,
Yet with sweet soul of method in their madness!
'Salvation Army!' well, they mean to save;
And in their own rough way, they do, no doubt;
And I would liefer fling wild words about
With them, than slip through life, a smooth-lipped slave
Of reputable forms. Far better with too much
Of zeal to swell, and hot aggressive love,
Than sit in cleanly state, and fear to touch
The clouted sinner, lest you soil your glove:
In this waste field, where rough hands blindly throw
Good seed, you slept, and taught the weeds to grow.

Blackie's article was a description of the Sunday night meeting in The Vennel. He approved even of speakers walking up and down, unconfined 'in a box called a pulpit', and of the marching-song hymns to keep the audience from falling asleep—an advantage he suggested need not be despised even by attenders at less 'disorderly' services. He warmed to the way the 'fair sergeants or whatever the title be' welcomed the kneeling converts, and assessed the service's impact on himself not as mere novelty of spectacle but as an 'honesty, directness, and smoking fervour' which without either hypocrisy or restraint dealt effective blows against 'our three great enemies, the World, the Devil, and the Flesh'.

This was a bit much for the more conventional McMurtrie. He felt he had to add a note to the article which, good editor and decent man that he was, he recognised he ought to print. He worried about the Salvationists becoming a new sect, about the dangers of a less upright dictator-general than Booth, about excessive if unconscious irreverence and 'no attempt at a better tone'. He feared the unwholesome doctrine of perfectionism was taking root among them and noted that not only were children encouraged to announce their conversion in public (a style by no means confined to the Salvationists, however) but that 'young women constantly preach'.

Other constant preachers clearly worried the good McMurtrie's conscience for different reasons. In 1884 there is a refrain in *Life and Work* as familiar as any chorus from the Salvationists or Charteris's favoured evangelists, Moody and Sankey: poor stipends for hard-worked ministers. Of the total number of parish ministers, wrote a Mr Thomas Barty, at least a third were not sufficiently provided for. More than three hundred had livings which, including the glebe, yielded less than £200 a year, the 'barest maintenance for a clergyman'.

Such ministers could never be free from the pressure of anxiety. They faced a constant struggle, a lifelong burden; and eventually found their worldly cares increasing, with the minister worrying that on his death 'those who are dearer to him than life must leave the manse not only in sorrow but in poverty'. If Mr Barty's dissertation on 'our underpaid ministers'—a plea for the annual collection for the small livings scheme and for a fund under the presidency of the Duke of Argyll—sounds like a far-fetched modern letter to the editor of *Life and Work* there are probably points to ponder in both the familiarity and the far-fetchedness. For the problems have not gone away, though some at least have been eased.

How badly off were these ministers on less than £200, out of which they had to meet expenses and what Barty called maintaining themselves and their families 'in a respectable position'? Comparisons are very difficult to make. For example, the cheap supply of domestic servants (perhaps not quite so cheap if they ate heartily in the manse kitchen), is one example of the difficulty in saying what £200 (less expenses) was worth then. A skilled engineering worker got rather less and probably faced periodic unemployment. Around 1890 a pattern-maker got just under £2 a week. An industrial labourer might get about eighteen shillings a week. The highest manual wages were in steel, where long shifts went with a relatively short life in the best-paid parts of the industry. A plate miller or roller could get £7 a week and even a steel shearer £4. Miners had about twenty-four shillings a week if one seeks a neat figure, but their earnings seem to have fluctuated violently. On the railways, stationmasters, who had free houses, might be compared with ministers: their

Victorian salaries ranged from £50 to £130. On the other hand it was an age of major differentials inside the ministry, as well as of class distinctions. These made it expensive for a poorly paid professional man to keep up the standards expected of him, though to judge by some of the low salaries in the schools most teachers did not really count as 'professional'. But the United Presbyterians would pay their ministers more than £500 a year in prosperous Edinburgh churches like Palmerston Place and Broughton Place, even in mid-Victorian times.

Quite apart from the traditional 'plums' among the parishes there were Church of Scotland charges in well-off areas of development which expected to pay the same kind of stipend. For example, there is the case quoted by the modern historians Drummond and Bulloch, of the Maxwell Church in Pollok Street, Glasgow, handy then for the newly developing area of Pollokshields, which opened in 1865 with a stipend of £440. In successive years it rose to £500, £600, and £700, of which £580 (like the UP stipends) depended on the giving of the congregation. Differentials created by such situations were, of course, even more valuable than their equivalents would be if they existed in the modern Kirk, for they were not swallowed up by a voracious Inland Revenue.

But at the time the thriving middle-class congregations were responding in what we would today consider the American manner, the country parishes were beginning to feel the effect of the hard times facing British agriculture, for stipends depended on crop prices. Although the Free Kirk and the UPs often fared poorly in the countryside in membership they drew on the committed, the generous, and sometimes the prosperous. Drummond and Bulloch have pointed out how in Haddington and Dunbar the Kirk's members in 1891 averaged about five shillings a head in givings and the Free Kirk and UP members about £2. They also give national averages which appear to contest a view sometimes encountered today that the Auld Kirk was not so far behind the other Presbyterians in its financial ethos as is usually believed. The figures fit in with the kind of exhortations often to be encountered in *Life and Work* for these Victorian decades. The national average of the Auld Kirk was 13s.2d.; of the Free Kirk £1.16s.2d.; and of the UPs £1.15s.9d. No doubt these figures reflect both the weakness and the strength of the established Church of Scotland, to use a term which *Life and Work* in those days disliked intensely. The weakness stemmed from large numbers of nominal members who gave little of their substance, especially as they assumed that the Kirk could be sustained by its endowments. The strength lay in the ability of the establishment—as revived by the generation after the Disruption—to reach large sectors of the Scottish population in which the Free Church and the United Presbyterians were weak, despite pockets of local strength which make it impossible to be dogmatic about their middle-class character.

But those like Charteris who had the strongest sense of national duty and national mission were the first to recognise how far the Kirk's strength was unequal to her task. They were also, very often, those like Charteris himself who were most anxious to honour the work and zeal of their separated Scottish Presbyterians and to rebuild the national church in a way which would allow them to rejoin it.

History, however, has its ironies. Charteris, the passionate advocate of reunion, was to find himself the foremost defender of the Kirk in a political battle against disestablishment in which his main adversaries were some of Scotland's other leading Presbyterians—notably the Free Kirk's Principal Rainy—and the Liberal politicians. Some of these, like Sir Henry Campbell-Bannerman, remained in the Auld Kirk, however lukewarm their attachment to it. Others were in the two main presbyterian churches outside the establishment. But the man who mattered most was no Presbyterian, although he was of Scottish descent. He was William Ewart Gladstone, the outstanding Anglican layman of his time.

Dean David Edwards, the Anglican historian and commentator who, until recently, combined his writing with the chaplaincy to the Speaker of the House of Commons, includes Gladstone in his selection of the 'leaders of the Church of England' of the last one hundred and fifty years. He was theologian as well as moral crusader—among other things a notable critic of the Papacy's claim to infallibility. But he was also a politician inevitably drawn into political alliances, one of which was with those Scottish Presbyterians outside the establishment who wanted a 'voluntary' church free of all state connection.

For several years the Auld Kirk's defence against this threat, which grew in the 1880's, reached its peak in the early 1890's and faded rapidly thereafter, was to dominate *Life and Work* and divert even some of Charteris's superabundant energies.

Before looking at this interlude, however, it is worth taking a wider view. The Scots of the 1880's were both an imperial and a missionary people. Even those who responded to Gladstone's attacks on some colonial wars (he was to fight others of his own), were proud to share in ruling India and eager to keep in touch with their cousins in the colonies. Yet even in the age of Britain's 'splendid isolation' they retained a sense of affinity with Europe which was probably stronger in Scots than English and stronger too among Presbyterians than Anglicans.

Chapter 3
The overseas interest

'The money available for division was £17. £10 was assigned to Jaffa Mission for the support of Katrina Jirius, and it was agreed to give £7 in equal parts to Darjeeling, Africa (Blantyre), and China.'

(From the report of the Juvenile Missionary Society in the St Bernard's Supplement to *Life and Work*, April 1883.)

The first substantial mention of foreign missions in *Life and Work*, in February 1879, is an untypical and unexpected one. It is an account of the life of the first Anglican missionary bishop, John Coleridge Patteson, an Old Etonian who went from Oxford to eventual martyrdom in Melanesia. He was not only an outstanding missionary but a notable cricketer, well enough remembered for the 'champion' bowler of a later English XI visiting Australia to want to bowl a few overs to him in private, for 'the Bishop of Melbourne does not approve of cricket for clergymen in public'.

That discovery is not dredged up as merely another warning against the dangers of taking episcopacy into our system. It is an indication that in its world outlook *Life and Work* was from the start missionary-minded but never sectarian. It set little store by the differences among Protestants, far less Presbyterians, and it rarely dwelt, at least in mission matters, on the vast gulf which divided nineteenth century Roman Catholicism from Protestant Christendom.

Perhaps *Life and Work* benefited from its co-existence during its early years with the dull *Mission Record*. Even when McMurtrie, the Kirk's foremost organiser at home of missions abroad, was its editor, it took a worldwide view. The new magazine, with its enlightened management by the wide-ranging Christian Life and Work Committee and its considerable editorial independence, obviously emphasised the areas of the Church of Scotland's direct involvement but it was far from confined to them. Perhaps the worldwide view came the more easily because the Scots took it for granted that they would be a far-flung people, not only in the colonies but in the United States, the Argentine, and even the Continent. It was a time when the

31

prosperous went by train on Cook's tours without losing the sense of wonder and excitement of their predecessors on bumpier Grand Tours. The Scots business and professional men who dashed off to see Rome or Washington (and, according to their memoirs and diaries, found little trouble in being introduced to the Pope or the President) had some of the same spirit as the younger men who went abroad to find fortune. And in those days they would find Scots churches or services not merely in Melbourne or Montreal or Buenos Aires but in Dresden, Venice, Florence, and Naples, as Baedeker helpfully recorded.

The Scots were a European people, and more conscious than the English in their religious experience—which was less insular than pre-imperial anglicanism—of the nineteenth-century importance of Germany. It may be that they picked up some bad theological habits in the process, but they were not the bad habits of isolation. Two of the first three editors of *Life and Work* had studied at German universities and McMurtrie, for all his commitment to the main mission fields, gave generous space to the French Protestants, whose influence under the Third Republic was higher than at any time since Henry IV, and even to the United States. There was also a strong strain of practical sympathy for the Italian Protestants (a connection which continues in our own time), and hopes, often exaggerated, that the rise of secularism in Spain would open the way for protestantism in the bastion of the Counter-Reformation.

It was also an age of missionary development. British India had a new stability as well as a new system of government in the decades after the Mutiny. China was opened up to European and American influences, one of which was Christian missions, whether the Chinese liked it or not. Africa was opening up, and Africans responded more readily than the Chinese.

There was also what must be called The Very Special Mission: to the Jews. That was a mission which was both a home and an overseas one, but it was a mission not only different in style but in some ways senior in prestige. 'First to the Jews' is a phrase which comes up time and time again in the first half of *Life and Work*'s history. Commitment to Jewish missions—which revived in the post-Disruption Kirk despite the loss of missionaries to the Free Church—opened up wide horizons for the Scottish church both in East Central Europe and in the Mediterranean.

By the 1880's only a relatively small Jewish population had gone to join the remnant in the Holy Land, making only about twenty-four thousand in 1882 according to some modern Zionists, though this figure almost trebled in the next twenty-five years. But the interest in the people of Israel went with an interest in the land of Israel, or Palestine. Ironically, in the light of later

Lebanese events, the main Victorian Church of Scotland mission to the Jews in the Levant was at Beirut (it was the Free Church whose Dr Torrance was working at Tiberias), but its ministers were eager to go to Jerusalem, a small city which was growing with Jewish immigration. (In 1889 it had twenty-five thousand Jews in a population of forty thousand.) Usually they landed at the steps of the Jaffa sea-wall after a sometimes choppy boat trip from the ships riding well offshore, anxious to see what traces there were of biblical Joppa. Nearby was the mission school of Miss Walker Arnott, which an earlier traveller described as one of several 'conducted as private enterprises by ladies of culture'. But the Kirk's interest in Jaffa was already strong. McMurtrie's congregation in St Bernard's, for example, were already backing it even before they could read about it in their fine new parish magazine. But Jaffa was an Arab town and Miss Arnott's pupils were mainly daughters of Christian families.

However, when in 1887 the Rev Thomas Nicol reported on his visits to medical missions in the Middle East, there were Jews as well as Arabs and

10. Joppa (or Jaffa)

Greeks in the school and among the patients who came to Miss Mangan's medical mission linked to it. Patients were coming from many parts of Palestine. However, it was in the Kirk's mission at Smyrna (in modern Turkey) that thousands of Jews were being reached, if not converted. The tracts and text cards were in the Mediterranean Jewish Spanish dialect, and there were text-cards in Hebrew for 'those who would take them'.

Nicol was a fairly practical traveller. Because he wrote of blind beggars, cripples and lepers (especially by the Jaffa Gate of Jerusalem), he made a more specifically Christian impact than some more literary travellers, for he made it seem both natural and necessary that the great Teacher should also be the great Healer, 'thronged by suffering multitudes', as part of the revelation of him as Saviour.

The literary and scholarly ministerial travellers abounded. None, perhaps, matched the great Free Church scholar George Adam Smith (later, Principal of Aberdeen) who in the early 1890's wrote the excellent *Historical Geography of the Holy Land*. Some were too scholarly about the Temple site, some inclined to show a rather forced piety in Galilee, though the fault may be of style and not feeling. One of the better contributors (in 1892) was Dr James Robertson of Whittinghame, one of many Christians—especially Protestants— to find the interior of the Church of the Holy Sepulchre disappointing and one of many Victorians to prefer other sites for Calvary. Rashly, perhaps, Robertson committed himself to accepting 'Gordon's Calvary' though he added the saving words 'if not here in just such a place'. But his real merit was a clear, descriptive style which deserves a place in an anthology of Victorian travels in the Holy Land. All credit to him, too, for ending his last piece with a warning against exaggerated emphasis on the value of seeing the Holy Land: 'There is indeed a gain . . . but the truth of the Gospel is a spiritual truth independent of place. The great message is known best by inward communion with the living Christ.' Robertson, Arthur Balfour's parish minister, was Moderator in 1909.

This inner religion was outward-looking. It looked beyond the main mission fields of the Church of Scotland—for example at the activities of a Mr Curtis who was a missionary in the Japanese city of Hiroshima (under not very clearly defined auspices) as well as at the 'private enterprise' Jaffa mission whose work is today carried on in a very different context by the Tabeetha School. Mr Curtis of Hiroshima had a father-in-law in Scotland who importuned McMurtrie, and the copy was as dull as the discovery of its city of origin is disconcerting. One or two titled ladies also seem to have been able to place missionary material which was not, to put it mildly, subject to the most exacting rigour of editorial selection and condensation, but perhaps part of the readership responded to the title more than to style. (Lady Grisell Baillie, first deaconess and a great home missionary, was another matter; like her brother Robert she was probably a saint both in the eyes of the Lord and the world.)

Even in the 1880's it is clear that missionary enthusiasm and fund-raising needed a bit of stimulation. An example of early 'answers to objections to missions' came in 1882 from Christopher Johnston, an Edinburgh advocate, and is better written than most of the genre over a hundred years since. He warned that missions were unpopular in the sense that every congregation had people who were not only indifferent but hostile. People were tight-fisted and felt missions remote. There was a 'materialistic spirit of the age'. But they also had another very Victorian objection:

> What with our steam engines, our telegraphs, and our telephones, we are so accustomed to rapidity of movement and quick results that we lose patience with every undertaking that does not move towards a speedy issue.

The Edinburgh advocate whose initials fit is almost certainly the later Procurator of the Church who in 1917 exchanged the style of Sir Christopher Johnston for the judicial title of Lord Sands and became the church's most prominent layman of the years before and immediately after presbyterian reunion.

Other advocacy for missions came (once McMurtrie was into his stride) in the serial story, though historical themes seem to have been more popular. Most of the advocacy, however, came from the men on the spot. They were in Nyasaland, in Darjeeling and the Punjab, and in China, although the Chinese coverage (which is among the best overseas material of the early twentieth century) is disappointing in the earlier period. In 1882 readers were being offered a far-fetched calculation that if protestant missions kept up the pace of the previous thirty-five years there would be one hundred million protestant Chinese by 1913. In 1898, still a bit heavy-handedly, the Rev William Deans of Ichang was explaining the infinite complexities of Bible translation in China. What is incidentally brought out is that the missionary had to learn the spoken language to preach to the ordinary people and then study classical Chinese—and its philosophy, morality, and political theory—to approach the educated classes whose scholars liked to read Bibles and tracts 'if in a good classical style'.

One obvious problem in missionary coverage, and indeed all coverage of church activities that cost money, was that to some extent the various schemes of the Kirk were competing for money. The political and diplomatic skills required of an editor of *Life and Work* before the co-ordination of appeals and the emergence of the freewill offering must have been considerable. The choice of what to put in the magazine must have been affected by all sorts of pressures (as it still is), and by consideration that publicity could mean the difference between triumph and tragedy for somebody's enthusiasm. McMurtrie was in a special position with the overlap of his foreign mission and magazine responsibilities, but any editor faced the same problem.

In 1890, for example, he let a very heavy-handed piece in from a missionary called Turnbull in Darjeeling. The mission desperately needed £13,000 to build a new mission compound because the existing one was threatened with disastrous subsidence after an even heavier rainy season than usual. Mr Turnbull and his colleagues, perhaps ready to snatch advantage from the jaws of adversity, had their eyes on a new site. It was the only one possible, it happened to be available, but the money was needed at once. Moreover, the 'Disestablishers in Edinburgh' were saying nasty things about the Kirk's unworthy record in foreign missions. It would all cost less than the price of building or restoring a single church at home:

> Darjeeling is as really a parish of the Church of Scotland as St Cuthbert's itself. Its two missionaries are her ordained missionaries, its 611 converts are her baptized children, and she is occupying the field with its 150,000 unconverted heathens to the exclusion of other Churches which would be only too glad to take her place and undertake her obligations.

The Punjab mission at Sialkot and Wazirabad had about 2500 converts at this stage. The part of inland Africa that was known as Nyasaland, (then British Central Africa, later Nyasaland again, and now Malawi), was another where the Kirk occupied much of the field, though with a happy arrangement which let the Free Kirk operate far to the north in Livingstonia. Fellow Presbyterians of the Dutch Reformed Church had an area in between, and one of their first missionaries was a Murray. But if inter-Presbyterian relations were amicable there were other troubles for the mission at Blantyre, whose name also marked the common devotion to the memory of Livingstone who had, despite a Presbyterian background, really been a Congregationalist.

In July 1890 McMurtrie picked up from the Blantyre Supplement to *Life and Work* an item in which the missionary Dr John Bowie, senior medical missionary in Africa, wrote of the 'deadly reputation which this part of Africa had gained', though he looked to a happier future and suggested that the main problem for Europeans was not a high death-rate but the 'loss-of-health-rate'.

11. First Church at Blantyre, British Central Africa

Most of the one hundred and fifty Europeans in the area had been affected by bouts of illness, some had been invalided home 'and I dare say many (more) should be invalided'.

The following March McMurtrie carried the telegram without punctuation:

'Doctor Bowie Mistress Henderson infant died of diphtheria.'

In April 'there was more of sorrow than in any recent issue.' Bowie, his sister Mrs Henderson (wife of the pioneer missionary Henderson who himself died at Quilimane on his sad way home), and her child had all died. Bowie had caught the disease sucking a tube in a tracheotomy in a vain bid to save the boy. He rose from his deathbed to perform the same operation in another vain bid to save his sister.

A few months before a minister-missionary had died too, Robert Cleland, a working man who at twenty-one heard the call to be a missionary through a sermon at Garturk Parish Church, Coatbridge. He learned his Greek verbs during his engineer's dinner hour—he was not in the alienated part of the working classes—and died at thirty-three. And yet the BBC tells us sometimes that the Bishop of Rome has created the first or the second Scottish saint since the Reformation!

But, said McMurtrie, five young ministers had volunteered for the place left vacant by Cleland. As he recorded the latest deaths he also announced that a minister, a doctor, a lady missionary, and a gardener had been appointed and would leave the next month.

The Auld Kirk worried about not keeping up with the enthusiasm of the Free Kirk—said to have received all but one of the original missionary band in 1843—and the United Presbyterians. From them came Mary Slessor, of whom the notable twentieth-century Scottish newspaper editor (and Presbyterian) J M Reid suggested: 'It is difficult to believe that any other Church could have produced a missionary quite like her'. She was tough enough to survive and self-confident enough to succeed.* In fact the style and enthusiasm of the missionary effort of all three Presbyterian churches had much in common, though when Charteris at the height of the disestablishment controversy sought something to praise in the other two churches he picked out the Free Kirk's support of poor congregations with help from the rich and the UP effort in foreign missions. 'All would be done in generous ardour by a united Church', he wrote. Certainly, the emphasis which Charteris or McMurtrie put on mission abroad, as well as at home, helped to maintain some sense of balance, charity, and perspective, as the politics of disestablishment came raucously to the fore at home.

In some ways evangelical zeal even gained strength from the difficulties and faction to which Scotland was a prey in the last twenty years of the century. As Charteris said in 1892 in a sermon which *Life and Work* reprinted:

> That Christ died merely for us, that we might have preachers and churches and ecclesiastical rivalries and aesthetic services and Guilds and parish halls, and sing our complacent hymns amid the roar of a frantic heathen world, is too awful to bear putting into words.

He feared then that 'fighting for our life as a Church' would poison the air in Scotland. 'But I think that if we meanwhile enter into the mind of Christ regarding our relation to the great wastes of heathendom . . . and if this old church, established by our fathers, were dissolved, we have a building of God, an house not made with hands'.

For a time it did indeed seem possible that the church of Knox and Melville, the church of Carstares, the church that Chalmers loved so much that he left it in law to save it in spirit, the church revived under the Macleods and

* See James Buchan's book, *The Expendable Mary Slessor* (The Saint Andrew Press, 1979).

12. Mary Slessor

Charteris himself, might be dissolved. Then its members would be left to choose between joining the Episcopalians, becoming a mere presbyterian sect without an ethos to match that of the Free Kirk or the UPs, and making what terms they could to fit into a church dominated by perhaps the outstanding prelate presbyterianism has produced, Robert Rainy, who had become principal of the Free Kirk's New College five years before Charteris founded *Life and Work.*

Chapter 4
The intrusion of politics

'The gravity of the situation lies in this, that it is now impossible for any Scottish Liberal to be true to the Church of Scotland and yet vote for a follower of Mr Gladstone, unless indeed he can find a representative who, while following Mr Gladstone on other questions, will oppose him in regard to the Church.'

(From *The Church of Scotland; her danger and her duty* by A H Charteris, June 1890.)

'Controversy and prejudice were the great blots on the record of the Church in Victorian Scotland . . . Her different branches were too much intent on dogma, and too little in love', write the notable modern historians Drummond and Bulloch, the latter of whom maintains the tradition that a scholar of distinction may still serve a country parish.

It is a fair judgment, especially if the Kirk is to be judged by its allegiance to its Head and not, say, by mere comparison with the Church of England. Indeed, up to a point the conscious effort of men like Charteris to reunite the Kirk and to maintain lines of communication with other Presbyterians was a tacit admission then of the force of that charge brought against the Kirk now with the historians' benefit of hindsight.

The dogmatic controversy was most acute in the Free Kirk and most significant at the time of the Robertson Smith case. One of the ironies of history is that the controversy was to intensify in political matters when it seemed to be dying down in some spiritual ones, or at least when the most furious doctrinal quarrel had become a kind of private fight within the Free Kirk. It produced, first, the departure from it of the Free Presbyterians, and then the bitterly disputed union of 1900 with the United Presbyterians.

In 1869 the Anglican Church was disestablished in Ireland, where it was the church of at most an eighth of the people, little more than half the protestant population. Pressure was building up for a similar disestablishment in Wales where, in a different denominational context, the same alienation of

13. Lloyd George. Once he got near the top in politics Mr Punch put him in the pulpit of John Knox.

the Anglicans from the majority existed. A young Baptist solicitor called David Lloyd George was reflecting on the rhetorical possibilities of the subject. In England many Free Churchmen, infected by the example of the United States and the liberal doctrines of the age, aimed in the same direction, though most of them supported the party led by Gladstone, the outstanding Anglican layman of his time and the gradual convert via the Peelites from the highest of church-and-state Toryism.

In Scotland the Disruption had been with no thought of disestablishment—that is, for loss of the traditional recognition by the state and the maintenance of traditional income from land. Chalmers, as much as his later admirer Charteris, stood for the national recognition or establishment of religion. The great majority of Scots thought of themselves as Presbyterians: one suspects that even the joke which ends 'but I'm a *Presbyterian* atheist' may really date from the age of Bradlaugh and the agnostic Huxley. The Roman Catholics lacked political power and, despite their largely Irish rank and file, were led by conservative Scots bishops. The Episcopalians, becoming more and more the 'English church' of colloquial speech as their genuinely Scottish traditions mingled with the effects of tractarianism and social climbing, were scarcely likely to press an issue which might be turned against their English brethren.

But two phenomena dramatically changed the outlook. The first was the move of the majority in the Free Kirk towards the United Presbyterians, who gloried in the 'voluntary principle'. They had drifted from the established Kirk (largely in the Original and Relief Secessions) and drifted into notions of disestablishment—and yet they had taken in tow the outstanding leader and political intellect of the Free Kirk, Principal Rainy. The other was the capacity of Gladstone, once so high a Tory, to become more radical as he grew older. And for all his scholarship and genuine spirituality, Gladstone had many of the political crafts of Lloyd George and Harold Wilson. He also had that power of convincing himself that he was doing the Lord's work, which bred the joke credited to Disraeli, the anglican Jew, that he not only had aces up his sleeve but claimed the Almighty had put them there. Drummond and Bulloch date the beginning of the 'pamphlet war' from the report of a UP committee in 1872, when Gladstone's reforming government was showing how significantly Disraeli's Reform Bill had changed British politics.

The Auld Kirk had taken alarm by the time *Life and Work* was established in 1879 and had an Assembly Church Interests Committee from 1882. An unsuccessful back-bench Bill was introduced in 1884 and the following year the Church Interests Committee had raised nearly seven hundred thousand signatures for a defence petition. But at this time Gladstone was approaching the great crisis of his career and his conversion to Irish Home Rule. Despite the lobbying of the UPs and the subtler pressure of Rainy (who was a distant relative of his own, and a cousin of the Perth Liberal MP Charles Stuart Parker), Gladstone drew back from Scottish disestablishment. By the time he really took it up again there had been a dramatic political change in British politics and in the structure of the parties in Scotland.

In 1885 Gladstone, though an old man, seemed set to lead the Liberals as a 'natural majority party' (to use an American concept) until he handed over to the Unitarian Joseph Chamberlain, his natural heir. But the Home Rule crisis saw Chamberlain smash the Liberal Party whose organisation he created. The Liberal Unionists, if allied to the Conservatives (which they did not mean to be but had to become) weakened, but did not break the Gladstonian hold on Scotland. They did, however, draw off some of the Liberals who would have resisted an all-out commitment to disestablishment.

Thus by 1886 the immediate threat of disestablishment had receded, for

Gladstone was out of office and Chamberlain was enabling Lord Salisbury to lead a Conservative government. But if Gladstone got back he was likely, if it suited his book, to yield to the radical Scottish pressure for disestablishment.

Here a minor mystery must be noted. Rainy and Hutton (the dominant figure in the UP campaign) sat on platforms with Gladstone or breakfasted with him. They listened to his table-talk and assumed he took the matter seriousy. Yet modern biographers of Gladstone, or historians fascinated by his dealings with the Irish question, take little or no note of the issue. That is not merely because they are generally English and therefore ill-versed in the niceties of the private feuds of presbyterianism. It is problably also because Gladstone personally was not very deeply involved in disputes of people whose concept of the Church he did not share. He rose from his deathbed to kneel before his clergyman son to take Communion in the Anglican manner. If he ever took the bread and the cup when Rainy presided it would have been because the spirit of Christ or of expediency triumphed over his doctrine; indeed, his private religious enthusiasm in the country of his ancestors was for the Tractarian Episcopal Church there.

The disestablishment argument gathers momentum in the 1880's and reaches a peak by 1890, sustained into the time of Gladstone's fourth and last government which began in 1892, when the Liberals squeezed just ahead of the Conservatives at a General Election which also produced forty-six Liberal Unionists and the eighty-one Irish Home Rulers customary at the time. But in 1894 Gladstone retired and the Government drifted to defeat under Lord Rosebery, whose modern biographers do not dwell at length on their subject's religious convictions. (He attended the kirk at Dalmeny and on occasion crossed the Almond by his own ferry to Cramond.)

What did damp down the disestablishment argument, however, was not the change of premier but the crushing defeat of the Liberals at the 1895 election and the integration of Chamberlain and his followers in the Salisbury Government, though in fact they still claimed to be a distinct party. From then on Charteris needed to say little about disestablishment and there was no need for McMurtrie to cull from the supplements evidence of the local enthusiasm in the parishes for 'church defence'. Charteris, ageing and ready to leave his Chair in 1898, turned again to hopes of distant reunion; Rainy turned his diplomatic or prelatic or jesuitical skills to the revived prospect of union between the Free Church and United Presbyterians. But to Charteris's credit he had never lost his passion for reunion even in the darkest and most bitter days of the disestablishment argument, which were probably almost past by the time of his moderatorial term in 1892. Perhaps his finest and most political polemic was in June 1890: 'The Church of Scotland, her Danger and her Duty'. Lest anyone underestimates the quality of the Christians who became embroiled in the political wrangle, it should be noted that the previous article in *Life and Work* is the last part of that life of the saint about whom his sister, Grisell Baillie, wrote: 'He looked up into Heaven, and as I do not doubt, saw Jesus coming for him'.

No Scottish Liberal could vote for Gladstone, wrote Charteris, and be true to the Church of Scotland, unless he had a candidate who would follow Gladstone in all else but church matters. That meant, incidentally, that in Midlothian, Gladstone's own seat, no loyal church member could vote Liberal at all, squaring his conscience with the hope that *his* Liberal might stand up to the Gladstone-Rainy alliance. In 1892 Charteris was to back a determined attempt to unseat the Grand Old Man there.

Gladstone had, in fact, jumped off one of his earlier fences; and Charteris attacked him as 'making light of the Church which cost Scotland so dear' and as drawing a loyalty of the kind which clung to the Stuarts. 'Scotland has always tried to identify a cause with an idolised leader.'

At times it was rhetoric—holding up the banner of the Reformation and the Covenant—at other times debating to exploit the weakness of the 'Voluntaries' who wanted the state out of religious matters but also wanted the state to 'sanctify the Lord's Day' and maintain Christian teaching in the public schools. At times it was plain political exhortation, asking members to say to all politicians and candidates: 'Hands off the old Kirk of Scotland . . . I shall not vote for you if you are a disestablisher.' The core of the argument was that 'religious equality' was a 'name, a cold shadow in the moonlight which its very devotees cannot grasp . . . national total abstinence from religion'.

In 1891 Charteris was writing of reconstruction, of closing superfluous churches after a few years, emphasising his second favourite theme: that the divisions of Scottish presbyterianism were a scandal but that 'Disestablishment would not end them: only union will.' Causes often survive reasons, and 'God's grace alone can put away the causes of dissension, which are so unreasonable.'

But Charteris was as vigorous a controversialist as any, though inspired by his favourite theme: that there was a need for national establishment (or recognition) of religion. McMurtrie's editorial selection, too, reflected a propagandist journalism to match the mood (or as they would have said) the need of the times. 'Large proportions' of Free Church people in Sutherland are noted as signing against disestablishment—which fitted in with the conservatism which was in a few years to take them out of Principal Rainy's church or, as the courts later said, to take him out of theirs. There were local polls or calculations of parliamentary electors and complaints that Liberal MPs took no notice of constituency feelings.

Gladstone's alliance with the disestablishers drove the Auld Kirk and Charteris into as political an attitude, even in the party sense, as the Scottish church has adopted in modern times, though it was matched by the Free and UP alignment with the Liberals. On each side, of course, large numbers of voters probably continued to support their traditional party or switched for quite different reasons, but the church machines were dangerously close to being geared to party machines. Not all the argument was on this level, for Charteris combined his passion, rhetoric, and command of words with a clear view, perhaps a prophetic view, of the dangers to the church in a secular state. If the 'Voluntaries' theoretically offered to equip the church better to survive and flourish in this new environment (the post-Constantinian era that East Europeans now talk about), they were naive and confused about the benevolent neutrality they expected from the state. But in other hands and with lesser spirits the argument degenerated—as it did on the other side. The Gaelic version of the Free Kirk *Record* and another *Life and Work* controversialist, Dr William Mair of Earlston (Moderator in 1897) were caught up in an argument about whether the Auld Kirk Assembly could open without leave of the Lord High Commissioner and whether Edinburgh was deafened by royal military honours rendered to the Queen's representative.

Another great name of the day in the Kirk, Principal R H Story of Glasgow University (and Moderator in 1894, two years after Charteris) got space to write some strange stuff about the effect of voluntaryism in the United States. To read his account is to see a strange vision of unchurched upstate communities where the protestant denominations have abandoned the field to the Roman Catholics, thanks to the ineffectiveness of 'voluntary' principles: but travellers abroad found it hard to keep off the temporarily obsessive topics. There was a spell when Norway (very fashionable as a tourist country, rather as Scotland had become) attracted attention in *Life and Work*. But even the travelogue-style pieces duly noted how strongly attached the people were to their state church, although priding themselves on being one of the most democratic countries in Europe. It had also to be admitted that they were 'not very zealous' in church attendance and 'not at all strict in Sabbath observance'.

Gladstone's last term is not a happy time in *Life and Work*. The quotations from the parish magazines read like party magazines. In Inveresk those who would barter away the national church are lumped with Esau 'who for one morsel of meat sold his birthright and afterwards found no place of repentance though he sought it carefully with tears.' In Chirnside they quoted John Knox's last message about the merciless devourers of the patrimony of the Kirk. It would take much space even to name all the ministers and laymen who had been thumping the table or the pulpit. Some optimists hoped that the Kirk 'had so many friends in other religious bodies' that the attack would fail. Others blamed the influence of 'atheists, secularists, the godless, and the indifferent'.

There were warnings about the danger of waiting till an election to mount a propaganda campaign—'a hopeless if not criminal plan', said an enthusiast who wanted to create a church defence correspondence column in *Life and Work* as 'more fitting than in the public prints'. He got his own letter in but failed to get his idea accepted in the magazine. Some of his views, however, caught on. In the winter of 1893-94 there were meetings, in Gaelic as well as English, in Highland parishes to be reported. In Kilmore, near Oban, 'everybody in the neighbourhood who was not disabled with influenza was present'. In Appin it was standing-room only; though in Lismore 'no meeting could be held till the influenza abated'. Some of the attraction was perhaps in the equipment and not merely the leaders of the 'crusade'. Despite arguments that the apostles and the martyrs of the Covenant would not have approved, the crusaders went with a magic lantern. In Ayr there had been forty-three meetings between October and Christmas to hear 'the history, work and defence of the Church illustrated by limelight'. The organiser of the campaign, Dr John Pagan of Bothwell, Moderator in 1899, had four hundred requests in a year for his own lecture.

The rules for such meetings were that nothing was to be said to which any other denomination or the members of any party could take legitimate exception, though a lot no doubt depended on what was meant by 'legitimate'.

Even the formalities of the General Assembly were overshadowed by the controversy—most notably in 1893, when the Moderator was Marshall Lang and the Lord High Commissioner was the Marquess of Breadalbane, a Liberal peer, in the Campbell line of one of the few Scottish aristocrats (the then Earl of Breadalbane) to support the Free Church at the time of Disruption in 1843.

In the ornate words of Charteris's biographer, 'it was discovered after the rites of hospitality had been exercised at Holyrood on the eve of the Assembly' that the Lord High Commissioner's speech 'had a conspicuous blank'. It omitted the customary pledge to maintain the Church of Scotland with its presbyterian government.

The reason, apart from the general commitment of the Gladstone government to disestablishment, was a promised first step in a Suspensory Bill which would have withheld stipends from ministers elected after its passing.

The man behind this, and the Lord High Commissioner's speech, was Gladstone's Scottish Secretary, Sir George Trevelyan, father of the great historian and himself a more formidable literary figure than a political one. He had repented of his break with Gladstone over Home Rule but seems to have been one of nature's losers; for he lost out in the fierce backstairs argument over the Breadalbane speech. There was a threat to take the matter to Queen Victoria herself, a Crathie communicant who was neither disestablisher nor Gladstonian, and Trevelyan had to back down. *Life and Work* made nothing of this at the time and merely 'added a sentence to what we might say at much greater length' that his Grace had contributed much to the dignity and efficiency of the Assembly. He had clearly been as relieved as the Moderator when the speech was restored to its traditional form. But Lang had sat with two speeches ready, one 'couched in the usual terms of graceful loyalty' and the other protesting against an unconstitutional and partisan action. Breadalbane included the customary declaration and the protest stayed in Lang's pocket, or wherever Moderators keep their alternative addresses.

But in the first issue after the Assembly there was no quiet 'Sunday Fireside'. Instead Charteris thundered against 'shilly-shallying about not voting', about the threat to the church, and about the need for foreign mission contributions to match the Free Church and UP effort in money as well as prayer. 'Prayers will not be very earnest if the devotee grudge the money.'

To add still more electricity to the atmosphere, 1893 was the fiftieth anniversary of the Disruption and the Free Kirk was singing its own praises very vigorously (as anyone who reads the jubilee *Annals of the Disruption* will discover).

To its credit the General Assembly of the established church recorded its admiration of those who had left the 1843 Assembly for conscience' sake. 'I have a kinsman's pride in the labours and sacrifices which constitute the history of the Church they founded', said Charteris in his St Giles' sermon as retiring Moderator.

But that sermon was an affirmation of the need for a national church, an attack, too, on those in the establishment who gave way to despair in the face of a 'strong stream of objection': 'But we shall resist it, for it is only a summer flood . . . we are the only possible meeting-ground of the scattered Presbyterians of Scotland.' Some day, he claimed, 'If God help us to weather this storm, we shall find ourselves the very Zion of Presbyterianism throughout the world.'

It was to come, but in a very different mood, a very different world from the one in which Queen Victoria went to communion at Crathie and

Gladstone, worn out at last, gave way to Rosebery. There were other tides, apart from the summer flood of the disestablishment campaign, which the church, not just the Kirk of Scotland but the Church of God throughout the world, was to find far harder not only to resist but to know how to resist and how to channel.

But within a year or two of the passions of 1893 the excitement subsided and the magic lanterns could be used for slides of Blantyre or Ichang. The Liberals not only lost power but lost cohesion; by the time they found it again Britain had gone through what seemed at the time a significant imperial war, had seen imperialism (one of the issues to divide the Liberals) reach and pass its zenith, and bred a new generation of radicals who gave a far lower priority to disestablishment. Moreover the denominational structure of Scotland had been changed by the merger of the Free Church and the United Presbyterians, at the cost of the alienation of a mainly Highland 'Wee Free' minority and a long-lasting lawsuit which gave Principal Rainy more controversy than even he bargained for.

New men were to take over in the new era. In 1898, the year Charteris left his Chair, editor McMurtrie retired after nineteen years as editor of *Life and Work*. He had also, since becoming foreign mission convener in 1885, been the Kirk's foremost advocate of the missionary cause, as his moderatorship in 1904 recognised. He died in 1912.

His successor was Archibald Fleming, a Perth son of the manse and Edinburgh graduate who, like many able ministers of the day, also studied in German universities. He was a rising and gifted literary minister, regarded as a *protégé* of the editor and imperialist poet W E Henley, and said to have been a favourite preacher of Queen Victoria in her last years. He might in due course have been expected to move from Edinburgh's Tron Kirk to somewhere even more notable. In fact he was lost to *Life and Work* but not the Kirk fairly soon because he went off to London as minister of St Columba's, Pont Street. As it turned out his main contributions to *Life and Work* during less than four years (the shortest term of any editor after Charteris) were in handling the incorporation of the old *Mission Record* (whose circulation had been 36,000) and through coverage of the war in South Africa which was already looming in 1898 and which was to be a far longer, costlier, and more painful affair than anyone expected.

But it would be wrong to take leave of the Victorian founding fathers of *Life and Work* with a chapter which concentrates on the feud which inevitably took up so much of their attention. It would be misleading, too, to give the impression that accounts of zeal for good works or missionary organisation can give a complete or even adequate picture of the life of the church in those days. As always the life and work of the church reflected the inner Christian lives of its people. At its worst Victorian piety was only too easily attacked as the hypocrisy which in some cases it doubtless covered. At its best it matched the Christian devotion of any age. Take, for example, the Baillies. Lady Grisell was the first deaconess. Her brother, Major Robert Baillie, was regarded by Charteris as almost an ideal elder. When he came to his 'mirthful, happy, joyous breakfast' he had already prayed and dressed with a devotional book open before him. At 9 am he conducted family prayers, then joined his sister in

14. Editor Fleming

a long intercessory prayer, after which she read the Bible aloud to him. Later in the morning he read alone, 'searching' the scriptures and preparing evening family prayers; and only after *evening* prayers did he read the morning newspapers.

> Every afternoon he spent (as an elder of Bowden in the Borders) in visiting his dear flock. He read the Bible in some houses, not all; he prayed in every house and with everyone, well or ill. He did not wait to be asked.

Some silly people outside (perhaps even inside) the modern church would call Baillie a religious fanatic; another church would start seeking miracles attributed to him and call him a saint. But the miracles were to be found in the revival of the discredited established remnant of 1843, and not least in the Committee for Christian Life and Work, conceived at a prayer meeting in Queen Street, Edinburgh.

It would be easy to point out that Baillie was a gentleman of leisure—easy but misleading; for every minute of the day was planned for God's glory and his work. At its best Victorian piety influenced all classes, especially when General Booth and others reached the poorest class. It could find expression,

15. R. M. Ballantyne

for example, in homely verses of people of powerful mind, passionate zeal, and no wealth or position.

Looking for the 1894 obituary of R M Ballantyne (who wrote six serials for *Life and Work* after 'Philosopher Jack'), the present editor came across a poem in Scots, probably in an Ayrshire idiom, in the magazine. Many such, to be honest, he has skipped, for nineteenth century popular literary taste is often not ours. Above Ballantyne's portrait was this 'Evening Prayer', and it was readable. It is about a kind and couthie granny, telling of a happy hame above where the bairnies dwell with Jesus free frae ilka taint of sin, ending:

> May the loving arms o' Jesus
>   draw us near Him as He whispers
> A hope of life for ever free frae
>   worldly care or strife;
> May we fa' asleep committin' our
>   souls into his keepin,
> Till we wauken i' the mornin'
>   born to everlastin' life.

The poet was J Keir Hardie.

Was it the J Keir Hardie of whom the world was to hear much more in another context? Apparently it was, for though there is only the name to the poem, the letters MP are added in the index, and Keir Hardie was elected for West Ham South in 1892.

Does it matter? But the name emphasises that the faith, the works, the idealism of Victorianism (often diluted and inevitably adapted), inspired much that mattered in our own century. Let us not judge those who diverted so much of their energy into Christian quarrels that mean little to us. They did much more, and they saw some things more clearly than we do.

It would be easy to highlight the weaknesses and limitations of *Life and Work* in these late Victorian decades as a full record of the life, especially the intellectual life, of the Kirk, far less the world Church. There is little, for example, about the Cairds, or about the German scholars whose names mattered so much at the time in the history of theology. There is little of note about religion and science, though given the dullness of many Victorian books on the theme that may be a blessing. (It was the Free Kirk that had the Christian man of science, Henry Drummond, still eminently readable, just as it was the Free Kirk which had George Adam Smith and, more controversially, Robertson Smith.)

But the nation's life is about people, not intellectual controversies. The

16. Professor George Adam Smith

remarkable thing is how much of what Charteris and McMurtrie put together speaks from the kind of experience which a century of scientific and technological revolution has largely left unchanged.

Chapter 5
An intrusion from Africa: The Boer War 1899-1902

'He whom angels guarded at Atbara and Omdurman fell at length, when his time came, at Magersfontein. The tale is all too harrowing to retell, for the day was another Flodden'.

(The editor of *Life and Work* on the death of General Wauchope of the Highland Brigade during the Boer War, January 1901.)

At the time the Boer War seemed a very great war, the first since Waterloo really to touch the life of the British people.

As things turned out it was soon to be overshadowed by a very different and much greater war. And as things turned out in South Africa itself, the people who appeared to have lost the war were soon well on the way to winning the peace and creating the new united South Africa after their own fashion.

But something of the Great Boer War, as Conan Doyle and others called it to distinguish it from the Majuba campaign of twenty years earlier, went into British history and tradition: Kipling's horsemen bound for Table Bay; the relief of Mafeking and the mafficking that followed; the goodbye to Dolly Gray and with it a goodbye to a century of splendid isolation and a decade of unbridled imperialism.

It was also to bring problems of conscience and involvement for the churches: it was, after all, a Scots Presbyterian, Sir Henry Campbell-Bannerman, who coined the phrase about 'methods of barbarism' used against the Afrikaners whose descendants today are so frequently accused of methods of barbarism by ecumenical and other church groups. Yet it was Scots Presbyterians with such names as Murray and Robertson who had maintained and renewed the Dutch Reformed Church after the British occupation of the

Cape. They had worked there when others had developed mission work among the 'Kaffirs' who were to be variously spectators and victims of the white men's civil war in South Africa, sometimes carriers of information and supplies as well as hewers of wood, drawers of water, and a source of labour for the mines which were so largely the occasion for an old quarrel becoming a modern war. Occasionally, as among the Basuto, they were participants on the fringe of the war or, like the future black editor Sol Plaatje at Mafeking, passionately committed observers. The battlefield was close to the mission field; and the Boers of the Transvaal and the Orange Free State who inherited Scottish theology (and in some cases Scottish ancestry) were at odds not only with the imperial government so imperiously represented by Lord Milner but with the British element in South Africa, including the Scots who formed the 'colonial congregations' there of the Kirk.

As Milner and Kruger, old enough to have been at odds with David Livingstone, prepared for war by trying to put each other in the wrong in long drawn-out negotiation, *Life and Work* was a pretty placid pitch on which a new editor was quietly playing himself in.

There was the quarrel of Auld Kirk and disestablishers, still rambling on despite the death of Gladstone, the Liberal internal quarrels, and the consolidation of the Liberal Unionists with the Tories to form a solidly-based government. In it Joseph Chamberlain, the Unitarian who once squared up to Anglicans over education, was Milner's superior and ally. The African references are more often to Blantyre in Central Africa than to the rand, though the great missionary Dr Stewart of Lovedale (a UF Moderator) had earned a few lines of favourable mention by coming out against disestablishment.

As war approached there was a picture of a brand new 'fifteenth century' spire at Craiglockhart in Edinburgh and support for an inebriates' home in which habitual drunkards might be sent, after conviction, for cure.

There was a minister's wife deploring 'the privations of the clergy' with few holidays, few books, growing families, and one unfamiliar verse to go with that refrain still sung today: the dread of the financial burden which sickness brought to the manse. 'No educated man', it was claimed, 'in other position is as poorly paid as the clergyman.'

As war approached there was also praise for a Jew in Odessa rejoicing (prematurely as it happened) over a retrial of the Dreyfus case, and said to have called for the revision of the verdict 'in another unjust trial which ended in unjust sentence of death long ago'. And as war actually began, and as the Boers swept into Natal to besiege Ladysmith, the Duke of Argyll was being thanked in *Life and Work* for presenting Iona Cathedral to the Church. 'It only remains for some generous churchman to undertake the restoration of the ancient building and beautify it once more to prepare it for the regular offices of praise and prayer.'

The Boer War was to mark the end of an era, and the British Empire was never to be quite the same again. But it is always easier for historians writing after the event to see turning points and watersheds of history. The war in South Africa made a fairly slow entrance into the monthly columns of *Life and Work*. Perhaps editor Fleming had already learned enough to reckon with the hazards of a monthly schedule; and at the end of 1899, as someone later said in another African context, it looked as if it might all be over in a matter of weeks rather than months—far less drag on into 1902. Moreover the British public was used to colonial wars in which the tribesmen put up a stiff fight—Fuzzy-wuzzy, said Kipling, was a first-class fighting man—before being efficiently brought to submission. But this white tribe of Africa, Calvinist cousins after a fashion of the Scots, were a tougher proposition. They were not only marksmen who had learned to use the cover of the *kopjes* but pioneers of a new kind of mobility and flexibility.

Chaplains, like generals, probably underrated them. The first impact of the war in the Kirk's columns is at second-hand. The editor quoted the magazine's 'Soldiers' and Sailors' Supplement' in the course of an appeal for £30 to send both supplement and a 'Soldier's Prayer-book' to South Africa. He quoted the kind of pun that ought to be a court-martial offence:

> Never injure a woman. Don't carry a spirit bottle into battle with a Boer: it will make your courage just like his—Dutch.

Even with the turn of the year, and the 'Black Week' of British defeats, there seems almost the exact opposite of what the instinctive approach of most churchmen would be today. Instead of the all-consuming urge to be 'relevant' there is a restraint that is almost a retreat into pietism, though this mood was not to last.

'In the state of public affairs assuredly there is much that calls for courage, thoughtfulness and prayer', wrote Dr Norman Macleod of Inverness (elected Moderator later that year) in the magazine's first article of 1900, after a few words about the dark shadow of war. But it is only as a prelude to an exposition of a very personal, even private, religion.

> Our highest blessedness must ever be found in the discovery of God's lifeplan for ourselves—in other words, in the secret guidance of the Almighty. How strong in its repose! How full of restfulness is such a conception of human life.

57

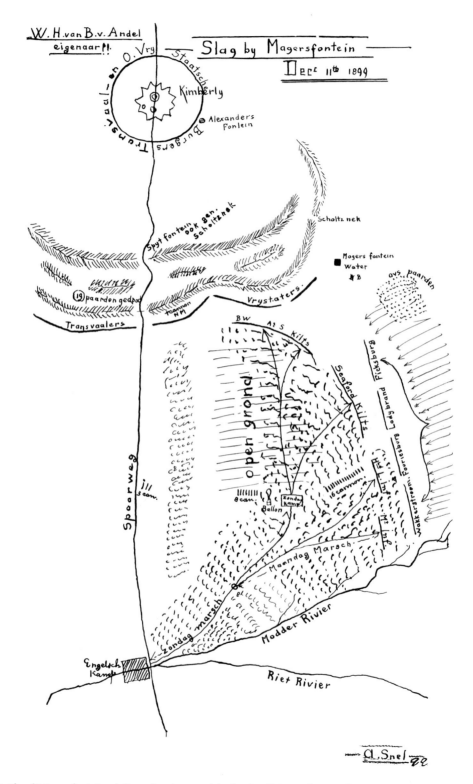

17. Battle of Magersfontein. A Boer sketch map of the battle of Magersfontein showing Highland Brigade positions.

Then the tide of war flows more strongly—carrying with it indifferent verse, that occupational hazard which all editors of *Life and Work* are bound to encounter; but still the editor seems to be resisting the tide of war-talk, although noting that it has been discussed 'from many standpoints' in the local parish magazines—still the 'supplements' in the idiom of the day. He had also, he said, 'able sermons' before him—a gentle word presumably addressed to those whose thoughts he didn't want to publish. But soon the consequences of the war are coming thick and fast; another appeal for the increased expense of taking on more military chaplains; talk of the 'great straits' to which Scottish ministers in South Africa had been reduced by the war; and reflections on heroism from a former moderator, Dr Archibald Scott, who believed that, 'forced into this war by dishonest and disloyal conspirators, we can only answer their appeal to the God of Battles by placing our army and our resources at His disposal.'

'Steady boys, steady' ended this flow of ex-moderatorial rhetoric. The first weeks of 1900 called for some steadying influence, especially after the battle that really brought home to Scotland that this was to·be a far more costly business in blood and tears than even the fiercest skirmish on the North-West Frontier. At Magersfontein, on the Free State frontier (the route of any force seeking to relieve Kimberley from the South), the Highland Brigade was thrown against a well-entrenched enemy—for war on the veldt at this stage was not quite as open as often supposed—and took terrible losses; and among the dead was Major General A E Wauchope, the brigade commander and a leading layman of the Kirk.

Wauchope, a midshipman before joining the Black Watch, was a politician as well as soldier and churchman. As Colonel Wauchope of Niddrie he had run Gladstone fairly close as Tory candidate at the 1892 General Election, the only occasion in Midlothian after the famous 1879-80 campaign there at which the Grand Old Man was under any pressure. He had given special pleasure to what might be called the establishment of the Establishment by his powerful defence of the Auld Kirk, though as an elder and 'constant attender' at the General Assembly he had made a virtue of soldierly brevity ('I am no theologian, nor am I an ecclesiastic; I am a soldier, I second the motion', ran one of his speeches).

'There was never a more honest, more gallant, more godly Christian gentleman', wrote editor Fleming in the review quoted at the beginning of this chapter of a biography of Wauchope rushed out a few months after his death. But an obscurer note immediately after the event about a crowded memorial service at Newcraighall (a parish with its pits as well as its laird) has its social

18. Padre Robertson

commentary as revealing as the praise given to the Tory Wauchope for helping distressed miners during a bitter coal strike of 1894. 'Is the Church built by the help of our dead friend, and meant for the use and benefit of the people, to be crowded for once and then to be deserted, scantily attended, disregarded?' That seemed to be the way of it.

But it was a few months before the Kirk's magazine had really caught up with events. South Africa was a long way off by the sea-route to the Cape; and the telegraph, so much used by that constellation of war correspondents in which young Winston Churchill shone so brightly, was presumably beyond the budget of the editor and his committee. Then, as now, a monthly had its problems as a news medium.

In fact it would appear that *Life and Work* was scooped after a fashion by the Kingussie supplement, which had got an account of the Highland Brigade's activities from its senior chaplain, James Robertson, just after the Modder River battle but before Magersfontein. *Life and Work's* own war news-coverage had only got as far as somewhere on the voyage out, with another Kirk chaplain, John Bird, having to share the Church of England service with the ship's captain on a troopship with drafts for English regiments. The reluctance to pose as an English clergyman left the main role to the captain, although he too was a Scot of the Auld Kirk. In fact the article was a bit padded out by reflections on the advantages of set forms of prayer. Chaplain Bird sounded a bit on the high side.

But while *Life and Work* was waiting for its news service to start functioning—editor Fleming had written to the Highland Brigade chaplain and was waiting for a reply—the war made its impact.

Ruskin was quoted on his 'strange and very dreadful' discovery: 'When I tell you that war is the foundation of all the arts I mean also that it is the foundation of the high virtues and faculties of men.' And 'a woman' supplied thoughts on the war for womenfolk at home, some of them apparently having their sadness 'deepened by an uneasy feeling that war is wicked and cannot be blessed by God.' She wanted them to strengthen their sons and husbands and brothers to do their duty and wrote:

> First, be sure that things could not go on as they were before the war. Without understanding the politics, we may understand that a great nation like our own has great responsibilities and that shame and ruin would soon overtake us if we cared only to be comfortable at home and were indifferent to oppression and injustice in other parts of the Empire. Mistakes have been made in the past—often from a weak dread of war—

but no human being can say 'I never made a mistake'. And unless we had as a nation deliberately turned our backs on those who trusted us we could not have avoided this war. If we read our Bible, we shall see how often war was used by God to work out His purposes for men; and we may believe that to-day He can bring from this terrible struggle the results of peace and justice for generations yet unborn.

Is there a hint there of the feeling that the Boers were oppressive in their 'native policy'? (though clearly the 'Uitlanders' are thought of as the immediate victims of injustice). And is there a warning about those who today, even over Africa, want to be relevant and committed?

It was April 1900 before first-hand material of real quality about the war was appearing in *Life and Work*; and again it was from Padre Robertson, who had appeared before Magersfontein in the Kingussie pages.

Journalistically, the style is old-fashioned even for 1900. 'Dear Mr Fleming', Robertson began, 'you must not think me remiss in not answering your note re contributions to *Life and Work*.'

But the despatch is timeless in some things; in others an important record of the mood of the moment after Magersfontein. 'The mail has just come in. There is angry indignation over the adverse criticisms passed on the Highland Brigade in some of the reports of Magersfontein', wrote Robertson, warmly defending the men he served, and adding under orders: 'I'm not to refer to General Wauchope'.

His role, he explained, was not just a chaplain's:

I am on Lord Methuen's staff and am not at liberty to send articles for publication. I might have stretched a point in the case of a church magazine, only, as perhaps you know, I was employed on duty outside a chaplain's province—despatch-riding and regarding prisoners etc, so I feel under a double restraint.

But Robertson had all too much a chaplain's sadder duties. He had written letters to next-of-kin (not just dictating and signing them) and he had to bear other burdens:

Think of my burying 176 after Magersfontein, the great majority of whom I had to handle and identify alone as the Boers would not allow anyone else near their trenches.

While the work had to be done a sense of duty kept him going, but reaction set in—especially as only he and a colonel remained of seven members of Wauchope's original brigade staff who messed together.

19. Fighting Mac: Sir Hector Macdonald

After crying out of the depths 'literally with strong crying and tears', he was cheered by communion, which he announced without preliminary notice or preparation, dispensing in the circumstances with forms of procedure, and inviting all to partake:

> To my great surprise, knowing how backward young men, Highlanders especially, are in coming to the Lord's Table, but to my heart's joy, over 250 stepped out and many more would have come if it had not been for the fact that they had to go at once on picket duty ... The heartening came most opportunely for I was sore, sore needing it.

Robertson also cheered up with the arrival of his old campaigning friend Hector Macdonald ('Fighting Mac') who took over the Brigade. The chaplain was a Speyside man who had already served in the Sudan and had been mentioned in despatches.

His South African service, which earned him not only a DSO but also an Aberdeen DD, is said to have made his name a 'household word' in Scotland. Later an Anglican chaplain reported that at Magersfontein Robertson risked his life under fire, especially in trying to find Wauchope's body: 'Why he was not killed in his fearless efforts I cannot say.' But he was spared to leave the Army in 1904 for a long ministry in Methven and survived till 1929.

The trivia of war flowed in now to *Life and Work*. There is a story of sermon notes captured by the Boers and then (in the idiom of a later Army generation) liberated by the British advance and then preached. The Cadzow Parish Supplement records that the minister's little daughter had written to 'Fighting Mac' about his wounded foot—'entirely at her own instigation'—and got a letter back beginning 'Dear Fairy'. The Bishop of Rochester gets a favourable mention for warning clergy and laity against standing Tommy Atkins too many drinks when he comes back from the war. (Many must have been the blessings called down on his episcopal head!) Later Lord Wolseley, who had been the Army's commander-in-chief and archetype of colonial campaigners, mingled an appeal for help for old soldiers with his own warning about 'intoxicating liquour'.

But once Kimberley was relieved and the tide of battle turned (and the war, quite wrongly, seemed all but over) there were siege survivors anxious to tell the tale.

Peter Milne had been the Colonial Committee's minister in Beaconsfield, Kimberley, and an 'irregular member of the town guard', Like most of the diamond town's white population he seems to have been an admirer of Cecil Rhodes. 'The native question', he wrote, was a source of anxiety, 'but Mr

Rhodes relieved the difficulty by starting relief works on which the boys found employment.'

He also had a view of providence which nowadays may seem simplistic:

> We could not fail to notice our providential escapes. Shells fell on every side of us, and of our congregation none was struck. Hundreds fell round our Church and yet they seemed to choose the vacant spots on which to fall.

As some towns were relieved others were occupied, among them Bloemfontein, the Free State capital. The Presbyterian minister there was James Craig, who took advantage of enforced leisure while convalescing from typhoid to record the anxiety and suspense of the British in Bloemfontein during the days of the Boer successes. He had been the first of the English-speaking ministers to get permission to hold services for British prisoners of war, his permit coming from a Free State official with the un-Afrikaans name of James Collins and the town jailor who turned out to be an old British soldier. He also recorded how the Scots of Bloemfontein had rallied to the support of fifty Black Watch and Seaforth prisoners from Magersfontein who were marched through the streets. The minister, the only Scot allowed to see them, brought tobacco, fruit, and £12 which an old Aberdonian had raised in a morning's whip-round.

But soon the tables were turned and Padre Robertson was being invited to preach in Mr Craig's pulpit, with a great crowd and choir joining to sing 'God Save the Queen'. However the British Army's losses were not mainly from Boer marksmanship or captures—though on the bare veldt isolated detachments went 'into the bag' as they did forty years later in the desert—but from fever. Illness spread from troops to civilians and by May there were five-thousand sick and wounded in Bloemfontein, with the old Boer parliament house, the Raadzaal, pressed into service as a hospital. Craig was busier than ever, finding his faith strengthened, he said, by the testimony of the sick and the dying.

Another report of hospitals came from the minister of Inchinnan near Paisley, the Rev R McLelland, who had gone to South Africa as an 'extra chaplain with the forces', and was sent at first to the base hospital at Rondebosch—an improvised affair of marquees in which he conceded things 'were capable of improvement in some important respects'. Although he claimed not to be casting any reflection on the RAMC, Chaplain McLelland was a forthright commentator, which may be why a careful editor pushed a later note from him to the foot of a column of 'Notes in Passing'. 'The care of the sick and wounded is yet far from perfection', he wrote, 'it is a most faulty state of matters to find as I did recently 256 sick men in a divisional hospital of tents intended for only 100 patients.' A little later McLelland was writing with feeling of the burial of Camerons killed at the battle of Spitz Kop, in what Britain now called 'the Orange River Colony'.

For a while the war coverage in *Life and Work* lost something of its sense of urgency. This was the phase in which the war seemed over, with total British victory in the field and annexation of the Boer Republics. There were also distractions: an appeal, for example, for the Central African *Life and Work* printed far to the north of the war at the Blantyre mission, and a curious intimation that the Sober Scot Society, described as an 'offensive and defensive allliance' against treating (and drinking between meals) and listing Professor Charteris among its vice-presidents, had changed its name to the Scottish Self-Control Society.

The magazine itself was much concerned with the incorporation at last of the *Mission Record* of the Kirk, while much mission enthusiasm that might have gone into South African peace-making was distracted by the Boxer rebellion and the perils of the Chinese uprisings. Notable events at home ranged from the death of Queen Victoria and the start of a new reign to the arrival of a Moderator (James Mitchell of South Leith) who 'is remarkable for three things; he gets up at five o'clock every morning; he is master of seven or eight languages, and he preaches in the good and wise old manner of our fathers right through the Bible chapter by chapter.' And the 'khaki election' had come and gone, leaving *Life and Work* more than content that 'for the first time in many years' there was a majority of Scottish MPs not pledged to support disestablishment.

Back at the war chaplain Bird, that lover of set prayers on the troopship, appeared again to convey something of the new phase of the campaign when the work of the chaplain was 'much interfered with' by the garrison's unrest at Barberton in the East Transvaal in face of the new guerrilla attacks. He was also a bit sour, if honest, in complaining that the attendance of soldiers at communions was 'disappointingly small'. (Perhaps they didn't like his style or his liking for set prayers). The secular tone and materialistic 'tone and temper' which he found in the Army made if difficult (he claimed) to get 'even well-meaning men' in the mood for the sacrament. But at another post he found not only soldiers but local 'English and Dutch' residents coming to evening services.

The Kirk's 'colonial Committee', which was in close touch with the South African Presbyterians, also had contacts with the army. In Newcastle, Natal, the minister, the Rev D McFarlane, was reporting in September 1901 that attendance of the troops 'fluctuates very much' because of the constant changing of units. He also caught the spirit of what was a civil war in white South Africa in noting that the war was not likely to finish in 1901, but he added: 'Colonists, many of them, think that if they could have their way it would be all over in six weeks. But they never got their way.'

Despite these hints of the jingo sympathies which were common in Natal his ministry also extended to the Natal Boers. He noted a wedding he conducted among a family in which 'two of the bride's brothers are now in prison for rebellion and the bridegroom's brother is a prisoner in Ceylon.'

Indeed as the war dragged on a surprising amount of goodwill towards the Boers begins to appear. Chaplain T A Cameron (from Farnell near Brechin but with the Gordons) found that being a Scots minister made his visits to Boer prisoners always welcome: 'The bond of a common Presbyterianism has its effect'. However, he added a bit of ritualistic jingoism to make up for this Christian humanity and reformed fraternity: 'They have been the victims of designing knaves who have not had punishment meted out to them in any way proportionate to their demerits.'

Cameron, who noted a little primly that he reported according to War Office instructions to the general at the Cape and not, as someone had tried to get him to do, to the senior episcopal chaplain, was really a Black Watch man. But his battalion had been broken up into details—a symptom of the guerrilla war—and he found himself with the Gordons. He also narrowly missed death in a train accident on the way north from Pretoria to Pietersburg.

Another chaplain to show increasing goodwill towards the Boers as time went on was chaplain Bird. Well before the end of the war (for publication in December 1901) he was writing of the Scots ministers in the Dutch Reformed Church and of the summing-up by an Anglican of Afrikaner attitudes: 'The Boers do not like foreigners, although they prefer Scotchmen very much to other nationalities, as being linked to them by the same church polity and creed.' He wrote of bridging the gap in South Africa, which he called one of race hatred. But he meant the gap between Boer and Briton, and in this piece never mentioned the word 'black'. He wanted the church to foster a spirit of brotherhood and thought the Church of Scotland might have a providential mission, which he didn't try to relate to practical suggestions, in dealings with the 'Dutch Church in Africa'.

What one misses in *Life and Work* is pro-Boer feeling of a more political kind, though this had never been absent from the radical wing of British politics. (It is, of course, a supreme irony of our own times that the ultra-right of jingo ancestry should find some sympathy with the Boers' descendants and that the liberals and radicals should often give the impression of hating not merely a South African attitude but the nation for whom the Boer War is the 'second war of independence.')

This was clearly a more sensitive issue for the editor of the United Free *Record*—still known as *The Missionary Record*—which had been formed with union of the majority of the Free Kirk and the United Presbyterians in 1900. Both churches had been more sensitive on the political issue, though there was a Free (later UF) regular chaplain, the Rev Thomas Murray, with the Gordons who fought in Natal and were besieged in Ladysmith. When the UF editor wrote of opinion being much divided about the war he meant, *inter alia*, that it was dividing his own Kirk. He also, thanks to the greater UF missionary interest in South Africa, allowed contributors to develop, in relation to South Africa, a theme about the value of missions in relation to cultural development, and its political implications, which is less obvious in *Life and Work* at this stage. Later it was to emerge in relation to India and to the Central African missions.

But attacks on white men's attitudes to black men in Africa are most evident after the Boer War had been won; and the most obvious targets are not the beaten Boers but the mine-owning allies of Mr Chamberlain who wanted to recruit in Nyasaland. By 1903 *Life and Work in Central Africa*, printed in Blantyre, was indignant and some of the indignation spilled into the parent magazine. Dr Hetherwick of Blantyre wrote in April 1903 that the South African colonist had 'notoriously failed with the native question' by failing to train Africans in 'habits of industry'. But one of his complaints about the exploitation of Africans in the mines was that wages were six times the local rate and would encourage men to learn new vices and be 'idle loafers' with money they didn't know how to spend properly. The women, he said, would be left to till the fields.

Life and Work took a rather Tory line with the denunciation of 'methods of barbarism' against the Boers—perhaps not so much because Campbell-Bannerman was an advocate of disestablishment but because of the powerful influence in print of the Army chaplains. Chaplain Cameron held services in Boer 'concentration camps' crowded with non-combatants and denounced the 'insane outcry' against them. The name, of course, had not the ghastly association of thirty or forty years later and it could be argued that the 'concentration' was not merely to cut the guerrilla-war commandos off from their support and sustenance but to prevent the civilian population from starving when the war became an attempt to isolate the Boers from their supplies. Cameron took the Kitchener line that the camps derived from a policy dictated 'not only by military necessity but by humanity' and hoped that 'we shall hear no more on this subject from hysterical ladies who would be better employed at home'. That was unkind and unfair to the great humanitarian Emily Hobhouse and it skirted what seems to have been the truth of the matter: that the Boer women and children (and many black 'displaced persons' in camps) were victims, like the fever-stricken soldiers the chaplains helped and buried, of the inadequacy of the medical organisation and knowledge of the time to cope with the problems of crowded camp life in South African conditions. There may have been a grain of deadly truth in his complaint that all the Boers had to complain of was too good and rich a diet. There was not a shadow of truth' he said, in the ruthless charges brought by 'those who seem to glory in traducing our army'. The soldiers, he said, were humane and generous as well as brave; and ready to share their rations and last bit of tobacco with Boer prisoners.

But perhaps chaplain Cameron should take his leave on a kindlier note. When he was at Pietersburg he preached at the black location with two interpreters, one for the Basuto and the other 'in the Kaffir tongue'— presumably Xhosa or a related language. The Africans, no doubt deciding that a little flattery would not go wrong, let him know they had debated whether he was 'a great English boss or a great Scotch boss'. 'I told them', he said, 'that I was no big boss at all, but a humble Christian, as I hoped they all were.'

But by the time the humble Christian chaplain had got into print the war was all over bar the final formalities of Vereeniging. For South Africa it was no more than the end of a beginning. For the Empire it was not exactly the beginning of the end, but things could never be the same again.

A different kind of era had ended while white men in khaki, or in floppy hats and shapeless jackets, chased or ambushed each other on the veldt. Though it did not make too much of the fact, the Auld Kirk was aware that Edward VII's lifestyle was by no means that of his mother, that devoted communicant of Crathie Kirk whose occupation was entered on the roll there as 'Queen'. There would still be royal chaplains but they were no longer likely to be royal confidants.

But something more important had passed with the Victorian age. The Church, and especially the protestant churches, were passing the zenith of their social and temporal importance. Young Mr George, the notorious pro-Boer, was soon to be better known for denouncing dukes and offering 'ninepence for fourpence'. Disestablishment no longer concerned him or others quite so much. The social-security ethic was to become more obvious than the protestant work-ethic.

The great age of church-building was passing. With the creation of the United Free Church, and the Highland emphasis among the Wee Frees, Lowland Scotland often found it had three kirks where two might do. And although the Auld Kirk commented cautiously there were many hints, some of them in *Life and Work*, that the UF union, combining voluntary enthusiasm with Chalmers' (and Charteris's) passion for national recognition of religion, might be a vital stage on the way to a reunion of the whole Kirk.

Chapter 6
Edwardians and after

'If not new, Socialism has entered on a new phase. The different schools are combining under more practical and human impulses, so that they seem less than formerly to be advocates of a perverse economic upheaval. Large sections of the Socialist ranks that inherit the hostile bias towards the Church begin to learn and appreciate that ideal passion for the service of man, 'the enthusiasm of humanity' which has always been a characteristic of the Church.'

(From 'The Church and Social Questions' by the Rev A S Martin of Aberdeen, *Life and Work*, October 1908.)

The new reign began in 1901. Although it was to create an atmosphere that we now think of as Edwardian it was to be the shortest tenure of any monarch from Victoria's accession to the present day—excepting only the uncrowned interlude of the later Edward.

But on the Auld Kirk's editorial throne the shortest reign was succeeded by the longest. Editor Fleming was called to be a fashionable London minister at St Columba's, earning English compliments as an enthusiast for church unity and (from *The Daily Telegraph*) praise as a 'popular and earnest preacher'. There is nothing, it is claimed, 'of the stern and dour aspect of worship at St Columba's that the Southron is too wont to connect with Presbyterianism'. But to Dr Fleming's future credit was not only his long ministry in London and his zeal for reunion of the Kirk, but his success comparatively late in life as a pioneer religious broadcaster. He was also an honest observer of London life. When he got there he noted that the continental Sunday had come to London, that eighty per cent of the population never went to church; and that there was more hope among the 'honest unbelievers of the working class' than the 'pleasure-seeking pagans who are found at the opposite pole of society.' He died in July 1941 not knowing that his kirk had been destroyed in the devastation of the great air raid of May 10.

In his place came Robert Fisher, who had not long since moved from the West Church of Aberdeen and was later to move again from Morningside in

Edinburgh to St Cuthbert's. Although he died in 1934, seven years before Fleming, R H Fisher was to remain editor of *Life and Work* for twenty-two years—roughly from the end of the Boer War to the end of the first Labour goverment. Another son of the manse, he grew up in Orkney and graduated from Edinburgh to be assistant in St Bernard's to its editor-minister McMurtrie. He was described as a mixture of moderate evangelical and high churchman, sympathetic to the high Scottish Church Society on worship but holding to a more traditional reformed doctrine. Late in life—too late—he turned down the opportunity to be Moderator of the General Assembly. He was

20. Editor Fisher

an individualist in some things but a hard worker on the Union Committee preparing the way for the reunion of the Kirk. He combined personal humility with a dislike, sometimes evident in his editorship, for place-seekers, climbers and ostentation.

Fleming bowed out with a few words about his recent troubles which made it sound as if he was none too sorry to go. The fusion of the elements of *Life and Work* with the incorporation of *The Mission Record* had not produced an ideal result', though it made it *the* magazine and not just *a* magazine of the Kirk. A symptom of the problem is a quarterly supplement made up mainly of records of financial contributions and statements of account. Notices in it had to be paid for but on at least one occasion it reached fifty ponderous pages. Another is the way the worthy but almost as ponderous 'News of Female Missions' became a kind of supplement to a supplement, the livelier *Woman's Guild Life and Work*, the ancestor of today's Guild magazine *Spotlight*.

There had been denunciations from rival quarters of the domination of 'literature' and of 'missions', and the Christian Life and Work convener, Dr William Robertson, in effect the chairman of the board, called it 'an exceptionally trying and critical period'. The lavish praise he poured on Fleming's departing head looks as if it gained some of its distinctive flavour from a good deal of grumbling that had been going on behind the scenes.

A clumsy but long-lasting compromise was the inclusion of a magazine within a magazine—the missionary 'In Far Fields' section whose eventual autonomy, with separate editor and even editorials, reflected the financial arrangements that paid for the extra pages, though it was 1909 before this arrangement reached the form which survived with little change for the twenty years till the reunion of the Kirk. The most notable of its editors, a writer of grace and distinction elsewhere in *Life and Work*, was the Rev. Dr Thomas Marjoribanks of Colinton.

But Fleming had an even larger ladle to dish out praise of his successor. Fisher's appointment, he claimed, automatically ensured the confidence and approbation of the church and aroused 'the most confident anticipations of an editorship of exceptional brilliance'. In fact the early years of Fisher's editorship are not very lively even by Edwardian standards. The new editor had to play himself in on this wicket that had rolled out awkwardly after the take-over of *Mission Record* and its obsessive recording in print of financial detail. He did, however, launch a *Life and Work* prize competition, the prizes being publication of winning entries and a guinea. (He reserved the right to publish other entries and pay nothing!) The first competition was a prize for the best suggestion for a competition and the firstfruits of the tree thus planted was an invitation to offer articles on 'The Helpful Sermon', subject to one condition: 'no names of living Scottish preachers must be used'. Later the competition moved on to the use of the psalms and even anthems in worship but in due time Miss Wilson, a school teacher at Abercorn, got her guinea and a column and a half. Her entry, a short story with a good deal of teaching in it, probably pleased the ministers since part of its moral was that unhelpful sermons might be the fault of the listeners and not the preacher.

The young people in the story tell their wise old auntie that they're too fond of criticising sermons. 'It's a bad habit', said Aunt Martha, 'and one that dies hard in us Scotch folk.' She could say that again! No doubt the grandchildren of the young people still do.

But editor Fisher had another reason for not moving far too fast in *Life and Work*. He had scarcely been a year in the job when he found himself lined up for a six months' trip to Australia, with leading lights of the Kirk to take his place in the Morningside pulpit and his assistant handling even more of the weddings and funerals than usual. The trip—four months at Scots Kirk, Melbourne, plus a round-the-world trip in the travelling, paid for by the

Australians—seems to have kept the Melbourne Scots happy while their minister, who had been Christian Life and Work vice-convener when he was in Callander, came back to visit Scotland after sixteen years away. Although Fisher used it to supply a year-long series of chatty articles about the voyage and Australia he had to let *Life and Work* tick over. A series on the twelve apostles succeeded one on the Twelve Prophets and Norman Maclean had a long-running serial, 'In Old Glengarry', about the aftermath of the 'Forty-five.

Fisher was, in fact, to show in time a vigorous editorial personality, though the qualities that shine through his bound volumes may not be the qualities that made him a popular preacher, lecturer, and writer in his day. Unlike the editors of modern times, even the ministers among them, he also had a parish to run. To his credit, and even apart from the Australian trip, he liked to see more of the world than Morningside and was occasionally to send parishioners or *Life and Work* readers encouraging messages from Biarritz or Britanny or Bad Homburg. He wrote a charming letter from Biarritz (where there were two Morningside families in his hotel) thanking his Edinburgh people for paying off the cost of the church hall.

In his early years, however, he was to some extent a prisoner of the decision to make *Life and Work* the voice of the church, in the sense of being the record of its committees' doings in the way the committees liked them presented. For a time that meant that the voice was less powerful and resonant than Charteris and McMurtrie had made it.

In its role as the 'record' it is fascinating and rich not only in church but in social and imperial history; but as journalism and literature it often falls short of what it might have been—and indeed what it was to be once Fisher, a slow starter, had got under full sail and into more open editorial waters.

He had a few *bêtes noires* (as he might have said himself, having a weakness for a foreign phrase): Roman Catholicism, in many of its expressions, and the Anglo-Catholicism which imitated it; love of luxury among the rich; and at times entertainment among the poor. But he could be more diplomatic than some of his editorial notes suggested. A classic piece of editorial diplomacy is his gentle answer to turn away the wrath of indignant ministers who thought their rejected offerings better than those which made the top spot in the magazine, the 'Sunday Fireside' sermon. It was, he explained, filled by invitation only, and inevitably some of what was offered but rejected was even better than what he had commissioned. In one of his denunciations of Roman Catholicism—inspired by what he called the natural joyful piety of the Festival of the Assumption of the Virgin in Brittany—he regretted that 'so much evident devotion should be spent in a worship with error at its root.' But he added a tactful touch: 'I have much less sympathy with Romanism than in earlier years, and probably much less than many of you have', he told his Morningside people. It is a touching vision: the Auld Kirk congregation there, ecumaniacs ahead of their time, lingering over the rosaries that their minister had grown out of. But it must have made them think that it wasn't really that the minister was at all prejudiced by normal standards, just that they were unusually enlightened.

But Fisher's 'high' side showed up when even in 1902 he gathered an 'excellent' congregation on a Thursday for a Christmas Day Service.

As an editor, Fisher had some unusual problems and highly individual techniques. *Life and Work* in those days had to pass what he called an ordeal of inspection. A committee of twenty-three received copies of the make-up and were expected to note typographical errors, factual mistakes, and 'especially to pass judgment on any subject of ecclesiastical policy'. It met for these holy purposes in the church offices, at 22 Queen Street, Edinburgh, on the twelfth day of each month; and the wonder is that the editor survived and that the magazine showed a good deal of life and character.

Fisher had printed forms with the formula 'The editor regrets that owing to the great pressure on the available space etc . . .', which were used, he said, 'whatever be the reason for rejecting a manuscript'. He had, he claimed, at least twenty times more than could be used, and he used relatively little unsolicited material. But he also had a locker known as 'the incubator' containing manuscripts, notes of possibilities, 'kind letters', and names of future writers.

When a contribution was accepted Fisher would 'work his will upon it—within certain well understood limits'. Alas, they were not defined! But contributions not accepted were often illiterate, lacked a 'tolerable English style, even when from educated people', or were 'ludicrously inappropriate to a Church magazine'. Not long ago, wrote Fisher in 1912, 'a picturesque and realistic account was offered of a Berlin music hall'. This was a formula for producing a stable, and at times even staid, magazine.

But though it was an age of gradual change in the church the early Edwardian years saw order and stability in the state and the social structure, despite the real and deep sense of loss when Queen Victoria died, inspiring poignant poems and leaden prose which the historian will not quote if he wants to keep in with his readers. Even the passions roused by establishment seemed to have subsided—partly because there could be no headway with a Tory government, partly because even Principal Rainy's abundant energies were fully enough occupied with the litigation which followed the creation of the United Free Church and the determination of the 'Wee Free' minority who abhorred the union with the United Presbyterians to prove themselves legally and morally the Free Church of Scotland. Fisher (and Fleming before him, and indeed Charteris) looked ahead to presbyterian reunion, but not yet. Both in church and temporal matters, however, there was an emphasis on things that would not alienate the minority of *Life and Work* readers who belonged to the UF Kirk.

There was practical as well as spiritual guidance for them. A feature of Fisher's early years was a good deal of medical advice, though this carried on an earlier *Life and Work* tradition. At times *Life and Work* reads like the modern home doctor with eminent physicians of the day pronouncing on degeneracy, eugenics ('when weaklings marry weaklings') and the need 'to strengthen during youth the inhibition groups of cells'.

Another physician, a Dr Hutchison who was author of *Food and the Principles of Dietetics*, was enrolled for a matter of considerable and indeed consuming interest to the Edwardians, what people drink. He began with tea, coffee, and cocoa but got round to alcohol to give Christmas guidance to the Auld Kirk in 1903, and perhaps to worry the more powerful abstinence lobby among the UFs.

Dr Hutchison had to tackle some problems which seem remote today. He had 'no reservation' in asserting: 'to persons in perfect health alcohol in any form is quite unnecessary', and he brought comfort to the tea-Jennies by assuring them that those who denounced the evil wrought by 'tea-drunkenness' were certainly wrong. High tea, however, he denounced as an assault on the digestion, and dyspeptics were advised to stick to China tea. And he wanted tea served in warm cups: 'No one thinks of serving soup in cold plates', and the water must be 'well aerated'. Tea drinking, 'in moderate quantities' won his support, and he gave a reassuring answer to his own question: 'Are tea and coffee a blessing to the race or a curse?' Coffee, in fact, gets relatively little attention: and cocoa (not for the first time in *Life and Work*) is occasion for a counter-attack on the extravagant nutritional claims of chocolate manufacturers.

But *Life and Work* was the Auld Kirk's magazine, not the Band of Hope's. Dr Hutchison was a temperance man but not, it would seem, a total abstainer. He 'humbly commended' his advice to those who took alcoholic beverages 'for no other reason than that they like them'.

Some of it is common sense, some social commentary—with warnings, for example, even in 1903, of the danger to women of taking drink to relieve depression, and admonitions never to take it before work. It is, he said, 'best regarded as a restorative after work is accomplished'. And, like Paul,

MASON'S
EXTRACT OF HERBS

For the immediate production of

BOTANIC BEER

A Nine-gallon Cask of Alcoholic Beer from a Brewery will cost you 10/6, but Eight Gallons of Beer made from

MASON'S

Extract of Herbs

Can be obtained for 6d., plus a pound or two of Sugar and a little Yeast.

THE FINEST BEVERAGE IN THE WORLD.

Inventors and Manufacturers:

NEWBALL & MASON

Hyson Green Works,
NOTTINGHAM.

If unable to obtain it in your neighbourhood, send 9 stamps for sample bottle; or samples of both Wine Essence and Extract of Herbs, post free for 15 stamps.

Every House-wife should use it.

We have more Extracts than MASON'S EXTRACT OF HERBS for Botanic Beer—DANDELION, SARSAPARILLA, HOPS, GINGER, GINGER ALE, LEMONINE, HOREHOUNDINE, CIDERINE, and WINTER EXTRACT, and MASON'S WINE ESSENCES; these we recommend for Children's Parties.

21. Botanic beer: elixir of life? Apparently the only beer ever advertised in the magazine.

Dr Hutchison advised a little wine for the stomach's sake:

> We are not all of us—particularly in these days—in perfect health and there are many especially who lead harassed and driven lives to whom a little alcohol at meal-times may make all the difference between good and bad digestion.

But on two points he is clear. Don't drink between meals; and take it only 'in dilute form'.

Later, Fisher's medical contacts developed other themes about good health, and even the inevitable aftermath of even the best of health. By the end of the Edwardian era *Life and Work* was offering cautious encouragement of cremation as a seemly, acceptable, and even desirable Christian means of returning ashes and dust to their own elements.

There was another area, where medicine, morals and social habits overlapped, in which Fisher evidently had strong views but also what now seems a Victorian reticence about expressing them too explicitly. He worried audibly but enigmatically about any fall in the birthrate. It is difficult at this distance to work out exactly when he is concerning himself about the then unmentionable mechanics of contraception—for his hostility to 'luxury' could link up with alarm about the low level not only of the birthrate (by Victorian standards) but of Christian liberality. For example: 'A Christian grace grows badly out of corruption. Self-sacrifice is not likely to be fed by cowardice and unnatural self-indulgence.' Cannot people give more to the church when they have to spend less on their families? Yes, they can but they won't, was the gist of his argument.

Such enigmatic exploration of potentially awkward topics was the exception rather than the rule in the Edwardian and early Georgian years, however. Under Fisher the bulk of the magazine was fairly earnest, placid, useful and predictable. It expounded Christian truth for those who were convinced or anxious to be reassured; and it had Lauchlan MacLean Watt switching from poet to serial writer. But as the house-magazine of the household of the faith it avoided real controversy within the church—and to a great extent between the churches.

The exception was the vigour of Fisher's own editorial expression, which occasionally led him into trouble, though he remained a bonny fighter even when cornered. For example he took a tactical beating but won a strategic victory in 1911 in a row with the Scottish-born son of the manse who was Archbishop of York (later of Canterbury), William Cosmo Gordon Lang. This seems to have been conducted on one side with a rather headstrong mixture of decency and militancy, and on the other with an extreme unction which seems to justify the cruel punning couplet written a quarter of a century later about Lang after the Abdication of Edward VIII:

Auld Lang swine
How full of cant you are

Lang was the son of a Moderator of the Auld Kirk's Assembly, J Marshall Lang of the Barony and Aberdeen University, whose first contribution to *Life and Work* was in 1879 and who was a friend of Charteris. Another son, less prodigal, was to be Moderator in 1935 in the reunited national Church, Marshall Lang of Whittingehame. But Cosmo Gordon Lang did rather well in the far country (as did a third brother) and became more exclusive in his attitudes—as well as higher in his theology—than many a native English Anglican. It is said, for example, that a year or two before, when Bishop of Stepney, he would not let John Buchan's father (a Free Church minister who went into the UF Kirk) join in the marriage service when the rising presbyterian novelist married an Anglican in his bride's church. Fisher responded joyfully but impetuously when another more ecumenically protestant bishop tore into Lang for a 'spirit of separatism which belonged in fact to darker times' and claimed that he had admitted that 'on his visits to his home he could not join in the worship of his father's communion'. Unfortunately the other bishop's good intentions had outrun his accurate recollection of what Lang had actually said in what Fisher called 'an amazing and saddening speech'.

By March *Life and Work* readers were learning of the pain the paragraph in January had given the Archbishop of York, the 'ties of memory and affection' with which he was held to the Kirk, and his 'sincere anxiety to remove what seems to be some serious misunderstanding'. As letters to the editor for publication were not accepted as such from archbishops or anyone else in those days, Fisher had the opportunity to fit the Archbishop's protest into a framework of his own, which included the actual text of a speech which Lang in a second letter had been forced to agree might be misunderstood.

Lang was getting a retraction of a sort (which he was asking for in stately language meaning much the same as its brusquer modern equivalent) but at the price of having to explain what he really did mean in the passage which had outraged the Bishop of Hereford. He should probably have spoken of 'full communion' rather than 'worship', he agreed, and went on to say that what he meant: '. . . was not the occasional joining in the ordinary worship of the Established Church of Scotland but such action as what is called the

Interchange of Pulpits . . .'

Why the interchange of pulpits with a father, brother, and umpteen manse relatives mattered so much or deserved capitals, another generation will find it hard to understand. So to his credit did Fisher, man of this time in so many ways and yet for our time too in his healthy plain protestant speaking and genuine ecumenism. Part of Lang's price for satisfaction of a sort was to leave Fisher the last word, which was to suggest that the presence of Hensley Henson (then canon and later bishop) at pre-Assembly functions and in St Giles' was worth more than mere expressions of friendliness. He also said of Lang, in a passage which shows that Fisher was not as unsubtle as he sometimes seemed:

> Though he has chosen to follow his career in the Sister Establishment—once so near in fellowship with our own Church—Scotsmen have regarded his high preferment with gratification; and anything like intolerance or arrogance in one whom they claim a special interest would have been a cause of regret to the members of his father's Church, as well as a cause of reproach to his own.

But *Life and Work* sometimes went in for lively journalism of a less personalised kind. The old pattern of drawings (and paintings that lost most of their merit in black and white) was varied by a photographic competition. The influence of Fleet Street also extended as far as arranging 'Answers to Correspondents'.

Fisher (who had resisted pressure for 'letters to the editor') could handle these more like an old-fashioned schoolmaster, complaining that some letters showed an ingenious quest after subtlety rather than any anxiety for knowledge. 'This column will not be continued as it does not serve a useful purpose', he said before launching into telling a guildsman why he should believe in the Virgin Birth—the answer amounting to a dissertation on Christ's uniqueness, sinlessness, and the role of the doctrine in 'keeping us near a belief in a God who is no slave of mechanism, but a Creator still'.

Other correspondents worried about whether *Chronicles* condemned modern censuses ('No'); whether a Christian could be a socialist ('Yes', though there is a proper *caveat* about what we would now call communism or Marxism); what the Creed means by descending into hell; whether all gambling is wrong ('sixpence per hundred points of whist'); this time the answer is hard to render as either 'yes' or 'no'.

Other correspondents got a briefing on the 'burning bush' emblem, on why some hymns were never sung, and whether conversion could come without a sense of sinfulness; and a businessman was given the answer he perhaps wanted to hear when he complained that he did so much church work on Sundays that he was more tired on Monday morning than Saturday night. 'Rest is even more of the essence of the Fourth Commandment than even unselfish activity.'

Problems of the manse also got an airing. Compared with our own times the Edwardian and early Georgian age seems a placid time. It seemed very different to those who lived in it. Even the financial stability and middle-class prosperity and security which we think the ministry enjoyed seemed very different at the time. In June 1913, for example, editor Fisher was thundering about the more thoughtful way some matters were handled in other branches of the Church—a turn of phrase which usually means the UFs. Some modern scholars challenge the view that the UFs were more zealous and successful at fund-raising: at the time Auld Kirk exhortations did not hesitate to hold up the separated but not very distant presbyterian good example—not just about raising money but about spending it.

Surprising though it may seem, Fisher claimed that it was not infrequent for a minister preaching outside his own parish to come down from the pulpit, return to the vestry, and leave 'without having spoken to an office-bearer or a member of the congregation and without receiving a word of welcome or thanks even from the beadle.' What accompanies this dissertation on the damage done by Scottish diffidence to high-strung sensitive men who received a cold *douche* of indifference after setting their souls on fire is perhaps even stranger: a claim that congregations often failed in such cases to pay railway fares, hotel bills—a sign of missing hospitality—and incidentals which might add up to two or three guineas.

But perhaps sympathy with this mean treatment of 'preachers of conspicuous gifts' may give place to the anxieties of more ordinary and sometimes obscure ministers whose wives had, even in 1913, real problems of making ends meet. When one manse wife wrote about these troubles (over the page from the complaint about silence and unpaid expenses), Fisher added that 'nothing will persuade the Editor to make known who this minister's wife is'. The tradition, the editorial determination, and the problems continue.

This lady of spirit noted that lawyers' wives were not expected to tout for business and that doctors' wives did not feel pulses and mix powders. But ministers' wives were looked on as unpaid assistants, 'saving the congregation the burden of a parish sister', and having to bear the lioness's share of the costs of work-parties and mission sales 'entirely disproportionate to her income alongside those of other ladies'. Even the fact that some ministers' sons went wrong was blamed partly on this overwork of the minister's wife as well as the minister himself.

But this anonymous madam, whose name was so prudently withheld, had some hard words for some 'very silly women who become ministers' wives', display foolish airs of imagined superiority, drop old friendships, and 'imitate the lady of the manor in externals at least as much as possible.' Others, it seemed, were a bit too ladylike in their own estimation for 'the delightful labours of helping to save the sisterhood of the weary and the lost while it is yet day'.

Instead, the manse wife should be a queen of tact and not 'what so many seem to think, the unpaid parish drudge'. No minister's wife had reached perfection but many had touched saintship. One of the anonymous minor prophetess's concerns was to warn ministers' wives off encouraging class distinctions and snobberies in the parish. This is perhaps an Edwardian and pre-war concern in a way that is scarcely apparent in the Victorian times. Perhaps then God seemed to have not only ordered men's estates but to have fixed social relationships. The Edwardians show a consciousness of class which perhaps reflects a new social mobility as well as what we might call a new and more sociological approach—and an interest, whether anxious, curious, or sympathetic, in socialism.

But much in the mood of the later Edwardian years was more concerned with social than individual dilemmas. 'Socialism—it is the word on everybody's lips', stated the 'Young Men's Guild Supplement' in 1909, though the tone of its material often seemed aimed at the kind of young men who went to Territorial camps rather than Fabian summer schools. The *Guild Life and Work* reflected the interest of the time in sweated labour and bad working conditions for women and girls, and offered glowing accounts of how much better they ordered these things in Bournville under the Cadburys. But there is a surprising reticence on the argument about 'votes for women'. This seemed to be a subject the Kirk (at least in *Life and Work*) preferred to avoid.

There are frequent mentions both of the semi-religious appeal and atmosphere of socialism and of a lessening of its hostility to the church. There is also—as might be expected in the years of reform which followed the Liberal victory of 1906—an acceptance of the pressures for political and state, rather than voluntary and individual, action to tackle poverty and social distress, though some of the main political arguments of the age, between free trade and tariff reform, for example, are hardly touched on. It was accepted that Christians would be divided, though *Life and Work* seemed to have a special respect for the much troubled Tory leader Arthur Balfour, whose views on religion and science got a good airing in its pages and whose retirement from the leadership after years of bickering produced an unmistakably genuine note of regret that was presented as something above politics. Clearly editor Fisher also regarded British naval preparations to keep ahead of the new German High Seas Fleet as something else that was above politics, though there were times when it seemed to split the Liberals as tariff reform had split the Tories. The great political confrontations of the Lloyd George budget, the Parliament Act, and the Irish Home Rule Bill are also shadows over the life of the nation rather than subjects to usurp the natural rights in the magazine of series on great preachers, famous churches, well-known hymns or even Annie S Swan's extended reflections on family life. And while there is much (especially in the Guild supplement) about women's working conditions and the need for women in the factory inspectorate, and even the higher Civil Service, there seems a studious determination not to be involved in the argument about whether they should have votes.

Much of the magazine's emphasis was naturally devotional and much was still literary. Literary style and social concern probably met and mingled most easily in 1910 when David Watson wrote some brilliant sketches of what poverty meant in personal terms. They are too well constructed to bear quotation. The printed word then occupied roles taken later by radio and television. Indeed in some ways the most journalistic coverage of world affairs comes in the reports from the missions and of the Kirk's connections (or even Fisher's personal interests) among the other protestant churches. For example, all through the Edwardian years there is a tremendous enthusiasm for the *Los von Rom* movement which was an aspect of German nationalist discontent with trends in the Austro-Hungarian dynastic and multi-national empire.

Yearly figures were given of secessions from the Roman Catholic Church and little analysis was offered of the complexities of the central European situation. One of the ironies of Kirk history is that this enthusiasm for the anti-clerical German nationalists of Austria and Bohemia (who by no means always followed evangelical lines) was to be followed in a generation by an enthusiasm for the Czechs, the arch-opponents of the German nationalists. There is little evidence in the pre-war *Life and Work* of much interest in the Czechs, despite their Hussite traditions, or the Poles, or even the large protestant minority in Hungary. Interest in Russia is tinged with a mixture of British constitutional dislike of absolutism, protestant suspicion of orthodoxy, and, as powerful as anything, evangelical sympathy for the Jews. Japan got some sympathetic coverage in the Russo-Japanese War of 1904-5, admittedly from a Mr Ballard living in Tokyo: 'we never see an intoxicated

D   83

Japanese soldier'. However, it was balanced with an account of a Russian Easter in the days when the Kremlin rang with the cry 'Christ is risen'. So may it be again, in God's good time.

To its credit, the Kirk was suspicious of those who persecuted the Jews. Throughout the years before the First World War, Kirk readers were expected to show their love for the Jews by learning about them, and by supporting missions to convert them. One result was that any *Life and Work* readers who read and digested the whole magazine might have an altogether exaggerated impression of the Jewish response to missionary efforts. Victorian and Edwardian missionary zeal always tended to exaggerate the impact of missions, partly in reaction towards those who openly decried them or secretly nursed a lack of enthusiasm. Nowhere was this more evident than in reports of Jewish missions in Eastern Europe, North Africa, and the Middle East, including Palestine. But any diligent reader would be fairly well informed about Zionism and would have been given an accurate (and sympathetic) account of the vision and legacy of Dr Theodore Herzl, who rated a three-inch obituary notice in August 1904. His work, including the effect on him of the Dreyfus case, had been written up earlier.

The emphasis on Jewish missions takes even the historian unawares. It reflected the evangelical revival of the nineteenth century and the biblical basis of Victorian and Edwardian religion, with a knowledge of the Old Testament which the modern Church has largely lost and without which it may be impossible to do justice to the New Testament. Whatever the 'historical Jesus' may be like—and it is likely he is closer to the Victorians' idea of him than to the new myths created in the name of 'demythologising'—he was a Jew. Our Scottish ancestors never forgot that; nor, unlike some continental Christians of various denominations, did they find it an embarrassment. But it was a challenge to share the good news of him and from him with the scattered people of Israel.

However, the emphasis on Jewish missions was only a part of the emphasis on world mission which probably reached its climax with the Edinburgh World Missionary Conference of 1910, though in retrospect that may seem a more important landmark in the ecumenical movement than in mission history as the Kirk's people saw it at the time. Mission to them meant converting the heathen, and it meant good works to help those in need or in darkness, whether they were converted or not. What may astonish the historian is not merely to discover this emphasis—its emotional impact is unexpected even when he comes intellectually prepared for it—but to discover the Auld Kirk's sense of anxiety, even guilt, about not being an even greater missionary Kirk than it was. This was one area of church organisation where the enthusiasm and the hard cash produced by the 'voluntary' principle probably put the Auld Kirk at a disadvantage. Indeed, modern words like 'crisis' appear in *Life and Work*'s Edwardian mission coverage, with warnings that sound only too familiar about the need for drastic cutbacks in work if the Kirk's people fail to supply the means to support it.

Perhaps particular reference is better than general analysis to show the role of foreign missions in the church of the time (and in its magazine). Successive issues of the 'In Far Fields' section of 1912, for example, are rich in intrinsic interest and themes indicating general trends and problems: In February 1912, the main 'foreign story' is an account from Ichang on the Yangtse of 'the revolution in China'. It is by a young minister called Forbes Tocher who was to see many more of the trials and uncertainties which overwhelmed Christian missions in China. He tells of Confucius' birthday, a few months before, 'the last day on which the supremacy of Manchu over Chinese was recognised in Ichang', for the next day brought a quiet

22. Revolution in Ichang

revolutionary takeover. The picture with the article is of a revolutionary banner waving outside the Rankine Memorial Hospital, and of its inscription: 'The Chinese character "han" which stands for the Chinese people, as opposed to "Man" for the Manchus.' When Tocher wrote '. . . this is undoubtedly a movement of the people and a movement of the rightful possessors of the land against alien masters . . .' he was presumably not thinking of an anti-foreign movement, such as the 'Boxer' rebellion had been, but of a protest against the Manchu dynasty. His words also belie any modern suggestion that missionaries, so vilified since the much later communist revolution, were anything but sympathetic to the Chinese people:

> The imperialists have shown themselves so incompetent to deal with the situation with which they are confronted, throughout practically every province of the Empire, that we prophesy nothing but success for the revolutionaries (or the republicans, as they prefer to be called) and although here on the field we have to observe the neutrality of foreigners, we wish for nothing else.

It was, he said, a movement of the forces of enlightenment and progress and a great challenge to the Christian Church—though the troubled times had forced the postponement of a great evangelistic campaign in which 'we were looking forward to a rich ingathering'.

In the same issue there is delight at the award of a decoration to Dr Graham of Kalimpong during the Durbar Indian visit of the King-Emperor (George V) and equal pleasure at a census in the Punjab which has shown a two hundred per cent increase in Christian numbers in a decade. (They now exceeded two hundred thousand.) They are, says the Rev William Dalgetty at Sialkot, mainly from the depressed classes—he preferred to say 'depressed peoples'—but 'judging from past experience they will not long remain depressed. Christ lifts the fallen, and raises the beggar from the dunghill to set him among princes.' Other Indian notes rejoice in Maharajahs who had banned drink among young people or sought temperance teaching in schools, and scoff at a Muslim discovery of 'eight relics of Mohammed and his family', including the prophet's purported shoes and last coat, the hair of two of his sons, and bits of the costume of his 'favourite wife'. Protestants in the Victorian tradition, well schooled in the Reformation's view of bogus relics, were as plain-spoken in inter-faith matters as ecumenical ones.

A month later the Kikuyu mission in Kenya is rejoicing in its progress among girls (a boarding-pupil called Njeri wa Ikenyua had been baptised as Priscilla), although there are some boys and girls 'to whom the mission discipline proves uncongenial'. But there are plenty of pupils, although boys' fees have gone up to three rupees, mostly paid through 'the equivalent in work'.

But there were problems with the bawbees at home as well as the rupees abroad. 'A word on finance' from the foreign mission convener has an alarmist content that belies the prosaic heading. Incredible though it may seem, a wet and stormy day at home had put in jeopardy the Kirk's mission work abroad. A likely story? Perhaps there was an element of exaggeration. On November 5 'churches were emptied of their congregations' by the fiercest storm for years. Unfortunately this was the day when the Kirk folk were to be told to bring the foreign mission money the next week. When the next Sunday came the weather was almost as bad. It, too, produced 'sparse congregations and these largely unprepared with their special gifts'.

The actual 'loss' seems to have been less than a thousand pounds, and the convener's only too evident intention was to get a better and less insecure method of raising funds, and to remove the majority of kirks from their dependence on an annual collection for their main contribution:

> The conquest of the world for Christ, and our responsibility for part of that conquest, are far too serious considerations for permitting the weather conditions of one Sunday to have any influence on the matter at all.

In fact the situation in 1912 seems to have been healthier than a few years before, though the people of the Kirk seemed in need of constant exhortation. The frequency with which *Life and Work* is used for 'answers to objections'—even though the objectors were never allowed to state their case—suggests that it was never easy to finance the Kirk's effort, even in the days just after Britain's political and economic zenith. Any prominent person who wanted a little publicity in *Life and Work* had a sure way to get it: let him say a good word for foreign missions. He would be quoted.

April 1912. There is a detailed account of Madras Christian College, a hearty welcome for pro-Christian comments by the Chinese revolutionary leader Sun Yat Sen, a note from Nyasaland on the difficulty of getting African Christians to read the Epistles as well as the Gospels (a problem some ministers say affects modern Scots), and a report of a missionary survey across the Nyasaland frontier into Mozambique with a suggestion that this undeveloped Portuguese territory might prove 'the Church of Scotland's Macedonia'.

The reader of these foreign pages would also find wars and rumours of wars, overshadowed though they often were in the mind of the British public by the internal troubles of the early years of George V's reign, in which the

Parliament Act crisis was followed by waves of industrial conflict and the fierce parliamentary confrontation over Irish Home Rule which Irishmen, Loyalist as well as Nationalist, were not prepared to see settled merely by vote of the British parliament. The main impact of the troubled times is seen unexpectedly in the regular reports of the Jewish mission—first at the time of the war between Italy and Turkey and then in the Balkan wars which followed. But the Balkans seemed a long way off and there was far more about Salonika than about Sarajevo in Austrian-annexed Bosnia. There was also a rumour that the Bulgarians were so sure of taking Constantinople from the Turks that they were planning to restore Orthodox worship in Saint Sophia's.

As 1913 ended, readers of *Life and Work* worried about these wars and rumours, even of civil war in Ireland. The outlook for 1914 was uncertain, despite the apparent ability of the Great Powers to prevent the turbulent Balkans from dragging them into war.

No-one knew what the next few years would bring in Ireland or in British politics. But the leaders of the Auld Kirk, and most of the leaders of the United Free Kirk, saw the way opening ahead to presbyterian reunion, though some legal obstacles had to be overcome. After the 1913 Assembly, when the Moderator, Dr Wallace Williamson of St Giles', radiated enthusiasm for Kirk reunion, an estimate in *Life and Work* was that, at the best possible pace, union might be possible in seven years. Clearly that time was likely to be stretched rather than cut: if anyone had predicted that the union would not come until 1929 no-one would have been all that surprised.

The surprises were to lie elsewhere. European civilisation (still none too certain whether American civilisation, if it recognised such a thing, was a part of it) was under strain. Before the year was out it was well on the road to self-destruction. And the young men that worried Fisher with their passion for the music hall, the cinematograph theatre, and the football crowd were to find a tragic outlet for their energies.

23. The Right Reverend The Moderator, Andrew Wallace Williamson

24. Ministers at war. A group of ministers serving with the Black Watch.

Chapter 7
The unexpected ordeal
1914-1918

'It can hardly be questioned that in spite of all the horrible anxiety the country is a more gracious place to live in than it was in December last, and life is more serious and worthy. The endless round of entertainments in which rich people spend their time, the sports and indulgences of poorer people are curtailed and everybody is the better for it.'

(From 'What the War has done already', *Life and Work*, December 1914.)

Life and Work for 1914 began with a prayer for the New Year. It asked God for help 'to adventure upon the New Year without anxiety or distress'; it asked for a knowledge of God's goodness, 'so that none of the uncertainties of life can disturb us and none of its opportunities of service find us unprepared.'

Save us, it asked, from falling backward into evil. And before praying for the spirit of charity and union to flourish in the Church of Scotland it entreated: 'Grant peace and prosperity unto our Empire in the coming year'.

But the uncertainties of life were greater than anyone recognised. Europe was about to fall backward into evil, enduring what must now surely seem to be the civil war of a civilisation. It was not only a terrible but also an unexpected ordeal. Britain was militarily ill-prepared in some ways (although not in naval ones) and the small, fine Regular Army was used up by the First Battle of Ypres in the autumn. But the people were even less prepared for the ordeal of a war that lasted four years and demanded commitment of millions of men to a battlefield whose realities their elders scarcely began to understand.

The August issue of a monthly magazine is one which editors approach with their usual diligence rather than special care and concern, except perhaps special care to get everything done further in advance than usual. For August 1914 the editor had a workmanlike edition well prepared, probably well before the Archduke Franz Ferdinand was murdered at Sarajevo on June 28.

The Balkans, and even the fears of war, did slip into the August issue that was so overtaken by events. Among the editorial columns of 'events and opinions' there was a note of concern and sympathy with the Irish Presbyterians—for Britain seemed threatened by civil war in Ireland as Sir Edward Carson's Volunteers threatened to set up a Loyalist Government in Ulster rather than accept Dublin rule—but war still seemed a distant horror. There were pictures of refugees and a devastated village, but in Bulgaria. And in the praise of a soup kitchen in Thrace, and Scottish beneficence, there is, or so it seems, an unwritten qualification: it couldn't happen here. War was something that didn't happen to us—certainly not in the way that it had scourged the Balkans. An army crossed Thrace five times in the Balkan wars, reported Mr Frew of the Church's Jewish mission, 'and acted like a scourge of locusts each time'.

But, if the editor had planned his own holidays for August, he made creditable rearrangements for the September issue. By good luck, or by a quickly improvised raid on the reserve galleys, he contrived to get a story about a colour-sergeant who had fought at Waterloo and was also a precentor. In fact or fiction—it isn't clear which— he dies hoisting the Union Jack after the last death-bed words: 'I maun be up tae hoist the flag'. It wasn't much but it was a gesture.

A minister also got a better showing in this issue than he could otherwise have expected for a piece on a Sunday at a Territorial camp and for his advice to those landed with a sermon at church parade, 'The preacher must be alert and bright, pointed and paperless.'

Even the Moderator's message after the outbreak of war managed to get in, sandwiched oddly between a note denouncing the sin of keeping windows shut and a tribute to a sheriff-clerk at Perth. The Moderator was Professor Thomas Nicol of Aberdeen. His United Free counterpart was Dr George Reith, father of young John, later Lord Reith.

But the editor himself had to tackle the most crucial problem: 'What would Jesus have me think and say and do?' It is a question every Christian must surely ask in such or similar circumstances. Not surprisingly, but quite honourably and very solemnly, he came to conclusions whose main principles (if not practical assumptions) he probably shared with the editor of *Leben und Arbeit*, or whatever title the German churches of the day favoured for their publications.

> A Christian man's conclusion may be that though war is always evil it may be a necessary evil and there are worse things than war.

It is hard not to be taken aback, however, when the puritan piety shaped in the century since Waterloo thinks of the sins of ease which, 'must have grieved

Jesus more poignantly than any horror of the battlefield.' Editor Fisher was perhaps a bit hasty in deciding what would grieve Jesus most, but we all make the same kind or error:

> Amid all the distress and agony which will be witnessed on the fair fields of France during the present campaign there will be no more gruesome and saddening spectacle than can be seen any night in Piccadilly in London or the Boulevard des Italiens in Paris.

The comparison is so incongruous, and in retrospect so absurd, that it dulls the effect of the serious attempt to warn Christian men against 'war with a light heart', to find consolation in the national unity brought by war, and to try to limit the horrors of war. 'Hatred and blind fury of blood lust have no place in civilised warfare', said Fisher. However, he developed a theme which, in the mood of the time, was greatly to his credit:

> Not all the gross violation of justice by which the enemy has violated international law will make us minimise our respect for German philosophy and music and science and our real kinship for their people.

That must have been among the bravest things said in 1914, its bravery understandable only in the context of the time and the absurdities of chauvinism. Perhaps it will more than cancel out the only too evident demonstration that, in 1914, the British people had no conception of what a real battlefield was like: and had letters to the editor been in fashion then there would no doubt have been complaints that he was unpatriotic in remembering Kant and Beethoven.

But war puts peaceful men in a quandary. Secular journalism in Britain did not enjoy its finest hour in the First World War either, not by a long way.

There were, of course, some bizarre touches with a specially churchy flavour which got into religious periodicals, though as far as *Life and Work* is concerned the worst of these journalistic atrocities were committed in the missionary reservation and thriving private empire of 'In Far Fields'. It managed to work up topical enthusiasm for what Admiral Beatty had said 'in opening a sale of work in connection with the parish church at Braemar'. However, this was not quite the 1914 battle-cruiser squadron's equivalent of Drake's game of bowls as the Spanish Armada approached: whatever Beatty said in praise of missions was back in 1910. Religious journalists are sometimes wise not to worry too much about their news being red-hot, but this was carrying things a bit far. So was the dissertation on changing military tactics and equipment which led up to the reflection, 'We may note a somewhat similar change in missionary methods.' (Were they digging communication trenches and sending out wiring parties at Kalimpong, and using gas if the wind was in the right direction at Calabar?)

But the real problem of men of peace in a time of war is seen not only in the over-topical allusions that probably seemed a bit silly even at the time but in the popular successes of the day in *Life and Work*. Lauchlan MacLean Watt, first evident in the magazine as a poet more than a decade before, and to be Moderator in 1933, embarked on a series on Highland regimental history. It was fine stuff, worthy of the traditions to which the Colours testify, but it raises a nagging anxiety that somewhere in German church archives there may be a rousing series on Uhlans, Jaegers, and the Prussian Guard.

A quandary of a different sort was created for Fisher by his great success of 1915: 'In the Trenches', a short story in May which sold extra copies—even the UF manses were crying out for them—and was later reprinted at a reader's expense. But it also produced earnest but embarrassing requests to know whether it was 'authentic history or not'. The editor claimed in a skilfully worded reply to these seekers after a very literal truth that he knew no more about that than the man in the street, had no *affidavit* about literal accuracy from the author, but had heard rumours current at the front among our own men and the Allies. He also added that 'he knows with assured belief that, in the sense in which truth is most valuable, the main purport of the sketch was profoundly true.'

The 'sketch' was still capable of causing a flutter more than sixty years later. Parts of it were close enough in style to the idiom which John Buchan gave his hero Richard Hannay in the wartime successors of *The Thirty-Nine Steps* to lead the present editor to try to work out just where Buchan (an elder at St Columba's Pont Street and son of a Free Church manse) was at the time the story was written, for it had a professionalism in its presentation that *Life and Work* sometimes lacked. But the professionalism came not from that son of the manse but from a pulpit. The author was the Rev William Leathem, then of Holburn Central in Aberdeen, later a chaplain and eventually minister of St Andrew's, Ottawa. It was, as his son explains, intended 'as a spiritual parable', but at the time it seems to have been in danger of becoming Scotland's equivalent of the Angels of Mons, though *they* were more of a stunt than a parable.

'In the Trenches' purported to be a narrative by a soldier wounded in an attack in which 'the big guns had failed in their work of preparation'. He is pinned down fifty yards from the German trenches but gently borne off in the arms of the Friend of the Wounded or, as the French called him, the Comrade in White of whom men talked in hushed voices at Nancy, in the Argonne, at Soissons, and at Ypres.

> And while he swiftly removed every trace of blood and mire I felt as if my whole nature were being washed, as if all the grime and soil of sin were going, and as if I were once more a little child.

The story ends with its narrator weak, lonely, and in increasing pain but recognising the living Christ by what looked like a 'shot-wound' in his hand: 'I have his promise. I know that He will come for me tomorrow.' The detail and setting are vaguely those of the Neuve Chapelle battle in March. The authenticity is of the walk to Emmaus rather than of the Western Front, but in these early days of the war it is the closest *Life and Work* comes to conveying that deep piety of the best Scottish Presbyterians of the day—found, for example, in Lord Reith's account of his father's farewell to him in a UF manse as he went back to France from leave a couple of months before 'In the Trenches' appeared.

As the war went on, sacrifices became only too specific, rather than an abstract concept. Even the hope that the end of the war might be in sight in time for the 1915 General Assembly was clouded over by the thought that this could only be secured by the loss of 'still more of our gallant men'. And it was only April 1915 when that was written.

Only 1915. To search through the *Life and Work* of the years that were to come until the Armistice is to read through a report from the Valley of the Shadow. This was a nation at war which only gradually realised how terrible war could be. Yet it was a war in which the distinction between soldiers and civilians was usually almost as marked as it had been at Waterloo, Zeppelins and the Lusitania notwithstanding. A people who knew not the ways of war and the techniques of propaganda was cut off from those so near and dear to them, yet in experience so far from them. This is evident in the literature of the trenches, whether written at the time or later, whether protesting against the apparent futility of the trench war or in praise of the comradeship it brought: in Blunden and Reith and eventually Henry Williamson as well as Graves or Owen or the insubordinate Sassoon.

By action as well as prayer the church tried to close the gap as well as comfort the dying and the bereaved, help the wounded, serve the survivors and send the reinforcements out from home to those who so often encountered the mysteries of war and death. Those who know the war only from one genre of its literature may reckon that the citizen army took a poor view of church and chaplains. A serious and fair historian would probably have to take a much more complex view, often assessing apparently contradictory evidence, perhaps finding the contradictions within the attitudes of the same survivors. There are still survivors who would find the view presented in, for example, *Life and Work* of the church's concern and involvement and the young men's response—in faith, doubt, or perplexity—more true or, at least, often more typical than the anti-chaplain streak in some literature.

Indeed the church may have done more to close that gap than the press or the politicians. Ministers as well as divinity students were to be found in the combatant ranks of the citizen army. Ministers well into middle age, too old to be chaplains, manned the Scottish Churches' Huts behind the lines (although three of the Huts found themselves behind the German lines in the March 1918 offensive). In 1918 one of them was editor Fisher, superintendent of the Huts in the Etaples area (Eat-apples to the troops); and among the Churches' Huts lay-workers was the editor of the UF Kirk's *Record*, W P Livingstone, who was already past forty when the General Assembly elected him in 1912. The fullest accounts of the Huts' work come in the 'Young Men's Guild Supplement' to *Life and Work* in which they took the place of the normal activities which were virtually suspended when the members joined up.

In 1915 no-one realised just how great the impact of war would be, even if eighteen parish ministers, fifteen assistants, and sixty-six divinity students of the Auld Kirk had gone off to the war and more than two hundred had volunteered as chaplains. A little later the 1st Black Watch had three ministers as well as the padre among its officers. Glasgow cathedral, perhaps melting down an old ploughshare, had presented ceremonial swords to two assistant ministers, one commissioned in the Seaforths and the other in the HLI.

This was no more than a reflection of the mood of the people of church and nation. In the congregation at Pathhead in Kirkcaldy, a family had eight brothers in the Army, five of them in the Black Watch. Notes begin to appear of officers holding short presbyterian services for their men in the absence of chaplains, suggesting that John Reith of the Scottish Rifles, eccentric though he was, was far from alone or even remarkable in this.

By May 1915 ninety per cent of the sons of the manse were estimated to have joined up and Lauchlan MacLean Watt was quoted as finding a Gordon Highlander 'who had folded up in his sporran a copy of Delitzsch's edition of the *Psalms* in Hebrew to read in the train.' From time to time there are also reports of the troops in France reading *Life and Work* 'from cover to cover'. Perhaps it was good. Perhaps they felt religious. Perhaps it reminded them of home. In the magazine the war becomes the subject matter for the much-used verse in Scots. Rarely tinged with greatness, such verse can still be rich in feeling—for example in A B Gillespie's 'Furlough', a rather churchy and civilian name for a leave from France:

> Then, swift ahint the pulse o' joy
> There stings a stab o' pain—
> I'll scarce hae welcomed back the boy
> Ere he maun gang again!
> Yet what would mony a mither gie
> Had she but sic a chance,
> Whase waukin' een can never see
> Her laddie hame frae France?

That poem also tells us, more eloquently than much prose, that in seeking the outs and ins of these troubles:

> Some haud it's for oor sins.

More pretentious verse ages more easily, for example, the attempt to set words about crosses on the Union Jack to 'Stand up, stand up for Jesus', ending up with perhaps its best lines:

> And red, white, blue fly signals
>   of love divinely shown.
> God make us less unworthy
>   to call that flag our own.

War brought minor inconveniences, such as a prohibition on reduced train fares for commissioners to the General Assembly. Then came the bitter losses recorded in every parish magazine. Here and there an elder's son or some other lad wins the VC but as the losses being to mount and more survivors win decorations—especially after a successful 'show'—they begin to get less space. Now and again something stands out as tragic even among the carnage. For the South Leith Church, disaster came before most of its young men were anywhere near the front. Twenty of them from the 7th Royal Scots were killed in the Gretna train disaster. There were also losses among those who had already made their mark in the Kirk's affairs. Colonel James Clark of the 9th Argylls, for example, was an Edinburgh St George's elder 'who had been consolidating a position in the General Assembly which had become very secure'.

The anguish of these days, the search for God's will and God's help, is evident in issue after issue. There is a quest for comfort and assurance of God's love that sometimes, through protesting and asserting too much, seems to betray unspoken anxieties. Sometimes the vintage from the grapes of wrath also has a bitter taste. Editor Fisher found himself arguing that only a small minority of engineering workers could be involved in Clydeside's wartime labour troubles but complained that a 'comparatively few slackers may disorganise and hinder progress. It is pitiful to think that such debased humanity can exist.' There were also moments that came intermittently until 1918 when he had a run round the editorial table and a kick at the Pope, who was accused of leaning towards the Germans and Austrians. This became most marked when the Irish Roman Catholic bishops aligned themselves against conscription. There were even moments when obscure disputes over the status and rank of chaplains revived old ill-feeling between Presbyterians and Anglicans—notably when a bishop was appointed 'Major-General' over 'Brigadier-General' Simms, the Irish Presbyterian (and later Moderator) who was principal chaplain in the British Expeditionary Force. On one occasion Fisher's copy on this argument was censored by the committee, which managed to delete a punchline. 'It was omitted in the interests of charity', Fisher retorted later, 'It might have been retained in the interests of truth.' He counter-attacked by having a go at the episcopal 'Major-General', who was accused of abandoning united services.

Fisher also found himself running into mild theological trouble about this time, though not for one of his stranger editorial comments in 'Events and Opinions' which tried the difficult task of preaching against Sunday work on practical grounds after conceding that making shells on the Sabbath was not only an 'act of necessity and mercy' but a 'really sacred business'. The General Assembly, however, had set up a commission on the moral and spiritual issues of the war. In July 1917, the month the third battle of Ypres (Passchendaele) began, he asked if this commission would have courage and faith:

> . . . to attempt some restatement of Christian doctrine in the light which the self-denial and suffering of the time have cast upon the role of a Righteous God and the sacrifice for mankind that was made by his blessed Son, our Saviour?

What exactly he meant was not fully explained, not even when he bowed before a storm of criticism. 'Nothing was farther from his mind', he insisted, than to question the doctrines of the incarnation, the resurrection, and the divinity of our Lord. He merely thought that the suffering and sacrifice of young men would make people more responsive to the gospel of the cross.

The suffering and sacrifice were only too evident, all the more after the New Army was thrown into the Battle of the Somme. One among the thousands upon thousands it claimed was a nineteen-year-old Gordon subaltern who had seen his father, Dr John Brown of Bellahouston, installed as Moderator a few weeks before.

But war is not only blood and agony and waste; it is comradeship, high spirits, hard work; for some it was routine work behind the lines: and for everyone in the BEF at some time or other it seems to have brought spells of boredom. How some of the men saw it, how the chaplains saw it, and how the Church Huts competed with the *estaminets*—all this is brought out in column after column in *Life and Work* itself, in the 'Young Men's Supplement', and in the 'Woman's Guild Supplement' which (though it concerned itself with the men too), includes some material well worth exploration by historians of the women's services:

> ... It is not a field of service for young girls from sheltered homes who have never known what it meant to rough it or to face life on their own. The khaki girl abroad must be prepared to face a life of hard work, unfamiliar conditions, few comforts, many difficulties and temptations ...

There is also, as one would expect from the Guild, a proper concern for the state of the kitchens and of the menu, including an honest account of army suppers: 'Remains of soup and stew from dinner are heated up, scraps of pudding mixed with more milk and recooked, or bits of meat minced and done up into rissoles etc.'

It is hard to come across much that has the quality of the best of Boer War writing. Too many contributors and committees were competing for too little space—for the magazine was showing signs of austerity both in size and quality of paper—and perhaps the awful scale of things was beyond them. But that, of course, is what historians have now generally concluded about the generals too, at least until the last year of the war.

There was little inclination, however, to criticise generals then. One of Fisher's stranger editorial notes even found cause for praise in the fairly advanced age of many of them and suggested that congregations might, after reflecting on the role of Joffre, Foch, Hindenburg, and Kitchener, think more kindly of ageing ministers. There was even a civil reference to a German general allegedly on active service at the age of eighty-one.

But Haig, a youngster of fifty-three years in 1914, was the favourite general. As a visiting Glasgow minister reported in April 1917 in the 'Young Men's Guild Supplement' after a visit to GHQ, he was a regular worshipper, 'a man of faith—a man who prayed'. He was also, of course a Scots Presbyterian and had an effective public relations man as well as preacher in the Rev George Duncan, 'still youthful and bearing lightly his weight of learning', which he was later to display as a professor and Principal of St Mary's College at St Andrews.

The war, which dominated the main magazine and supplements, also forced its way into two distinctive areas: the serial story and the missionary reservation.

In the final instalment of one of the serials, the Canadians 'maintain a furiously accurate fire with their magazine rifles, every bullet finding at least one billet in human form'; they also do a lot of bayonetting in a style which confirms what the author's view of the relation of ammunition expended to wounds inflicted might already have suggested: that he was not embarrassed by too much up-to-date military experience.

Our hero, alas, is wounded by the 'Hun' whose life he had spared, but his batman is at hand: 'before the dishonoured caitiff could congratulate himself on what he had done he was pinioned in merited death to the dust.'

The title of this tale by William Swan? 'The Two Manses'—one Auld Kirk, the other United Free. Our hero is from one, our heroine from the other, and the course of true love (aided by such improbable coincidences as the heroine being at hand in a base hospital to help the wounded hero) seems much tangled with hopes of presbyterian union. As the hero says, a column before the wedding, at which the bride wears her nurse's uniform, 'The Churches are not quite united yet, Hetty, but we are soon to be.'

Hetty may just possibly have had a sense of humour, though her beloved keeps muttering gentle nothings about a great movement that is to renew the vitality of Scottish religion. 'Terms', she tells him, 'may not be quite so blissfully easy to arrange as they are with us.'

There we leave Ronald and Hetty to make the most of their brief leave, barely resisting the temptation to add a few more lines of dialogue, ('Do you think, dearest love, that when Church union comes it will be as sweet as this?'), and noting that the popular Mr Henry Farquhar is about to offer 'Heroes All', a serial with a seafaring setting, and, before it is done, minesweeping and flotilla action in the North Sea.

War brought other problems to the missionary emphasis which was embodied in the separate editorial 'In Far Fields'. It affected some missions and missionaries directly. There are reports of Nyasaland meetings to demand that German East Africa should not be returned to its old colonial rulers, denunciations of German native policy, and incidental references to dislocation of normal missionary arrangements. When South African troops came to Nyasaland, for example, they spread the practice of tipping, and according to the Rev J F Alexander in October 1916 they tipped too much. He feared that one result of the war might be to make Nyasaland a military recruiting ground for other parts of the Empire. The war, of course, distracted attention from missions. The vigour of the article in *Life and Work* about the missionaries not being forgotten has an over-protesting air about it. In September 1915, for example, it was being admitted that 'in some parts of the country it is being found difficult to organise missionary meetings; the anxieties and bereavements of the war are preoccupying the minds of the people.' What enthusiasts were inclined to call 'the romance of missions' was 'fading into dullness before the vivid and lurid lights of war.'

But as the war went on one sector of the mission-field became a battlefield. From 1915 much of the Middle East mission work, mainly aimed at Jews rather than Muslims, ran into very practical difficulties. Turkey, which stretched from Thrace to Sinai and the Persian Gulf, became Germany's ally. And after the failure of the brilliantly conceived but mismanaged Dardanelles expedition the main confrontation between the Turks and the British Empire was on the frontier of the Promised Land.

Chaplains began to write home that in the desert 'dwelling here has awakened the interest of the men in Old Testament history and they are all eager to hear about Abraham and his wanderings, Samson and his exploits etc.' Exaggeration? Perhaps. But while the present editor was writing this chapter a short comment in the magazine of 1978 produced a long letter from an old soldier who wanted the modern Israelis to stay in Sinai. Few of the Scots soldiers who passed that way now remain; but those who have met them will testify that they took a lively and often a biblical interest in the lands where they fought so well and left many of their comrades.

In fact the Turks, despite their terrible reputation, were by later standards reasonably tolerant of the Christian missionaries within their gates and power. Property was taken over but some work continued. 'In Jewish Fields', a page which went its own way within 'In Far Fields', is for a while taken up with scrappy and even contradictory news of the work at Constantinople, Jaffa, Beirut, and Smyrna. But two new notes soon begin to sound. One is of indignation at the Turkish treatment of the Jews, many of whom fled as refugees to Alexandria in Egypt (another centre of the Kirk's Jewish work). Some rabbis were displeased when *St John's Gospel* was used as a textbook in English classes offered to these refugees by the Kirk's evangelist there. Mild though the Turks' action was in comparison with the persecution of the Christan Armenians at the time, it was bad enough; it was also to have a bearing on some later arguments about Jewish presence in Palestine. Arab propagandists who want to take 1917, the year of the Balfour declaration, as the year for calculating old-established Jewish rights in the Holy Land— leaving aside the older-established rights of biblical times—pick a year when Jewish population was quite abnormally low. The ten thousand refugees at Alexandria, incidentally, were Hebrew-speaking. The 'sweet accents of the sacred tongue' were said to cause surprise in the Alexandria streets.

The second note, one of hope that swells into triumph, is the reaction to the realisation that something dramatic and even world-shaking was likely to happen in the Holy Land. It did, though we still do not know where the events that flowed from Turkey's choice of the losing side will lead. They have led so far to the British conquest, the mandate, the creation of Israel at the end of the mandate, and the wars that have followed.

As early as 1915, 'In Jewish Fields' was rejoicing in the news of the formation of the Zion Mule Corps, said to consist of Jews driven from Jerusalem by the Turks 'whom they naturally detest'. The news was eagerly picked up from a letter to an American Jewish newspaper, with obvious propaganda intentions, from the Dardanelles commander, Sir Ian Hamilton, who called it the first purely Jewish unit of the Christian era.

Mr Asquith too was winning approval for himself by claiming that Turkey's entry into the war 'had rung the deathknell of Ottoman dominion not only in Europe but in Asia.'

The excitement was not only in the Jewish section but in the main part of the magazine. Fisher's 'Events and Opinions' asked:

> What is to become of Palestine? Into whose hands are the Holy Places to be committed. Are the ransomed of the Lord to return to Zion? Or the dreams of the crusaders to come true?

As the questions suggest, there is some hedging, arising from a Christian uncertainty about the outcome of the Jewish argument between Zionists and their opponents and about the way the new Zion could be protected, 'for it could never hope to become a Great Power'. In fact Fisher was more inclined to ask questions than give resounding answers. He later seemed happy with a Palestine treated as part of the British Empire for the foreseeable future.

To most politicians, generals, and strategists—especially the 'Westerners' who resisted every diversion of men and resources from France and Flanders—the Palestine campaign was one of the 'sideshows'. To a large section of the Scottish Kirk, as well as those Scottish soldiers who bore the heat and burden of the day in fighting the Turks and the flies, it was a matter of passionate concern. It has been said that Lloyd George presented the capture of Jerusalem by Allenby's army in 1917, not long after the last mud and blood of Passchendaele, as a Christmas present for the Welsh chapels. Those who delve into the excitement over the Holy Land and the impact of the war on the Jews may wonder that the Kirk itself did not eventually put in a bid for the mandate of Palestine.

'All the romance of the Crusades is recalled', wrote the editor in *Life and Work*, glossing over the fact that some of the Crusades were distinctly unromantic and none was distinctly reformed in its Christianity. 'Sir Edmund Allenby is a fortunate man; his name will be remembered as long as Christian folk think of the sacred city of our Lord.'

Nothing seemed 'more refreshing to the heart' than the knowledge that 'the hateful domination of the Turks over the Holy Places of our faith is ended—and ended we trust for ever.' But in the winter of 1917-18, as the German divisions trundled westward from Russia and the British Army lengthened its front in France, there was a sore need for refreshment of the heart. The triumphal picture of the Damascus Gate in Jerusalem faces a long list compiled from parish magazines of honours and awards, beginning with a VC for Lance-Corporal John Hamilton of St Leonard's, Dunfermline. The casualty roll as such had been dropped, presumably for want of space. There are about a dozen deaths in action or active service in the St Bernard's parish magazine, bound along with *Life and Work*, for the last quarter of 1917. Even the honours were punctuated with notes that this or that hero had been killed since, or was reported wounded or missing.

Just as the Christians of Britain rejoiced in the capture of Jerusalem, the war in Palestine, still to roll over the rest of the country, very definitely became a military sideshow. For the Germans were preparing the offensive in France which locked the British Army in a long continuous battle that began as its greatest defeat and ended as its greatest victory, and as a still costlier campaign than the slogging of the Somme and Third Ypres.

But as the war reached its terrible climax in France there was a theme in *Life and Work* which was not only a logical follow-up to the capture of Jerusalem but the first step to a permanent enrichment of the life of the Scottish church and for that matter of the Christian diversity of Jerusalem.

It was in the last issue before the Armistice of *Life and Work*, in the 'Jewish Fields' page that the Rev Bruce Nicol of Skelmorlie wrote of the corners of Palestine that had become forever Scotland, with more than a hint of regret that Allenby had not given the Scottish troops the chance to be first in

THE LAST CRUSADE.

Cœur-de-Lion (*looking down on the Holy City*). "MY DREAM COMES TRUE!"

25.   The capture of Jerusalem (as seen by Bernard Partridge and Mr Punch)

Jerusalem. The piece was primarily a mission exhortation: 'Christ must be enthroned in Palestine', but it linked the cause to the commemoration in the fullest sense of that word of the 'price that Scotland paid for Palestine's deliverance'.

From such a profound mingling of experience—of hope, pride and tears—came St Andrew's, Jerusalem, the kirk and hospice looking across to the walls of the old city, over what in a later war was a truce line and no-man's land between Israel and Jordan. The main appeal for it comes in February 1921, though it was a joint Auld Kirk and United Free plan even then. Since then there have been more tears and hopes deferred, more to be proud of and some things in the last days of Empire to be ashamed of: but the Scots who passed that way have a worthy memorial.

But in 1918 men and women still wondered not how they would remember but when it would all end. After the Balfour declaration, 'In Jewish Fields' wrote words that probably seem more significant now than they did at the time (especially as the Kirk hedged its bets later when the National Home ran into Arab resentment): 'In all their wanderings the hearts of this homeless have turned to Palestine as their true home.' It saw the Jewish return as the fulfilment of prophecy and said 'all right-minded Christian folk will rejoice over the prospect of seeing the Jews once more restored not only to their ancient home but also to an acknowledged place among the nations of the earth.' Probably most Christians, however right-minded, gave more thought to the coming of the Americans, the conflict in Russia where the Bolsheviks had overthrown the original Revolution, and the long, last battle in France.

Editor Fisher, that good man ready to pack his valise for France, still found time to say the orthodox things about national rededication, to underline the war's impetus to reunion in the Kirk, to record without too much flattery Lloyd George's visit to the General Assembly, to denounce easier divorce, and to demand that parliament show as much respect for the rights and conscience of Presbyterians in Scottish education as it did for Roman Catholics. When the first Russian revolution came he was politically cautious and spiritually prophetic, warning of a danger that the 'faith of Russia and her dreams and her mighty passion for the Infinite' might be 'chilled into material'. After the overthrow of the democratic revolution he was to become an outspoken critic, in the mood of the day, of Bolshevism. As for the entry of the Americans into the war, the welcome is cordial enough, perhaps tinged with an unspoken feeling that they might have come sooner. Eventually, of course, there was to be a certain pride that President Wilson's moral idealism was so obviously related to his presbyterian faith.

It is probably fair to say that *Life and Work* fell away as the war drew to a close in 1918: there are signs of war-weariness, as well as paper shortage and of economies in fighting a losing battle to keep the basic price at a penny. Fisher also had his commitment to the Huts. As the year goes on a good deal of 'filler' material is used in 'Events and Opinions'. When the armistice came, just in time for the last issue of the year, the column led off with that hoary standby, the crosses on the Union Flag compared with the harsh German and Austrian eagles. A new lease of life was given to the old thought by attributing it to a chief's sister in South-West Africa who didn't want the Germans back after the South African conquest. The column wandered off into a dissertation on good manners and prompt answering of invitations.

But somehow a few inches were hacked out of the first page, where the 'Sunday Fireside' was occupied by the 1915 narrator of the 'Comrade in White', W H Leathem, meditating on the words of the *Epistle to the Hebrews* about Christ as 'the forerunner for us entered'.

'The horrible nightmare of four and a half years is over', said the leader, 'men rubbed their eyes and could hardly believe themselves awake.' People had gasped in wonder at 'the daily growing record of change' as Bulgaria, Turkey, and Austria collapsed and 'it was seen that the chief enemy was in the toils and must soon be overcome'. There was no bombast and not much joy in the tone: after thanks to God the obvious thought was the cost of war and the fresh tears that would flow with its ending.

A few pages further on were notes about plans for a new serial by Quintin McCrindle, articles on Scottish emblems and Scottish wildlife, plus 'some historical papers too long withheld.'

But nothing would ever be quite the same again in the magazine, in the country, in the church—indeed in that civilisation which generally still thought of itself as Christendom and had been so grievously wounded in its civil war.

Chapter 8
From Armistice to Reunion
(By Way of General Strike)

'We are uniting very soon in Scotland to form a great national Church in a reaction of co-ordinate freedom with the State . . . We Presbyterians have always been in touch with international life . . . From Geneva, and from Edinburgh its offspring, the spirit of modern democracy has gone out into the world. For example, President Wilson, President Masaryk of Czechoslovakia, and Governor de Horthy of Hungary are Presbyterians.'

(From an article in *Life and Work* by Professor W A Curtis on Presbyterians and unity, January 1921.)

After the war nothing was ever quite the same again. War had brought the churches together. New trends in society made them cluster together, even if there were times of irritation.

In the Kirk the ten years after the Treaty of Versailles led the two churches through the legal and practical preparations for reunion. While others were absorbed in promoting or resisting the emergence of Labour as a party of government and worried about the General Strike or the gold standard, the kirks ensured that there was a consensus as well as a constitution for their reunion.

But this same decade that began with the arguments of peacemaking ended with the economic depression which, among other things, revived the political prospects of an Austrian-born fanatic (due to become a mass-murderer) who had done his soldiering with the Bavarians. Further east it brought consolidation by the victors in the Russian civil war and a quarrel among the heirs of Lenin. An unpleasant Georgian, once a divinity student but also due to become a mass-murderer, defeated a Jewish intellectual who had turned out to be an organiser of victory in the war of Whites and Reds. It brought a new turbulence in India, where European and American slogans about self-determination were taken up by a barrister, part saint, part politician, whose lifestyle made unkind critics call him a naked fakir. America decided to experiment with prohibition and bootlegging but not the League of

Nations. Although America was isolationist where Europe was concerned, British concern for American susceptibilities helped end the old alliance with Japan, which looked ambitiously at China, where a new breed of nationalist revolutionaries were aligned with communist ones and resented the western influence which had brought (among other things) the conditions in which missionaries tried to make the Chinese Christian.

It turned out fairly quickly not to be a very brave new world. Sometimes it seemed a tired, weakened, embittered world; sometimes (as in some of the new countries of central and eastern Europe) it showed how quickly those who shouted loudest for their own freedom denied it to others or defined it to suit themselves.

By the autumn of 1919 President Woodrow Wilson was politically and physically a broken man and not, as he had seemed for a year during his second term, the presbyterian prophet in power. When Professor Curtis took the pan-presbyterian view of the world quoted at the beginning of this chapter, the great Scotch-Irish Southerner was already a spent old man as well as a lame-duck President, waiting to drag himself to Harding's inauguration and letting his wife look for a new house in Washington. Masaryk, indeed, whom Curtis claimed as a Presbyterian, was President in Prague, a genuine liberal patriot. But the way in which Curtis bracketed him with 'Governor de Horthy', the admiral in a landlocked Hungary and the regent who kept his Hapsburg king from claiming the throne, was a warning about generalisations in the new Europe. Horthy had his virtues—and he was, in fact, a reformed Hungarian Christian—but he had little in common with Wilson or Masaryk and only too much in common with a breed of nationalist politicians who paid off old scores if they were recognised as among the Allies, and waited for a chance to undo the work of Versailles and other treaties if they were listed among the losers.

But for a time it may have seemed bliss to be alive, and earnest Presbyterians found comfort not only in the League of Nations which Wilson had shaped (but which his country declined to join) but in the mood of Czechoslovakia and its protestant revival. They also found it in news of such tiny reformed churches as the one in Lithuania or of evangelical growth in such improbable places as the Polish Ukraine.

From the perspective of history, perhaps the most unexpected thing about *Life and Work* in this immediate post-war phase is that the Great War was such a long time fading away. The world was slow to recover from the impact of war and in its aftermath British troops still stood guard on the Rhine, the Dardanelles, and even on the Caspian Sea. In 1920 ministers still found a tolerant editor ready to find space for wonderful things they remembered from their days in France.

Well into 1920 it was still recording war honours proudly noted in parish magazines—mainly Military Crosses and other medals, including a Russian Order of St Stanislau which gave satisfaction to Glasgow St Vincent, if not to the *de facto* regime that was winning the war in Russia, despite half-hearted allied 'intervention' on its fringes. In 1920 readers were also being served potted regimental histories—presumably because many of them were both proud and interested. They read, for example, about the Royal Scots Fusiliers' blue facings, bearskins in full uniform, tartan trews, and diced glengarries, as well as of the regiment's changes of title, 'never we hope to be changed again'. That hopeful minor prophet got it wrong. When a French reformed delegate spoke at the 1920 General Assembly his DSO and MC attracted as much note as his fine command of English.

Beside the honours was a regular heading on the gleanings from local magazines: war memorials. About fifteen or sixteen new dedications might be mentioned in a month. They come as bronze tablets, stained glass windows, pipe-organs, Celtic crosses of polished granite, even crosses by the wayside, perhaps fit presbyterian calvaries for men who passed the wayside shrines of France and Flanders on their one-way journey up the line. We take them rather for granted today in the kirks; we gazed up at them from the front pews where the primary Sunday school sat and we saw new names added later; but at the time a vast emotional effort went into them. Tens of thousands of the Kirk's young people were among the Scottish dead; a note in *Life and Work* added the more precise statistics that among them were fifty-four ministers and probationers of the Scottish presbyterian churches, sixteen of whom had been chaplains, and fifty-two divinity students. The bugles' last, sad notes were slow to fade.

Editor Fisher of *Life and Work* was by age and temperament more inclined to side with those who found the brave new world uncongenial, and wished that the madness for change could have died away with the madness of war. But he had a deep feeling for the distress brought by the discovery that a land fit for heroes to live in was more easily invoked than produced.

He wrote of the great ache in Christian Scotland over energetic, efficient, willing workers who found their families on the verge of starvation—for the post-war boom was over and unemployment was rising, especially in the heavy industries. He wrote of the serious winter, with 'danger in it also'.

Hotheads are full of revolutionary ideas that find inspiration in Russia . . .

But the great common-sense of an educated people will not be governed by the idiotic frenzy of such hotheads.

Warning against those who 'coldly declared' that economic law must rule, he wanted the church, for all the difficulty of knowing what to say and do amid such distress, to retain a human heart unfettered by scientific rigidities. How odd today, when a few ministers think that they have discovered some economic laws divinely revealed to Karl Marx, that the warning about scientific rigidities probably needs to be aimed in a different direction!

That was Fisher, an old-style conservative growing old, at his best. When he wrote on the 'pictures' he probably approached his worst. He was also the 1920's equivalent of the modern minister who has strong views about television, even sound views, but who admits he never actually sees much of it.

It is the testimony of those who know the 'Pictures' more intimately than the present writer knows them that in most places where they are shown they are entirely harmless. At times perhaps stupid as a penny 'novelette' may be but generally of a good moral tone.

Yet was he a prophet? Some recent but undefined disclosures in America were a warning against 'the coarsening and degrading type of picture in which all sorts of immorality are made familiar.' They might, he thought, be horribly destructive of the public conscience if they were demoralised. With a sigh, he turned to wonder if Scotland's young people could be incapable of the sustained attention and enlightened curiosity which led an educated man through Sir Walter Scott with such a romantic delight.

Fisher had his critics. He defended himself against those who wanted detailed accounts of church work at home and abroad, and perhaps of their own and their friends' activities. Some important critics also apparently accused him of sectarian intolerance, to judge from the vigour with which he rebutted the charge. Roman Catholic attitudes to the Sinn Fein terrorist campaign in Ireland had certainly roused him to fury. 'This magazine must repeat its testimony against the malign influence in Ireland of a corrupted branch of the Church of Christ.' Even when he found something to admire in Roman Catholics, such as 'the zeal for their religion' which sent sixteen priests from Maynooth to China on St Patrick's Day 1920, he qualified his kind words about their enthusiasm, 'Would that it were equally strong in those who hold a more intelligent faith'.

But Fisher was no more an isolated eccentric than he was a bigot. The

110

flavour of the United Free Church's *Record* is also of concern about Roman Catholic pretensions in Scotland, perhaps tinged with some resentments of what Scots, like the English, felt was Irish extremist betrayal during the war. And the Scots minister in Paris worried about protestant parents sending their daughters to convent schools there. He asked Fisher's help and offered to recommend sounder schools. He did not appeal in vain.

But there were times when Fisher seemed to be drifting out of touch with much of post-war Scotland, too concerned about the girls who went to school in Paris or Lausanne or about the need to convince other girls of the dignity of domestic service. (There had been one hundred and seventy-five thousand girls in domestic service when he became editor.) Yet even as he grew old, and thought of the retirement that illness was soon to overshadow, he was able to be humorous as well as gracious. His literary interests and his sense of humour linked up when he decided that it was not profitable to inquire what was the worst line in English poetry—and, of course, proceeded to do so. He decided it was a dead heat between bad lines in Burns: 'Edina, Scotia's darling seat', and 'There all her charms she does compile.'

He also had practical problems to deal with. There was a year when *Life and Work* made a loss. As the price of paper and printing rose a worried committee cut the size to sixteen pages, including three of 'In Far Fields'. Even at that, the price had to go up to twopence in January 1921, following the example of the UF *Record* and the heavier Scottish dailies.

The wonder is that Fisher stayed on so long, finally retiring when he was in poor health at the end of 1924, worried about Scotland being flooded by the Irish—whom he found 'delightful in their own country'—and indignant about communistic Sunday schools, though reassured that 'no party of propagandists so entirely devoid of humour can ultimately succeed'. He was by this time perhaps more tolerant of Roman error (especially if not intoned with an Irish brogue) in face of modernism and atheism; and perhaps reassured too by twenty-four pages per issue and a nice shiny paper which after more than fifty years looks neater and cleaner than the modern newsprint of a few months ago.

Perhaps, too, he was reassured to see a Labour government come (and go) without much inclination to imitate the Bolsheviks. If God (whose ways we so poorly comprehend) disposes of matters appropriately, the present editor will some day want to talk over many matters with Fisher, a Mr Standfast among editors, and a Christian patriot and gentleman of his time, who also felt and shared the timeless love of his Lord.

There were times in the aftermath of war and the last years of Fisher's editorship (as there have been since) when Britain seemed to have lost its sense of balance, compromise, and fair play. But it is worth quoting a philosophical kind of historical article written in 1921 by Professor Rait of Glasgow, later Principal Sir Robert Rait, which has also a sense of political perspective:

> If some of the demands which we have to consider seem to us to overturn the foundations of society we have to remember that the demands made before 1832 seemed to many good citizens to involve no less a catastrophe … There is something behind such widespread industrial unrest as exists to-day, something that we must discover before we can apply the remedy. No agitation can flourish without some feeling of injustice to support it, however wildly that feeling of injustice may be exploited by professional agitators.

Rait found himself telling his readers how much worse things were after Waterloo. To read his stately prose, worth a place in an anthology of Scottish history, is not just to understand his own argument but to get a new insight into the alarm, anger, and perplexity that produced it. Fisher didn't react so philosophically, but a mark of a good controversial editor is sometimes knowing when to hire a philosopher.

To succeed Fisher came Harry Smith of Old Kilpatrick, a minister with an unusually broad range of literary gifts. He had edited the children's 'Morning Rays' for nineteen years and he had acquired a reputation as a General Assembly sketch-writer, editing the *Laymen's Book of the General Assembly* for ten years in times when such volumes could be marketed and presumably sold at half a crown. He had for most of Fisher's editorship appeared in *Life and Work* as essayist, historical writer, and devotional host at the 'Sunday Fireside', a task he tackled with more lightness and grace than many of the equally worthy but often ponderous divines commissioned by Fisher. He was also a Scots poet (found in the anthology *A Book of Twentieth Century Scots Verse*) using a North-east dialect:

> Baith wark an' play are noo near by—
> Gin they be a' then far hae I?

Fisher took his leave in the January 1925 issue, graciously conceding to his critics that the magazine 'may' have been too literary and 'may possibly' have not dealt sufficiently with the church's work but not really conveying any suggestion that he meant his farewell admission. He added a kick at the modernists, who claimed all the intellectual honesty for themselves, and at Bolshevism, among whose crimes he listed (quite correctly) the murder of

112

ministers of religion. Growling at those who did not 'consider Bolshevism the evil anti-Christian thing it is', he went to his overshadowed retirement. He lived on till 1934, but never recovered his health and, since latterly he lived in Oxford, he was cut off from church life and old friends.

The next month the gentler Harry Smith substituted 'Views and Reviews' for 'Events and Opinions' which, he said, seemed to belong to his predecessor and should not be appropriated by another. The same issue also recorded a presentation to Charteris's successor as convener of the Christian Life and Work committee, the Rev Dr William Robertson. He had been a member of it

26. Editor Smith

for forty-five years and convener for thirty of them, and therefore, in a sense, chairman of the company that brought out *Life and Work*.

They went in for long service in those days; but times were changing—changing most obviously in that the men who held responsibility in the Auld Kirk in the 1920's expected to have to integrate with the other great part of the Kirk, the United Free Church of Scotland. It was appropriate that 1925 opened with a thundering 'Sunday Fireside' oration from the greatest architect of reunion, Dr John White of the Barony in Glasgow. Later in the year he was to be Moderator (as he was again when the kirks united) and was bathed in the purple passages of Smith's sketch-writing. White laid down his duties as Moderator at the end of the Assembly 'with confidence intensified'. A year later, a sign of the times, Smith assured his readers after the Assembly how well another Moderator, Dr John McCallum, would perform 'those varied and widespread duties that now fall to the lot of the Moderator.' In trying to play a variation of a familiar theme—and any editor knows that problem when Assemblies and even Moderators begin to seem much alike—a couple of turns of phrase had caught the way the moderatorial office was changing from a short-term chairman of a long working conference to an archbishop on a one-year contract.

Smith had ideas: one of them was to break with what was becoming the dead hand of the serial story, though he replaced it with 'two series of sketches from ladies who wield graphic pens', one of them Mrs Isabel Menzies of Tobermory Manse. He was slipping back a bit by 1928 when a six-part serial by Ethel F Heddle ended with 'a wedding never to be forgotten in Kilspindie, the marriage of the young laird with Pansy.' 'Gair Folk' by Barbara Ross McIntosh also developed into a serial, as near as made no difference, and followed the tradition of having the lower classes speak Scots—which, of course, they did. Whether it was good Scots is a matter of opinion:

> I'm gaun hame they're aye tellin' me; but I'm nae ready an' I'm feart the Lord winna want me in his bonnie big hoose.' His voice trailed away but his eyes remained fixed on me in a troubled glance of questioning . . .

Younger ministers also squeezed into the seats at 'Our Sunday Fireside', though some of them turned out to be young men who, though less than ten years on from ordination, could sound awfully like old ministers. One was Charles Warr of St Giles, moving enough on the walk to Emmaus: 'The knowledge of Christ must begin the simple round of common life, and if there we cannot find him we shall find him nowhere else'; but authoritarian, imperious even, when he put elders in their place (or so he thought, and there were not letters to the editor to tell us what elders thought!) in 1928. Warr wrote, 'He has no part in the celebration of the Sacrament . . . the function of the elder is administrative and is in no sense ministerial . . . nor has he anything to do with the form or conduct of public worship . . . the eldership is not like the ministry a scriptural institution.' The word ordination, in that high view of the High Kirk, is reserved for ministers, and uttered with an awe which it would be hard to find today in many Anglican and even Roman Catholic utterances.

Smith, probably from both temperament and inclination, lacked Fisher's eagerness to comment on public affairs. Fisher responded to events with opinions; Smith, for whom almost everything—or everything he wrote about—seemed delightful, gracious, dignified, discerning, charming, distinguished, or refreshing, took pleasure in reviews and was sparing in views. He reflected the enthusiasm of the time for the League of Nations, deciding that 'manifestly the blessing of God is on it'; and in June 1926 he had to venture rather further into opinion than usual. It was hardly necessary to explain to readers why *Life and Work* reached them so late:

> Everyone knows what the whole country has come through. The General

Strike, so long threatened, has been tried and has proved it utter futility, as an argument of any kind, not even of force still less of reason.

On the most important church issue of the time circumstances reinforced his temperament and inclination. There was some exhortation of the Auld Kirk's members on the coming union and a good deal of cautious commentary on the progress of the United Free Church's processes after the last legal barriers had been overcome. Reunion also stirred the literary enthusiasm of Lord Sands, the Judge who was the most influential Kirk layman of the day and a major diplomatic as well as legal negotiator in the union discussions. (He had also tried his hand at a serial story of a sort.) But the Auld Kirk waited with a kind of restrained anticipation, well aware that a word out of place would become the small change of the wrangle going on among the UFs as a minority resisted the reunion: a small minority that hoped to be a big minority and which, skilfully handled, might be whittled down to a tiny one. The Kirk watched, prayed and waited. Inevitably its magazine to some extent marked time, for one of the things that could never be quite the same again after reunion was *Life and Work*.

27. John White of the Barony

Chapter 9
The Reunion of the Kirk

'A historic thing was done. It has deeply touched the heart of the Scottish nation. Will it be accompanied by a new chapter in the religious life of the people?'

(Dr John White, first Moderator of the General Assembly of the reunited Church of Scotland, in *Life and Work*, January 1930.)

Since the end of the war the two main parts of the Scottish Kirk had been increasingly acting together and not merely moving together. In the last years before the union they had also been planning together. Before they became the reunited Church of Scotland the Auld Kirk (or 'establishment') and the United Free Church already thought of themselves as sister-churches.

Certainly the UFs found this a happy phrase. To refer to 'our sister-Church' avoided a reference to the 'Church of Scotland'. The UFs were happy to use the old name once the new church was formed by reunion. But some of them found the term sticking just a little in their throats when it still referred to that part of the Kirk which had kept the old name and patrimony in 1843.

As the union approached the editors and managers of the two main church magazines also thought of coming together.

The United Free equivalent of *Life and Work* was *The Record*—to which could be added for a long time the description which made up the full title: 'of the home and foreign mission work of the United Free Church of Scotland'. By 1929 this had been simplified to *The Record of the United Free Church of Scotland*—and at the union was added, with the necessary deletion, to make the full name provide the sub-title of the united magazine.

The *Record* was a polished and skilful production, more topical and in the late 1920's more journalistic than *Life and Work*, and much less literary. Indeed in some ways it was closer than Harry Smith's *Life and Work* to the later magazine of the Kirk and even to the present one. *Life and Work*, thanks to the long editorship of Fisher and the way Smith had brought a different

DIVISIONS AND RE-UNIONS IN

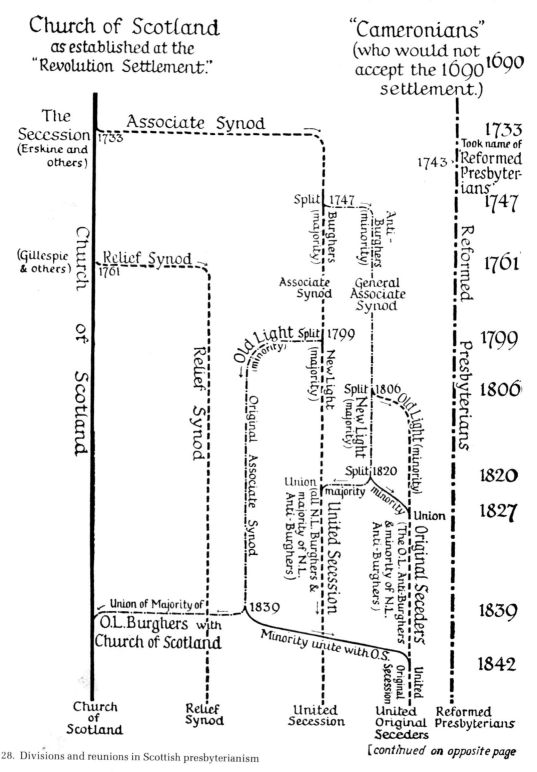

28. Divisions and reunions in Scottish presbyterianism

[continued on opposite page

Scottish Presbyterianism

continued from opposite page]

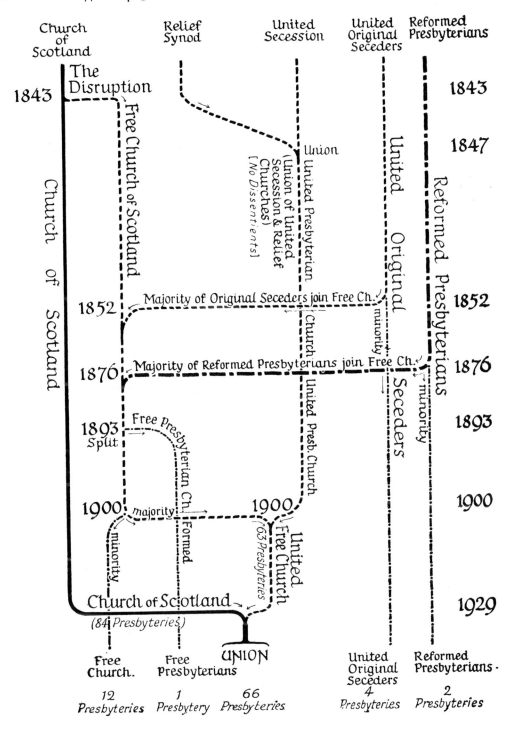

Church of Scotland   Relief Synod   United Secession   United Original Seceders   Reformed Presbyterians

1843 — The Disruption

1843

Free Church of Scotland

Church of Scotland

United Presbyterian (Union of United Secession & Relief Churches) [No Dissentients]

United Original Seceders

Reformed Presbyterians

Union — 1847

1852 — Majority of Original Seceders join Free Ch. — 1852   minority

United Presb. Church

1876 — Majority of Reformed Presbyterians join Free Ch. — 1876   minority

1893 Split — Free Presbyterian — 1893

1900 — majority — Free Presbyterian Ch. Formed

1900 — United Free Church (63 Presbyteries)

1900

minority

Church of Scotland → — 1929
(84 Presbyteries)

UNION

Free Church.	Free Presbyterians	UNION	United Original Seceders	Reformed Presbyterians.
12 Presbyteries	1 Presbytery	66 Presbyteries	4 Presbyteries	2 Presbyteries

temperament rather than a new formula, had remained fairly close to its old-established style. The *Record* expressed the strong journalistic personality (which went with much personal reticence) and the readiness for change of its editor, William P Livingstone, who had been elected by the UF Assembly in 1912, beating three ministers and commanding the then modestly reasonable salary of four hundred pounds a year. The UF Kirk also had a publications' manager, Alexander McKellar, who took over the work in the reunited church till his death in 1937. He had previously been London manager of Collins, the publishers.

29. Editor Livingstone

The *Record* reflected the character and interests of the UF church. Compared to *Life and Work* it was more militantly aligned with the temperance movement and seemed to hanker after prohibition. Compared to Smith's *Life and Work* (though not to Fisher's) it was more militantly protestant. It was even more passionately mission-minded, though Livingstone also edited a purely missionary magazine called *Other Lands* for the UF kirk, and was ready to clash with government and white settlers who seemed not to give priority to black African interests. It was more forceful than *Life and Work* on disarmament (though it is hard to say if this reflected a real difference in policy and not merely in editorial style), and because the UF kirk depended even more on what its people gave it had even more emphasis on money and giving. When the kirks joined in 1929 the majority of the one million three hundred thousand communicant members came from the Auld Kirk but the figures for giving (as Livingstone presented them in the month of the union, October 1929, when his *Record* was for three months 'of the Church of Scotland') showed that the UFs gave £1,500,000 the previous year and the Auld Kirk less than £900,000.

The *Record* also had far more emphasis on the union than *Life and Work*.

When a man is about to be hanged, said Dr Johnson, it concentrates his mind wonderfully. Although most of the UFs thought that they were to be married at reunion, and not hanged, the argument had a stimulating and concentrating effect, very evident in the *Record*. As the official magazine it was frankly propagandist, trying to whittle down the minority against reunion, as well as to encourage and reassure the doubters. There were a few doubters in the Auld Kirk but they formed no real opposition; in any case they had nowhere to go. The result was that the *Record* had a passionate sense of purpose which reflected and stimulated Livingstone's editorial powers.

Livingstone, from North Queensferry, began his working life in the burgh assessor's office in Edinburgh. Later he was attracted to journalism after a meeting with Annie S Swan and edited an office magazine before taking a job as 'official reporter to the legislative council in Jamaica'. He became editor there of *The Daily Gleaner*, a *Times* special correspondent in the Caribbean, including Haiti, and returned to be a chief sub-editor in Fleet Street. He was also a good opinion and feature writer who brought not only professional skills but a certain toughness (despite his diffident and withdrawn manner) and even thrawnness to his job. At one point he had all but thrown up his job in a battle of brinkmanship with his publications committee and its manager, Alexander McKellar, over who was to provide the blocks needed for better quality photographs. He was 'instructed' to get them from a London firm and seemed ready to ignore the instruction and take the consequences, though the quarrel was patched up. Yet in a very Scots way he combined this with an inner serenity.

As the negotiations for the integration of the publications work of the two churches went on he was also an advocate of radical change in church journalism. He had already been allowed by the UF publications committee (though with a bad grace recorded in a frigid minute) to give a helping hand to the weekly and financially strained *Scots Observer*, edited at first by a fine Scottish journalist of mildly nationalist inclinations, William Power, and later by Jack Stevenson, a minister who was one day to be editor of *Life and Work*. For a time in 1929 Livingstone himself acted as editor. The *Scots Observer* took a Christian view of the secular Scottish world and was commended—very generously in the case of Harry Smith's *Life and Work*—by the two pre-union kirks.

Livingstone, probably aware that the *Scots Observer*, which had church backing, was attractive but not viable in the long run, clearly thought of an 'official' church weekly. He lost the battle. When the two kirks decided to unite their monthlies and keep them in the magazine format, and as monthlies,

30.   1929: union at last

Livingstone's welcome for the decision was less than whole-hearted, despite his complete commitment to reunion. He wrote in the last *Record*, December 1929, that 'some hoped that so favourable an opportunity would be taken advantage of to make a fresh departure and provide a new type of magazine but it has been decided to proceed very much on the old lines.' Perhaps this was wise. Even with John Buchan as editor, a *Scots Review* had foundered in pre-war days. The *Scots Observer* was doomed. Yet if it was ever to succeed 1929 was the time for a fair chance and new start.

Before proceeding on these lines together (as settled in 1928) the two magazines proceeded on them separately for a little longer. But as *Life and Work* entered the reunion year, which was also in its own jubilee year, a sign of the times was that the UF Moderator, Dr Harry Miller, first-footed 'Sunday Fireside' in January. 'We have come to the meeting of the ways', he wrote. 'We have the right to hope that the witness of God's grace and power by a united Church will be clearer and stronger than ever.' He wrote serenely of God's guidance and expressed a widespread sense that the two churches had never really ceased to be one. The picture of the Sma' Glen above his piece was captioned 'The Gathering Storm', but it was a false alarm.

At the adjourned General Assemblies, whose approval of the basis and plan of union was recorded on the opposite page, the UF minority had been forty-eight. It was to be whittled down to less than half that for the final gesture, despite the passionate campaigning of the Rev James Barr, as attached to 'voluntary' principles in religion as to Labour ones in politics. He had been MP for Motherwell since 1924 and was later, after defeat in the national government landslide of 1931, to return for Coatbridge. *Life and Work* recognised Dr Gordon Mitchell as an Auld Kirk equivalent, who held that the union compromised the historical position of the national church, but he had raised only seven votes in the Assembly. It fell to three at the next Assembly.

As the actual time for union approached—with further Assemblies in May before the union ones in October—it was all over bar the formality, the emotion, and the ceremony, at which the Duke of York (later George VI) was Lord High Commissioner. The Moderators, Dr Joseph Mitchell and Principal Alexander Martin of New College, worked on their call to prayer, published (with slight differences in punctuation and house-style, viz: 'reunion' and 're-union') in both magazines.

Life and Work offered a Hymn of Union by W S Crockett, meant to be sung to 'Duke Street':
Now through the ever-changing years,
Behind the sundering and the strain,

31. The reunion procession

Thou comest, Lord, to wipe our tears
And build our broken walls again.

Livingstone in the *Record* was not a great one for ministerial verses. However he printed as the first 'note and comment' of the month, under the heading 'Union', the second paraphrase, 'O God of Bethel'.

The *Record* made no concessions to the minority who stood out to be the UF Church 'Continuing' and who remain in being today. Its September leader on the 'Supreme Event' saw it as a divinely inspired duty, a work expressive of the mind of Christ, and an act of loyalty not only to him but to all those who for his rights had 'endured the pain of schism only because they suffered from the still deeper pain of a conscience outraged by denial of the rights of the Redeemer'. The long exile is over. The Temple is purified. Another Zion rises on the old site. In the one hundred years of church journalism since the foundation of *Life and Work* there is no finer and nobler writing than these last words before the reunion, which all but restored the unity of the Scottish reformed church. Fifty years later we still await a few dear but awkward friends.

The union came. The formal act took place, after the service in St Giles', in the improbable environment of what was and still is a 'bus garage, the Edinburgh 'Industrial Hall' in Annandale Street off Leith Walk. It was a 'veritable cave of the winds' which had been transformed under Sir D Y Cameron's artistic direction into a temporary assembly hall able to take twelve thousand people, all the commissioners to what had been two Assemblies (less the continuing UF remnant) and a great army of spectators of whom most were really eager participants. There were ten pages of purple prose in *Life and Work* from Smith's favoured sketch-writer, the Rev Gordon Quig of Monifieth. The *Record* ran to twenty pages of pictures, drawings, and Livingstone's text to the 'descriptive and pictorial diary'. He had already brought out a commemorative issue to take the place of the October number. It is a historical document presenting the facts and the outlook of the united church as it saw itself and including a notable diagrammatic attempt to show the processes of secession, disruption, and reunion in the Scottish presybterian tradition.

This union to-day is the latest and largest but not the last. We have not got the final instalment. There are fragments of the old Reformed Church of Scotland yet to be assembled in one house. And until they are within that house there surely cannot be a true discovery of God's will for the wider household of faith.

Wise, and perhaps still relevant words from the closing address of the first Moderator of the reunited General Assembly, John White. Not till that homecoming will there ever be a mood and occasion to match that one of which the editors of 1929 made so much.

Now, as hero and heroine might have said in an old-fashioned *Life and Work* serial: 'My dear, not only we but our churches are now united: and their magazines very soon will be too!'

The union of the magazines, professing to include the best features of both, was delayed for practical reasons until the first issue of 1930 as *Life and Work—The Record of the Church of Scotland*. It was to be 'New series, Volume 1', though despite all their good intentions the Auld Kirk side emphasised the continuity and the UF one the new start. For some years the new magazine existed in annual bound form in both the red binding to match the old *Life and Work* and the black one to match the old *Record*, with the black one vigorously lettered 'Volume 1' on the spine from 1930.

Who was to be editor? The graceful Smith, coming up to five years in Auld Kirk office, or the dedicated and perhaps awkward professional Livingstone, who had served the UF Kirk so well since 1912? The Auld Kirk had never in its fifty years with *Life and Work* risked a layman. The reunited Kirk evaded the problem by appointing Smith and Livingstone as joint editors. It looked a formula for unhappiness but in fact it did not last long enough for the trials and tribulations of Gilbertian editorship in the manner of *The Gondoliers* ever to become fully apparent. The aim appears to have been for Smith to handle 'general literary matter' and Livingstone the rest. Shortly after the first new-style *Life and Work* had appeared a 'severe nervous overstrain' forced Smith to give up. However, he remained minister of Heriot and later was again convener of the Publications Committee—he had been joint convener after the union—even offering to act as interim editor during an awkward phrase after Livingstone retired when there was indecision and perhaps difference of opinion about his successor.

There had been some practical problems in coping with the new magazine. It had a vast circulation when the two former magazines were combined (nearly two hundred and seventy thousand at first) and continued to use both the printers of the separate church magazines, R & R Clark and Morrison and Gibb, both of Edinburgh. They gave way in 1939 to McCorquodale, of Glasgow, who continued until a move to Dunfermline in 1977.

The technical processes were explained by 'a printer' in June 1930, setting out to answer the question why *Life and Work* should go so early to press (a familiar question now as then), and starting with the familiar truth: 'Most people who read *Life and Work* do not realise how considerable a journal it is.' Although the article—an admirable account of the printing processes of the time— does not go into detail about distribution (a surprise, as this is the main reason for the relatively early printing date each month) he does make clear what went into the parcels, 'Young Scotland, Greatheart, the Scottish Sunday School Teacher, Morning Rays, and the Man's Own Paper'. The latter had, four years previously, replaced the 'Young Men's Guild Supplement'.

One of the problems of integration was that different editorial practices had been followed in the different churches. In the Auld Kirk it appears that the committee were still accustomed to 'revising the proofs'. The mind boggles, though at least one ocasion on which this censorship became publicly known was after Fisher's wartime campaign against anglican arrogance where chaplains were concerned. Perhaps Livingstone also boggled. The printer's account of his work six months after the magazine union implies that the editor and no-one else handled the proofs, except of course the advertising manager and staff.

One result of the union of the two kirks and two magazines was to make the twopenny *Life and Work* (postage 1½d, 1d to Canada) an important advertising medium. If more recent market research is any guide this must have been in face of the hostility of a section, small but sometimes vocal, of the readers who disliked any 'secular' advertising. (As far back as 1909 Fisher was telling this section that he would drop the advertisements if church funds provided the extra three thousand pounds they then brought in.) There were only two major differences then from present practice. One was the grouping of all advertisements together, which allowed their deletion from the bound volumes. The other was the acceptance of advertisements which today would seem to be at odds with the ethics of the advertising industry and the inclinations of both editor and Kirk committees, though there was a 'censors' committee' which rejected at least one 'anti-rheumatic tea'.

In October 1931, for example, at a time of severe trade depression there was a 64-page magazine, plus the four buff-coloured cover pages (instead of the old pink and to be replaced by blue in 1933). It had twenty-one pages of advertising, including a patent remedy, still on sale but making more modest claims, which purported to 'rejuvenate your arteries', fortify the heart muscle, and 'correct your blood pressure'. Ten years later it was toning things down, but still producing devotees with wonderfully 'strong hearts'. Other advertisements were, by modern standards, xenophobic and inclined to 'knocking copy'. 'Who wants dumped oats for breakfast?' asked a well-known

BECAUSE

1. Ours is the quickest way.
2. Nettoyage à Sec is world famous.
3. You know the exact cost.

FIXED PRICES.

COSTUME 5/6
COAT 5/6
JUMPER SUIT 6/-
FROCK 6/-

Keep up your
New Year Resolution
—— to save

Whatever resolutions you shed
when enthusiasm cools, never
lose the saving habit. The time
will come when you'll be glad
you kept it up.

Savings
CERTIFICATES

You can buy Savings Certificates in single
documents representing 1, 5, 10, 25, 50,
and 100 Certificates, costing 16s., £4, £8,
£20, £40, and £80 respectively. They can be
obtained from any Money Order Post Office
or Bank, or through a Savings Association.

Why do Mexicans
Revolute?

POSSIBLY it is the hot, peppery
tamales they eat. No doubt they
would "let off steam" in some more
civilised way if you could bring them
up on Scott's Porage Oats.

For these splendid breakfast oats build
sound and active brains as well as strong
and healthy bodies. They are the finest
of all oats—the best that even Scotland
can grow. And everyone knows that
Scotland's oats are without an equal for
quality and flavour.

*Yet, weight for weight, Scott's
Porage Oats actually cost you less
than imported oats. Look for this
name on the packet you buy.*

2 lb. 10ᴰ   1 lb. 5½ᴰ
FULL WEIGHT WITHOUT PACKET

32. 'Why do Mexicans revolute?' The magazine had few Mexican readers, and advertisers had more scope then than now.

name, denouncing Russian and other imported oats, 'often of very inferior quality'.

Elsewhere a lady from Tillicoultry writes to say that she was a poor cripple when she went to doctors and was only sorry she hadn't turned sooner to some philanthropist who offered rheumatic remedies free (well, on trial anyway!) He claimed to have cured many of the worst cases even of rheumatoid arthritis.

But the Kirk's own agencies were outspoken in their advertisements. The Continental Committee of the day began a quarter-page: 'With their backs to the wall Continental Protestant Churches are fighting the organised and well financed forces of Bolshevist Materialism and Romanist Aggression.' Their kith and kin of the colonial missions began their appeal for money: 'The sun never sets on the British Empire', and went on to say that 'Scots folk have settled to serve the world by their industry, character, and grit'—presumably even in South Africa and Rhodesia.

But the new magazine had been well and truly launched. To vary the metaphor a bit, the two old vintages had been poured into the new bottle.

Not surprisingly the first words in the restyled magazine were from the driving force of reunion and first Moderator of the united church's General Assembly, John White. The 'Sunday Fireside' had become 'For the Quiet Hour'. Whether anyone who really wanted a quiet hour would have invited John White in is arguable, for he stands out as a man of action rather than meditation. His meditation was on how action might be arranged.

'It is not merely a new year that is before us: we have entered into a New Age.' To respond to it White wrote in terms which often apply to the doubts and depressions of our times; and he wrote of the call to the middle-aged— 'young folk cannot work miracles just because they are young'— and of a dangerous surrender of intellect which led to indolence of the spirit.

'A new age'. For the Kirk it meant a lot of encouragement to think about the reunited church as a whole and not as a concordat between two great forces of the past. A few pages after White's 'forward call for the quiet hour' there is a piece obviously meant to introduce the next Moderator, Dr Andrew Bogle, to the Auld Kirk readers who knew little of his work as the UF Home Department Secretary. But fairly soon the emphasis on thinking as one became less obvious, for the union was going well. Unlike some further-fetched unions more recently canvassed, of course, it was between two churches which shared the same doctrine and order, and very largely the same ways, though some historians suggest that much in the modern Kirk's way of doing things in committee and congregation owes a great deal to the practice of the old UF Kirk.

'A new age'. The men and women of 1930 thought of it in terms of disarmament, of acute class divisions in society, of the break-up of the old party system (for a second Labour government, still without an absolute majority but stronger than the first, had come to office four months before the reunion). They thought of it in terms of temperance reform, for the failure of American Prohibition was not obvious and the 'dry' Hoover had apparently won a significant victory over the Roman Catholic and 'wet' Al Smith in November 1928; of the impact of the 'Oxford Group' Buchmanism, later to become Moral Rearmament; of slum clearance, which probably seemed and was the most soluble of the social problems of inter-war Britain.

A determination to widen the horizons of the Kirk and of the new *Life and Work* appeared in the September magazine when the Labour Under-Secretary of State for Scotland, Tom Johnston (later Churchill's wartime Secretary of State), wrote an article about slums which took first place in the magazine. Given Johnston's reputation in these days (he had quite recently specialised in polemical class warfare as well as social reform and had written some brilliantly unkind things about the Scottish upper classes), the more

33. Social problems in Glasgow—cartoon satire in the 'new series' *Life and Work* after the Union.

remarkable thing was not anything he actually said but that he was there to say it.

Some of it was and still is horrifying to read: accounts of 'three adult daughters and one adult son all occupying the same bed, and of other similar cases in the Scottish cities; of a Dunbartonshire village with eight dry privies for seventy houses, of an acre in Edinburgh with one thousand three hundred and ninety-three inhabitants and infantile mortality amounting to a 'massacre of infants such as Herod never knew.' There is also a counter-attack on the idea that if poor people were given bathrooms they used them as coal bunkers, and what our generation may find an altogether too sweeping assumption that people never make slums—a reaction to what Johnston called the 'smug economists' who blamed the tenants and not the housing.

'Public opinion is the great policeman', Johnston wrote, turning the eloquence that once rattled the skeletons in aristocratic cupboards to an almost prim pride in clean lace curtains and geraniums in window-boxes.

It was the time when the Locarno pact seemed to promise peace in Europe; when unemployment was severe but there were hopes that recovery was just around the corner; when the relatively placid mood of the 1929 Labour government (and Tom Johnston's welcome to the official magazine of the Kirk) suggested that acrimony in politics might gradually subside.

But ahead lay the deepest time of economic depression: the break-up of the Labour government when its leader, Ramsay MacDonald, went into coalition with his opponents and was reviled as a new Judas by his old supporters; and the rise of the dictators.

34. Sir Winston Churchill

Chapter 10
The gathering storm

'The most helpful thing that can be said is that since Germany has regained in her own way what she regards as necessary for her self-respect as a nation, the realities of the situation will force statesmen of all countries to resolute, unremitting, and combined endeavour after security, disarmament, and peace.'

(From *The Church of Scotland and Peace* by Dr J Hutchison Cockburn, May 1935.)

'But we must also learn to confess that in the past our own country has in some measure been guilty of the wrong-doing with which Italy has been charged to-day . . . we must first ourselves renounce the principle of unfettered national sovereignty and the armaments by which it is maintained, accept without reserve the principle of an international order based on justice, and be ready for the changes involved in such an order.'

(From the *Church of Scotland Ministers' Peace Society Manifesto*, published November 1935.)

The 'Gathering Storm' was the title of the picture that rather incongruously ushered in the reunion year in *Life and Work*. It is also the title of Churchill's account of the 1930's, the first volume of his Second World War series. But storms can begin to gather with a cloud no bigger than a man's hand.

In the Alps, around Berchtesgaden, say, the visitor may waken to an apparently cloudless sky, and breakfast while a few white puffs gather far above the mountain-tops. By early afternoon the sky is like a West Highland day that could go either way. Then, quite soon, it is clear that the storm is gathering. There is nothing to do but to await it and prepare, and to bear it when it comes.

The 1930's were a bit like that, though the literary tricks should not be taken too literally. Hitler for a long time seemed a cloud no bigger than a man's hand, but the indifference, complacency, blindness—there were elements of all these in the British reactions to events in Europe—can partly be explained by serious distractions. They included the wrangle over India, which set Churchill as far apart from the Conservative leaders of the day as Enoch Powell has been in our time; the painfully slow recovery from the worst of the depression and of the hopes that imperial preference would not only bind the Empire together but revive the British economy; Japan's adventurous exploitation of confusion in Manchuria at first and then in the rest of China; Mussolini's challenge to the League of Nations over Abyssinia at a time when he was still reckoned closer to Italy's old allies of the West than to Hitler; the passions roused by the Soviet Union under Stalin, which some people like the Webbs hailed as 'a new civilisation' and others, like Malcolm Muggeridge, discovered to be a system of cruelty, half-concealed by vigorous lies and much self-deception.

This is the world that is reflected in the shiny pages of *Life and Work* in the 1930's. Before we judge its response, reflecting the Kirk's response, we need to make two massive allowances. First, we have to see the leadership (or lack of it) from the church in the context of the mood of the nation and the quality of its leadership (or lack of it), not merely among those who held power in the national government but in the alternative government. Secondly, we have to realise how sadly defective our own assumptions and preoccupations might seem a decade from now. In fact the Kirk and *Life and Work* emerge, if anything, a bit better than the nation as a whole. But before moving to the supreme issues of the time it is as well to look at the development of the magazine and the life of the church.

In 1934 Livingstone retired after a term which (if one counts the *Record* as well as the 'new-series' *Life and Work*) roughly equalled Fisher's. Despite his gentle demeanour he had his enemies (his committee once refused to meet his expenses of £27 to go to a major international presbyterian conference in Budapest), and perhaps there were some ready enough to see him go in 1934, though his decision to retire must have been linked not only to his own health but to the fact that his wife was dying. She died ten days after being there to receive R F Dunnett, whose interview-profile of Livingstone in December, 1934, is not only one of the best pieces of journalism to appear in *Life and Work*, but almost the only picture we have of Livingstone as a personality and not merely a professional editorial presence. He was reticent in some things—among them his exact age (nearly seventy when he retired)—and surprisingly little known despite the popularity of a series of books which he wrote about missionaries. The most popular of all (about Mary Slessor) was translated into at least eight languages. A revised edition of it appeared as recently as 1967.

That interview, gracefully but reluctantly granted, revealed a lot about Livingstone, about church journalism and even about the church itself.

Was it really back in 1934 that an editor of *Life and Work* reflected that the church 'is in a very difficult period just now with the prevailing weariness of spirit, the overthrow of authority, and the pressure for change and readjustment'? Or noted that 'old loyal subscribers die off and one fears that their place is not taken by the younger folk'? Or conceded that 'an ambitious journalist unless he has a special call to the work' could find special difficulties in the editorship, when the 'fact dominating the situation is that the magazine is the official organ of the Church and that in a Church composed of individualistic Scots there is no common mind—there are are as many minds as readers'? The editor, said Livingstone, 'has a large intractable mass of

35. Editor Carstairs

official material to deal with—usually appeals for money more or less camouflaged'.

But Livingstone earned a tribute quoted later: 'No church ever had a better editor or a better magazine.' He was a very fine Scottish journalist. Although he reappeared in 1937 to serve the church as 'press agent' (in effect setting up a press office), that should be his epitaph. He died in 1950 aged eighty-five. His last book, on Shetland, where he retired to live in his son's manse, appeared when he was eighty-two. He had even become a reader (ie lay preacher), and acted as a *locum* in Shetland.

The 'intractable mass of official material' was to be thrust on to an unexpected successor.

After some hesitation in high places Livingstone was succeeded by another editor from the UF tradition, but one whose experience was outside Scotland, and outside both the parish ministry and journalism. The Rev George Carstairs, a man of great intellectual gifts, had been for thirty years a missionary in India, where he had turned his hand to much besides preaching and teaching, proving himself as an administrator. He was to develop this versatility in *Life and Work* and also become a religious broadcaster of note. It was also said of him that he had one essential qualification to be editor of *Life*

135

and Work: in Lamb's phrase 'he put up with the calls of the most impertinent visitor'. He was also credited with revelling in new tasks, new points of contact, and new problems, of which he must have found many, pitched into *Life and Work* as he was. But some people thought 'it was a waste to use this grand missionary as an editor'.

Carstairs' appointment avoided one perennial problem of *Life and Work*. It was easier for him than most people to meet the reasonable demands of the Kirk's immensely powerful missionary interest and to resist its unreasonable ones. But some of the skills of journalism, as well as the diplomatic problems of the Kirk's editor, he had to learn as he went along, though he could not go too far wrong keeping to the framework which Livingstone had constructed— and not only in missionary matters.

When Carstairs took over in 1935 *Life and Work* was still at that summit of its importance which it had reached after the reunion. When the tumult and the thanksgiving of 1929 died away, life in many congregations went on pretty much as it had done before reunion. The readjustment which Charteris had foreseen forty years before could not come quickly. The changes brought by union at local level gave some kirks absurd parish boundaries which had no real community meaning. How could they if three kirks originally built for separate denominations were in one high street? They also brought others anxiety about their future once 'union and readjustment' had reared its sometimes ugly, but often inevitable and urgently necessary, head. The printed word, however, was both a practical form and a visible symbol of the new unity. The united General Assembly met once a year; *Life and Work* appeared monthly, recognisably in continuity with both the Auld Kirk's magazine and the *Record*. Then as now, but in a special way in the mood of the immediate aftermath of reunion, *Life and Work* well expressed the complementary roles of the 'Church' as local congregation linked to community, national Kirk of Scotland, and Scottish province of the universal Church of Christ.

As the 1930's began it seemed that the Kirk's sense of belonging to the universal Church, and to the international reformed tradition within it, would continue to be most strongly affirmed through involvement in the 'mission field'.

That included India, where Gandhi was saint, politician, and symbol of a new India; it included South Africa, on which Livingstone had taken a strongly liberal position, though interest was fitful and criticism restrained by the standards of more recent times; it included China, where Chiang Kai-shek had been the ally of the Communists before becoming, thanks to his wife, the hope of the Christians as well as the focal point of resistance to Japanese encroachments. The union of 1929 in Scotland ensured that in the 'new-series' *Life and Work* there would be as much emphasis on Manchuria in the north as on Ichang on the Yangste. It even included the mandated territory of Palestine, where the enthusiasts for Jewish missions hoped and argued, sometimes in the face of all the evidence, that the development of the 'national home' would be accompanied by a fresh Jewish response to Christianity. They tended to see the secularism of so many Jews as an intermediate stage on their way to discovery of how the law was to be fulfilled.

But it was the affairs of Europe that were to dominate the 1930's. It is easy now to see the moment after which these affairs were never the same again, tempting to turn up that time in print—in *The Times* or *Punch* or *Life and Work*—and judge how editors and readers reacted. Sweeping judgments they could be, if we forgot about being judged and our own inability to look ten years ahead and be sure what will matter above all, and what will matter not a docken.

March 1933. In a monthly magazine it was the first time for reaction to Hitler as a man of power and not a man of words merely. *Life and Work* that month had a leader on 'The Church and Social Questions' that said very little but was meant as an introduction to a long report on unemployment by the Church and Nation Committee. It had some practical proposals for alleviating the worst effects of the depression, about allotments, carpentry and cobbling classes, and club rooms open all day. The mixture of theological and economic opinion is much harder to follow, and there is no need to try. But one of the lines of progress it tried to outline was 'cultivation of the international mind'.

The Woman's Guild was more concerned about gambling. Maintenance of the Ministry was worried about ministers who were not only underpaid but late in getting what was their due: £300 a year would mean far more to our ministers . . . were they to receive £75 at the end of each quarter.' The main Jewish mission interest was in 'notable baptisms in Tiberias'.

Hitler passed, it seems, unnoticed. But he was to thrust himself on the notice of everyone soon enough.

The Kirk of Scotland, and for that matter its magazine, were to emerge creditably—more creditably by far than some others in both church and state—before the final enforced, belated, and ineffective British and French surrender to the inevitability of war in 1939. The last pre-war years produced some notable Christian testimony in deeds as well as words, and some of it was nobly expressed in the printed word. But anyone who studies either the spiritual or the political mood of Britain in 1938-39 is liable to be disappointed, distressed, even shocked when he looks more closely at the years when Hitler might have been stopped, and Germany perhaps redeemed without the fire, blood, tears and martyrdom of the war years. Only if we could be more certain of our virtue and judgment today, however, might we dare cast our stones confidently.

It is, indeed, hard to look back and say that at such and such a moment the Kirk awoke to the peril—just as hard with church as it is for nation.

In February 1933, indeed, one of 'an energetic group of younger Scots who are dissatisfied with things as they are', had noted that in Germany paganism had become a cult. He was George MacLeod of Govan. Yet as one reads through the next few years, including reports of passionate General Assembly debates on pacifism, the same MacLeod is scarcely among those ready to stand up to Hitler in the way that eventually proved inevitable. But this was no lonely eccentricity. In 1933 it was the Rev J W Stevenson—a superb journalist and Christian—who led a bid to renounce war in any circumstances; the following year the noble spirit of a future moderator, Archie Craig.

What of the old, the wise, the established men? They had the caution of their wisdom. At the end of his moderatorial year in 1933 Professor H R Mackintosh of Edinburgh added a mention of a visit to Berlin after an enthusiastic account of the 'quiet confidence' in Prague of the ageing President Masaryk and the 'breath of a new time' coming over the Christians of Hungary, where ten thousand elders were about to gather in conference. And in Berlin?

> We found people very conscious of passing through a revolution . . . The victory of Hitlerism was obviously regarded in Christian circles as a welcome change from the antecedent regime, though no attempt was made to palliate outrages perpetrated on Jews, or to ignore the obligation to watch vigilantly over the independence and liberty of the Church.

Yet Mackintosh was a notable scholar, deeply versed in German thought.

In fact *Life and Work* was shortly to record, for a brief spell, attempts to 'palliate' those outrages that led to the holocaust and even to give space for arguments that the independence and liberty of the church were not really in danger.

In April 1933 one of the Kirk's continental bursars at New College, Carl Herlyn, led off a series on youth in the continent with an account of young people's support for Hitler, whom he seemed to see as leader of a back-to-the-land movement . . . 'it looks as if youth in Germany is well on the way to better things'.

This kind of view was also passed on by an able and honest young witness,

W M Macartney, who represented the Kirk's young men and women at a peace conference in Geneva in 1933 and who was later to be convener of the Kirk's Publications Committee and a successful missionary and minister at various points between Aberdeen and Vienna, including Africa. The German Christians at the conference had startled the others by their vigour and unanimity. They claimed a new era had begun, that all classes were behind the revolution, and that the Jewish persecutions were only one aspect of it. Their story was that

> Most of it was private vengeance on middle-men and others who had incurred deep hatred by their wrong-doing: the part played by the State was to mete out retributive justice.

But Macartney noted the deep division that ran through the conference, especially over the power of the state which the Germans saw as holy and powerful, 'the clenched fist of the right hand, providing the opportunity for the nation to do the will of God'.

The difference remained to the end, said Macartney, and could not be ignored, though some of his elders in the Kirk were prepared to try.

In April 1934, at a time when editorship seemed weak and uncertain with Livingstone's resignation already tendered, a Paisley minister was given a platform in *Life and Work* to support the German Christians (in the technical sense of the term) through whom the Nazis hoped to keep the Protestant Church under control and attack the 'academics' who were to form the Confessional Church. The minister concerned, remembered for his flamboyant style and flair for publicity, is long since dead. He was no doubt a good man and may well have repented of his hopelessly misinformed enthusiasm for matters he totally misunderstood. (His name, for the record, was David McQueen.)

With little doubt, this was the most outrageous article ever to appear in *Life and Work*. There have been others which were partisan, short-sighted, intolerant, hopelessly misguided, dull or obscure beyond all bounds of tolerance. This one read exactly as Dr Goebbels would have wanted it written, even in the inclusion of the 'world peace' theme and the argument that the regimentation under the 'German Christian' Reichsbishop was really quite like the union of the Auld Kirk and the UFs. A Nazi propaganda technique then, like communist ones then and now, exploited every weakness, vanity and jealousy. It was most effective—as communist propaganda has always been too—at second hand, from those who don't carry party cards but serve the party's purpose.

36. Hitler: the man's the gowd for a' that' (see page 141).

The Nazis themselves had exploited jealousy of the Jews. Their enthusiastic well-intentioned, misinformed, fellow-traveller in Paisley responded suitably, getting his facts all wrong in the process, and blaming the Jews (or lapsed Jews) for a situation in which 'obscene literature could be obtained as easily as a morning paper' in Berlin, the 'moral sewer of Europe'. (Our generation has learned that given the conditions and the public attitudes this can happen in nominally Protestant and nominally Catholic countries with scarcely any Jews to lapse. We have also seen other rival claimants emerge to lay claim to unpleasant titles.)

> What is denied the Jew in Germany is the privilege of every Jew becoming 'professional'. He may supply his quota . . . All Jews will not now escape manual toil.

Hitlerism, claimed this misguided minister, whose modern counterparts are advocates of communism, had brought moral and political stabilisation and Hitler's dictatorship had only just averted a communist takeover. (In fact it led to the takeover of what was once the heart of Germany, especially protestant Germany.) Germans outside the 'movement', he claimed, were a 'negligible quantity in numbers. This is to be attributed to the personal character of Hitler himself, who has proved to his fellow-countrymen that "the man's the gowd for a' that".' It was well written, for the minister was one of those, apart from Stevenson, involved in the *Scots Observer*; and Burns, let it be noted, can be quoted in pursuit of any kind of unctuous rubbish.

Of course this nonsense was quickly replied to, though the devastating retort by Dr John McConnachie, a Dundee minister who was a translator of Barth and had a German wife, was headed only a 'note' on the earlier article. The Confessional Church was properly honoured even if not given much support. The facts about the persecution of the Jews were made known. The Moderator in 1933-34, Lauchlan MacLean Watt, led the Commission of Assembly in deploring the 'grievous violation' of religious freedom in Germany and in praying for the dispelling of the menace of anarchy, violence, and pagan unbelief—though these were, of course, the pillars on which the Nazi regime was built.

The Kirk's Jewish mission lobby had protested even earlier. By December 1933 much of its enthusiasm for events in Alexandria or Transylvania had been supplemented by a passionate concern for the fate of German Jewry and of 'non-Aryan' Christians, those of Jewish or part-Jewish origin, though it still laboured under the delusion that 'quiet and courteous representations' had most influence for good. This was the public start of a long and honourable, even if tragically inadequate, theological and practical alignment with the persecuted Jews and 'non-Aryans'. It had a special emphasis on the relief of Jewish Christians, not because it distinguished between the victims of racial persecution but because they were ill-placed to receive any help from the international Jewish demonstrations of practical solidarity.

Yet with all the advantages of hindsight it is easy to ask why the Kirk did not do more and say more sooner. The low-key response at first to the Nazi persecution of the Jews seems out of character with the long-standing passion (admittedly sometimes looking like unrequited love) of the Jewish mission lobby. The answer is an unexpected one. The Kirk missed the significance of the new barbarism in Europe's most culturally and technically developed state, in its early stages, because it was already sadly resigned to anti-Semitism as an unpleasant (and, it hoped, temporary) fact of European life. Poland, Roumania, Austria, and even the central European country the Kirk knew best, Hungary, all had thriving anti-Semitism of their own. For the moment the pro-Jewish Christians deplored the spread of the poison to Germany. But their sense of German culture and civilisation conditioned them to think at first that the danger would be less in Germany, or at least that Nazi anti-Semitism merely spread and worsened an existing problem. It took time—precious time—to sense the new dimension of horror and to realise that the most extreme and austere reformed doctrine of man's depravity, irrespective of his cultural and technological pretensions, was to be demonstrated as only too true.

Even when *Life and Work* settled down under Carstairs, perhaps its most internationally-minded editor, it could still reflect the reluctance of some people in the Kirk to believe the worst and prepare for it. Sadly, perhaps because of Carstairs' cautious liberalism on India and Churchill's passionate hostility to self-government there, there is no sign of support for the outstanding political prophet of the age. In his response to Hitler, Churchill was the supreme realist; in relation to politics and public opinion, and not least church opinion, it was Baldwin, Ramsay MacDonald, and Neville Chamberlain who were the realists.

There is a paradox about the mood of the church, even though that mood in the Scottish Kirk was never as pacifist as in some other protestant churches: there was always a John White to answer those who asked what the 1914-18 war had achieved save pointless slaughter. He told the pacifists it had secured their freedom to try (without success) to commit the General Assembly to total pacifism.

But the paradox is there: the Kirk which had tried to give courage to endure in 1914-18; which had comforted the mourners; which had served a nation in arms; which had recruited its ministry very largely from the company officers of the citizen army, became more pacifist as Hitler created the conditions in which only effective rearmament to back resolute diplomacy could have averted war. Indeed the pacifists, in Scotland as elsewhere, were recruited from the survivors: George MacLeod and Archie Craig had both won Military Crosses by 1918. They knew at first hand what they wanted to avoid. They didn't know how, but in that they were not alone.

Indeed from about the time in 1934 when illusions about Hitler's internal popularity began to fade, the focal point of Christian concern moved away from Germany as such to a more abstract argument about collective security in which for a time Italy (and later Japan) had more attention concentrated on them than Hitler. Yet as late as 1936, when Carstairs quite rightly regarded the Confessional Church as the backbone of Christianity in Germany he could print a piece from some daft 'minister's wife' who had been to church in Berchtesgaden. She wrote a flowery piece in which with perhaps unwitting irony she described the Sunday scenery in the phrase of the poet Heine, who was being purged from the anthologies because of his Jewishness, '*So hold und schön und rein*':

> And on a wooded hillside above stood the modest house towards which the eyes of the valley folk turn many times a day—the home of their much loved Führer.

This, however, was a bit of isolated nonsense. Far more typical of the time is the November 1935 manifesto of the Church of Scotland Ministers' Peace Society, which appeared in the same issue as Carstairs denounced the Abyssinian war as bestial and inhuman. It passionately supported the League of Nations, yet could not support 'any form of violent or coercive sanction'. Even the majority view, put earlier by a future Moderator, Dr J Hutchison Cockburn, seems far more concerned with the theory of collective security than the reality of dealing with dictators. 'We must be pro-peace as much as anti-war', he wrote. But his deliverance the same month at the General Assembly had tagged onto it the absurd misjudgment, (taking the Lord's name in vain too), that 'God is leading the nations towards the definite and final renunciation of war'.

Mussolini had until then attracted little kirk attention, although (especially on the more robust UF side) there had been some alarm at his concordat with the Vatican, and the condition of the Italian Protestants. (The Italian who contributed to the symposium on youth in the European

churches—glory to his Waldensian integrity—avoided all praise of his government.) But the League of Nations' fiasco over Abyssinia distracted attention from the preparations and intentions of Hitler, despite the deep involvement of the pro-Jewish lobby and the consistently good coverage of affairs in democratic Czechoslovakia, especially after the arrival in Prague of a young minister called Robert Smith. There were also two major distractions caused by Japanese aggression in China and, after mid-1936, by the Spanish Civil War.

To the credit of editor Carstairs, *Life and Work* kept its head over the Spanish War. It yielded neither to the pressure to see it as a Christian crusade, a widespread view among British and Irish Roman Catholics, nor to line up with a Republic which as the war went on fell increasingly under communist domination. There is horror at the bombing of Guernica, reporting without comment of claims that the Republic encouraged religious freedom (though it was indisputable that some of its partisans, even when in alliance with the Catholic Basques, burned churches and persecuted priests and nuns.)

Carstairs, the intellectual conservative-liberal ex-missionary, showed in a special way the liberal democratic West's sense of being not only under pressure but under siege. Nazism, fascism, communism—yes, and Roman Catholicism—all seemed to him (and to most of the Scottish Kirk) as tyrannical, and as deviations from true Christianity even when they were not frankly pagan or atheist. To Carstairs' credit is an authoritative though infrequent coverage of Soviet matters, despite the Kirk's lack of direct contact with Russian Christians. Even when Soviet diplomacy veered towards *détente* with the West in the Litvinov era there were no illusions about the persecution of religion or the value of the various 'guarantees' of religious freedom before and after the Stalin Constitution. Nor was there any illusion about the cruelty and misery which Stalin's policies, in Lenin's amoral tradition of brutality, had brought to millions of people in the Soviet Union, and especially in the Ukraine. Early in 1936 Dr Adolf Keller of Geneva contrasted Soviet material achievement with its cost in human life and misery: 'There is no doubt that the Christians of Russia have to pay the largest part of this price and are still paying.' The words could be used again today.

The following year a bright young Bridge of Allan minister, Dr William Neil, later to be well-known as a New Testament scholar, looked in on Moscow on his way to the Far East (from which he wrote some of the liveliest *Life and Work* material of the decade). He visited the anti-God museum and found it full of quite fatuous exhibits, though he also blamed the Orthodox Church for pre-revolutionary ikons that smacked of black magic. Moscow he found a drab place of queues, shabby dress, cloth bunnets, unpainted buildings, dull shops. 'Nobody appeared to be bursting with enthusiasm and zeal as we were led to believe.'

Carstairs was sceptical of such an ally and of propagandist claims that a communist-dominated Republic was the real hope of the handful of long persecuted Spanish Protestants. But Franco, a Catholic crusader, seemed not merely the ally of expediency of Hitler and Mussolini but the expression of a Roman Catholicism scarcely less at odds with liberal Christian values. After all the Pope co-existed with Mussolini's Italy, and through the concordat gave it a blessing denied to the Savoy monarchy after 1870 (and ex-editor Fisher would have added, denied even when Italy was at war in 1915-18).

Where was there hope? In the West the great democracy was still isolationist. But there was another East in which Carstairs found encouragement. In India the move towards self-government accompanied a rise in influence of the old depressed classes. Moderate Hindu politicians showed signs of Christian influence. And in China, for all the chaos of the 1920's and the Japanese aggressions of the 1930's, there seemed hope for liberal democracy in which the Chinese Christians and the remaining missionaries might have an influence out of all proportion to their numbers. It never occurred to men like Carstairs that they would be denounced as agents of imperialism, for the new challenge to China was not from the West but from the expansionist Empire of Japan.

Certainly the missionaries made mistakes. One, only too evident in the *Life and Work* of the 1930's, was to underestimate the potential of the Communists. But another (as it turned out) was to commit themselves to Chiang Kai-shek as both liberator and unifier of China. Perhaps their later disaster was much more directly related to their identification with the losing side in China's own conflicts than with the more distant sins of imperialism.

The story of the Chines missions until the early 1950's as told in *Life and Work* and the various *Records* merits a book on its own: perhaps a book that can only be written from a perspective yet to be achieved in conditions that are still to develop, under God's providence, after who-knows-what cultural evolution, revolution, and counter-revolution in China. It needs conditions in which there is not only freedom of thought but of two-way travel, for Christians and others, between China and the West. But what has been, as the song says, is past forgetting.

As the 1930's saw the storms gather over Europe there were troubles enough for the Chinese missionaries without the added anxiety of rumours of war at home. In 1931 one of the main centres of the Kirk's activity, Manchuria, was turned into a nominally independent 'empire' which in fact was a Japanese dependency.

A year later Dr Jean McMinn of the Kaiyuan Women's Hospital was writing of a desperate situation there in a 'sad, sad land' where the people have had sorrow follow upon sorrow. Banditry followed the 'terror of the occupation'; so did epidemics, especially among children. She also added in a matter-of-fact way: 'We have had a good many gunshot wounds in old and young.'

But within a few years the Mukden Medical College was having to cope with Japanese 'advisers' and (in 1935) what Dr W A Young called 'a term of persecution'. But matters had eased when he wrote in January 1937, though his conclusion may not have pleased 'advisers' more concerned with politics than medicine.

China was no longer a house divided against herself, he wrote, 'To-day no single factor in the Far East is of more far reaching importance than the unification of China under the Christian president, Chiang Kai-shek.' Chiang was to be praised soon in an editorial note for his Bible-reading. Chinese Christians were to be lauded for their steadiness after the Japanese had launched what was virtually a war on China. They were also credited with fighting against the Japanese and praying for them. A note written in 1938 from Ichang, the Auld Kirk mission on the Yangtse, recorded a relatively unusual development in difficult times: 'The RC mission is co-operating cordially—a great joy to us.' It also noted a lull in air raids after a gruelling time in February and March, but the typing of that paragraph about the lull turned out (as a postscript noted) to have been interrupted by one that was 'more violent than usual'. Ichang, however, was to be badly damaged before falling to the Japanese in 1940.

Very occasionally *Life and Work* also had information about parts of the Chinese borderland untouched by war. A young scholar called J K S Reid got into Tibet—though not very far—and compared the pastoral visitation techniques of the lamas with those of Scots ministers. The main differences, it appeared, were that in Tibet the clerical visitor was shown into a room alone where he blew a trumpet as a prayer; that money changed hands; and that the Tibetan visit lasted a day and a night. The common factor was that tea was often served in both countries

But even while the shadow of Hitler fell over Europe, while the bombs whined and children screamed in China, and reasonable men tried to measure the infamy of Guernica against the shame of burned churches and murdered priests in Spain, (and truth became not only the first but the most frequent casualty in war), the life and work of the Kirk went on in Scotland. From the perspective of history even the work of church extension, or arguing with the brewers' advertising, or pressing to have the racing columns blacked out in public library newspapers, or exhorting potential future editors of *Life and Work* then in Sunday School to hand over their pennies for twin girls in Calabar—all these may seem distractions from spiritual preparation for the awful test which might come (as it did) or might have been averted. But whoever lives in the perspective of history? After all, on the day before the end of time or the Last Judgment there will be babies to baptise, funerals to be held, mourners to be comforted.

The greatest internal achievement of the Kirk in these years was one little evident in *Life and Work* at first sight: the consolidation of the reunion and the relatively rapid and genuine integration of the two kirks into one. But, Dr Watson might say, there isn't much mention of the point. 'And that, my dear Watson', replies Sherlock Holmes, 'is the very point: there was no need to mention it.' There was apparently no need for special exhortation in *Life and Work*, in contrast to the constant need for exhortation of a financial kind, with a predictable crisis yet again for foreign missions at the depth of the great depression. Maintenance of the Ministry needed a good deal of exhortation too, and got it. The development of the fund and its distinctive management within the Kirk is another achievement recorded, albeit unspectacularly, in *Life and Work*.

The other great achievement, church extension, lent itself to more effective journalistic treatment, and got it. There are pictures of braw new kirks in new areas—for church architecture in the 1930's was probably better, relatively speaking, than most other forms of architecture—and signs of a genuine pride, mixed with real relief and heartfelt thanks, that the Kirk more or less kept pace with the movement of the people. Not all of them, of course, wanted to come to kirk on Sundays. A great deal of clerical wind blew through *Life and Work*'s columns on the best way to deal with those who started off as 'hikers' and gradually became recognised just as hikers, without the inverted commas to express ministerial surprise in face of new notions and new trends. It was, of course, a dramatic trend: as dramatic in its way as the package holidays that took post-war Scots to the Costa Brava and not just the Cobbler.

These were also the years of the most dramatic of controversial parish ministries in the modern Kirk, that of George MacLeod at Govan, merging into the years of the formation of the Iona Community. They were also the years when the Kirk was so well served by the BBC (which had a broadcasting monopoly and a sense of standards hard to imagine now) that it forgot how lucky it was. In a different situation the church would have prepared itself to use broadcasting as it had used the printed word; indeed, in a more open broadcasting situation a Charteris of the inter-war years might have been pressing for a radio 'Life and Work'. But instead of a new Charteris, there was John Reith in London, son of the UF Moderator of 1914. In the 1930's there was also in Scotland Melville Dinwiddie, a controller who (like Reith) had a fine war record but had been parish minister before turning to broadcasting. The attitudes and influence of both are to be found in *Life and Work*, usually less remarkable for what they say than for the atmosphere of serene confidence and assured authority in which it was said. And it was a mutual confidence. The church was glad—perhaps complacently glad—that broadcasting was in such good Christian and even presbyterian hands. When, for example, Dinwiddie was interviewed for *Life and Work* in 1933 the criticisms he had to handle (without too much trouble) were of including 'so-called secular music in our Sunday programme', and even 'light music'.

Reith had been all but canonised by the late 1930's, though it had not always been so. When he wrote for the UF *Record* just before the reunion he responded with some asperity to an editorial compliment, suggesting that some ministers didn't recognise the 'ally of proved power' that they had in the BBC. 'Simplicity, sincerity, energy, beauty of form and reference to the personality of Christ': this was Reith's formula for effective religious broadcasting. By the late 1930's however, the 'conservatism and timidity' with which Reith had chided church leaders for their hesitation in responding to the BBC's readiness to help the church had probably gone into assuming that monopoly was the safest policy and that the BBC could always be depended on.

MacLeod of Govan was, to some extent, trying to renew the parish system to reach the people who were more regularly reached by Reith's Christian broadcasting. In 1936 he wrote at length about Scotland's 'churchless million', writing of a typical Glasgow street in which in 1880 only five hundred of six hundred and fifty 'contiguous protestant houses' had a definite church allegiance. He had found that by 1936 the figure had fallen from five hundred to one hundred and seventy-five and that only ten were connected to the church whose parish it was: 'The remaining 165 households are connected with 23 churches scattered throughout Glasgow.' Then followed the Govan formula for parish evangelism which had reached its climax at Easter 1934. It included a readiness to mind the shop on Sunday morning to let the shopkeeper come to kirk (what a contrast from those who wanted to ban light music and secular in Sunday broadcasting), and the discovery that even

38. Iona: an early picture before the Duke of Argyll's gift, the first rebuilding, and the Iona Community's restoration.

inarticulate members can be better ambassadors for Christ than a professional ministry. 'It takes an unemployed man, still proud of his church and his churchgoing, to convince an unemployed non-churchgoer that he will really be welcome in the suit he is wearing, if only he cares to come round.'

Two years later MacLeod's vision was fixed on Iona as well as Govan. In three articles he explained what the Iona Community was, and what it wasn't. No, it wasn't a rebellion against the church. No it wasn't a return to Rome—and MacLeod went on to explain that he intended 'precisely and acutely the opposite of a return to Rome'. No, it was not visionary or 'playing at being Franciscans' or aiming at poverty, far less celibacy. No, it wasn't a one-man band. It was an attempt to relate work, worship, religion, and community to try to preserve the essential truths for which our presbyterian forefathers died, in an environment unlike any they knew.

More surprisingly, to those who have known the modern community's emphasis (as well as his own view of the last fifty years), MacLeod insisted it was not a pacifist community, though he hoped that men of strong views 'for or against that solution' would join and not be afraid to hold their views. 'Its emphasis is neither pacifist nor otherwise', he said.

The argument about pacifism still divided the Kirk albeit unevenly, as Hitler's rearmament proceeded, as the Luftwaffe and tanks tested equipment and techniques in Spanish battle conditions, as the Führer prepared to force the confrontation from which the German Army drew back—the follow-up of annexation of Austria with a propaganda campaign using the Germans of Bohemia, Moravia, and Slovakia to break up the liberal democratic but inevitably nationalist state of the Czechs and Slovaks.

This time the mood was different. The most effective dialogue was between Professor G H C Macgregor, taking the line of a minority report on peace and war to the General Assembly. The reply—it was called such—came from Principal D S Cairns. By now there was a clarity in the debate. Men were prepared to go to what others thought unthinkable lengths to avoid it. The debate may not mention Hitler; everyone knows it is about him.

Macgregor was arguing as a response to Hitler in January 1938, that if people would only live here and now by the laws of God's kingdom it would 'break in upon them and take them unawares'. Far fetched? But like the pacifists of our own time, when weapons are still more terrible and probably able to destroy all life on earth, he argued that 'modern war cannot be reconciled with fundamental principles of the life and teaching of Jesus Christ'.

Macgregor argued skilfully, exploiting to the full the mess that the moderates of a few years before had got themselves into by depending so much on idealistic arguments about the League of Nations. They had joined the pacifists in abhorring purely national defence. Now that the League was a dying duck it seemed—in logic at least—that they must join the pacifists.

The majority of the Kirk had no intention of doing so. Indeed, when the failure and disastrous betrayal came in the later summer of 1938 it was because the politicians' nerve and judgment failed.

Cairns, in a magnificent piece of debating in print, set out the case for national defence and defensive alliances, though he had to appeal to sentiment rather than reality in arguing that the League was not dead but merely temporarily defeated. Against the pacifists he used the argument that renunciation of the lawful use of force would mean abandoning all justice and executive power within the state to non-Christians, since an ultimate resort to force to keep the peace is part of the state's internal structure as well as external relations. He also deployed an argument which in the light of later experience was to prove tragically ill-founded. Macgregor had argued that the church would either have to retract brave words of the General Assembly about never bombing civil populations in a 'defensive' war or declare herself wholly pacifist; Cairns claimed that to accept this inevitability would be to play into the hands of 'the baser element in our nation'. Area bombing was to prove Macgregor only too right. But would the kingdom of God have taken Hitler unawares if the surrender of Munich had been repeated again and again?

Ironically, there may be an argument that we have stood aside and settled for *détente* with Hitler on his terms. It might just be argued that far less human misery might have followed than was brought by the war and its aftermath. But it is an argument that depends not on the Spirit of Christ but of a Laval or a Quisling or, come to that, of a Stalin. For Hitler's fellow dictator and mass-murderer was to try exactly such a course between the non-aggression pact of 1939 which sealed the fate of the Poles and the German onslaught on Russia in June 1941.

Munich came. There was no false joy in the Kirk, at least as seen through *Life and Work*. The crisis came and passed between issues; and when it was past, for the moment there was an honourable sense of shame at the fate of the Czechs. Perhaps the saddest note in *Life and Work* from that period is not the comment on the great events, decent compared to, say, *The Times*, obviously as uncomfortable as it was uninspired, but a passing mention in an account of the trials and tribulations (not the last) which the Evangelical Church of Czech Brethren faced after Munich. It was not only the Germans (and in Slovakia the Hungarians) who destroyed the fabric and morale of the Czechoslovak state: at Teschen the Poles joined in. The strong congregations there, it was reported, 'have practically ceased to be'; and a Czech minister arrrested by the Poles was said to have died in hospital after maltreatment. Such is fallen human nature.

The Poles, till then, had been little mentioned in *Life and Work*. The tiny reformed church across the border in Lithuania had probably got more coverage, though Poland rose in some estimation when it was reported from an international temperance conference there that a hundred thousand Polish boy scouts had taken the pledge.

Poor Poles. They were to know soon (and they know still), the tribulations they joined in inflicting on the Czechs. And when those boy scouts grew up they were to face more terrible trials than the temptations of vodka.

As 1939 began there were a few illusions left. The Woman's Guild New Year message looked back on the year of Munich and reflected 'how wonderfully we were delivered from difficulty and perplexity'. But as the lights that had flickered so long now faded in Europe—all save the Light of the World—Carstairs reflected that 'hard as faith may sometimes be, the despairing doctrine of the meaninglessness of life is the most incredible of all.'

The routine went on: 'The beadle's work'; 'Life in the Buchan manse years and years ago;' 'Tinkers' children'; 'Are tracts out of date?' Then suddenly there is a piece of dazzling splendour: 'The Thoughts of a German Refugee'. Published anonymously, it was by Bernhard Citron, a Berliner who had taken refuge in Budapest where he encountered the Scottish mission and exchanged a nominal Judaism for a Christian commitment. When he died early in 1978 he had been able to read in *Life and Work* his last thoughts on Germany and Berlin, for he had been to the previous year's *Kirchentag* and had met a survivor of his family. He was to become a much-loved minister in Fife and one of the characters of the Kirk. It could have been said of him that he was a Jew like Jesus; but despite his Christian faith in a Scottish setting he never lost either his German accent or his German ways of thought and expression. Yet in 1939 he had to write of a Germany that persecuted him, that denied his right to the culture in which he had been brought up and which he loved. He had fled to Budapest with Goethe's *Faust* in his pocket but now he wrote of his search for a new spiritual home. Yet he wrote early in 1939 as the persecution went from bad to worse that 'the Jew is always faithful to the country where once he was happy . . . If some of them settle in other lands—for ever or a short time only—they shall try to be loyal and sincere to the history and traditions of them: but it must not be thought that it is easy to separate ourselves from the land of our birth. Germany can take away our German citizenship but Germany cannot make us non-German in spirit.'

For him the only spiritual home was 'the Kingdom founded by the greatest son of the Jewish race . . . Whom some of us call the Son of Man.' He was glad and proud not to deny his race and the traditions of his family 'because the race is persecuted, not the faith only'.

> And we must not be ashamed if other people who knew us before mock at us, thinking: 'They are full of new wine'. Thus the misfortune of losing our country and roaming through the world may be exchanged for the blessedness of finding a safe home which has not been granted by any human authority but only by Christ Himself.

While some found that safe home, others were taking trains home while the storm that had gathered so long was about to break. Dr Alex King, once of the Scots church and mission in Budapest and later with the parent committee, was on his way across Europe just before the murderers in Berlin and Moscow concluded their alliance to let the war begin. (In fact war had begun before Carstairs could publish this brilliant vignette of ordinary people thrown together in one compartment, just as war was about to thrust them into such separate compartments.)

In Vienna Jewish refugees boarded the train, seen off with tears after partings still more poignant than anyone really knew at the time. At Würzburg there entered a German, pale as a ghost, but suddenly 'the ghost began to talk':

> Apropos of nothing it addressed itself first to me then to the compartment in general. It boasted the invincible might of Germany, it prophesied war and the alliance of Hitler and Stalin, the downfall of England and the triumph of German arms . . . He declared war by directing a few vigorous nods in my direction and aiming an imaginary rifle at the girl in the opposite corner, with a 'poof-poof-poof' to heighten the effect. He brought his machine guns into action by swinging the invisible weapon about and brrrrr-ing for all he was worth. This *Blitzkrieg* came to an end when he stood erect, raised an arm, and shouted '*Deutschland Hoch*'. Then he collapsed into his corner, obviously mortally stricken, gasped 'England', and significantly drew his finger across his throat.

The 'ghost' was a warrior back from the Condor Legion in Spain, for he went on to boast to King of 'a great time with loot and Spanish ladies'. When he left at Ashaffenburg a Czech in the compartment turned to King and said:

> 'Now you know what they are like'.

King ended with the scene at Aachen where the unfortunate Jews were weeded out to be 'thoroughly searched before being allowed to leave the Fatherland'. He had argued with the Czech that it was an exaggeration to say all Germans were like that; and at Aachen he found 'natural feelings of a decent German heart' breaking through.

But the time had come when natural feelings were at a discount; when German decency would reside in a handful of people of the quality of Goerdeler, Stauffenberg, and Helmut von Molkte, and a little-known academic called Bonhoeffer who might have stayed in America to escape the dangers of Europe. The German Army, that had thought of stopping Hitler if the West had stood firmly behind the Czechs, prepared to strike east; and farther east still Stalin, the devil's other disciple, waited to strike the dying Polish Army in the back.

Chapter 11
World War: 1939-45

'There is no civilisation which has an absolute right to live in the sight of God. All civilisations live despite their sins by God's long-suffering kindness and mercy . . . We must therefore stand resolutely against this monstrous evil which threatens to destroy the whole of civilisation. Our uneasy conscience must not weaken our resolution.'

(Reinhold Niebuhr, the American theologian, writing in *Life and Work*, December 1940.)

War came as no surprise in September 1939. The reprieve that was merely a stay of execution had been bought by shameful betrayal at Munich nearly a year before. The grinding of the ruins of Czechoslovakia into the dust; the stridency of Hitler; and finally the Nazi-Communist pact—these had, long before the formality of ultimatum, prepared the minds of the people for war. When the wan, sad voice of Neville Chamberlain announced the declaration of war on a Sunday morning at church-time he merely ratified a decision already made in men's and women's resignation to the inevitable.

Years of fear made the reality less terrible even before it became apparent that, except for the Poles, there was to be an unreality about the opening phase of the war.

And for the people of the Scottish church there had been something more than the ordeals of judgment and conscience which all Christians had faced as the unthinkable became increasingly likely. For they had been brought closer than some, and not least through the pages of *Life and Work*, to the trials of the Christian resistance to Nazism from which many martyrs were to be drawn, and to the already far more terrible ordeal of Jews and 'non-Aryans', among them many German Christians. How terrible that ordeal was to be few, if any, could conceive.

But when war came on that Sunday morning, when *Life and Work* should have been in the pews or at the kirk doors, there was a different mood from 1914, partly because of the ghastly memory of the First World War, made worse by the nightmare fears of bombing, even more because no-one was taken by surprise.

There were perhaps some misjudgments: 'Never in the history of the world has a war been entered on in a less warlike spirit. Neither in France nor in Britain has there been a trace of jingoism', wrote Dr Carstairs. 'Those who passed through Paris or the provinces of France on the eve of war found men preparing with zeal but without zest', a nice verbal distinction which perhaps concealed the different states of morale in Britain and France.

But it is not the misjudgments—all editors make them, and usually in less spectacular circumstances than those of world war—which bring a certain sense of frustration and disappointment in reading the magazine for the Second World War years. Carstairs was at his best in the years before the war and seemed to fall away after 1939 in his command of what, under the impact of rapidly changing events and in face of practical problems of paper shortage, was a difficult task. He was ageing; and quite soon there were honourable distractions of the Home Guard, an experience which must have added to the zest with which he published the passionately anti-Bonapartist, anti-invasion sentiments of Thomas Chalmers.

Perhaps, if the apparent contradiction is permissible, he was always a better editor than a journalist. The pressures of war, and of space, tested his weak points. Carstairs believed in a rather dignified idea of progress made possible by stability. He believed in idealistic Christianity and rational argument. But war has little dignity, no stability; it compromises ideas as expediency dictates new allies and dubious tactics; it is the negation of rational argument.

However there are two reasons, unconnected with the virtues and limitations of a particular editor, which probably explain the contrast between Fisher's lively if often short-sighted 1914-18 coverage and Carstairs' duller response to events of 1939-45. One was that the primacy of wartime communication had switched from the written to the spoken word, in its radio broadcast form. The nine o'clock news mattered more than the Fleet Street dailies; and even a religious monthly was touched by this cooling breath of change. The other was that decisions taken before Carstairs succeeded Livingstone had made *Life and Work* rather more the magazine of the church offices and committees than had been the case during Fisher's reign. The pressure on space at the time of the 1929 reunion, and the prospect of all the old UF kirks (as well as the old establishment ones) seeking a corner for their local news and views, had all but banished local items.

Perhaps there was also a new sense of being security-conscious, though rules and precautions did not always make sense. When, for example, Jack Stevenson, a future editor but then minister of Culter, wrote under his own name about the coming of Poles to Scotland he had to use the name of a

39. 'Huts and Canteens': a lifeline—a 'five-storey hotel' on the Belgian border, 1940.

fictitious parish. The Germans, it was apparently assumed, would read *Life and Work*, but would not have had the prudence or initiative to invest in another of Charteris's legacies to the Kirk, *The Church of Scotland Year Book*.

Later, when the bombing started, John White's list of presbyteries in which churches and manses had been destroyed or damaged (with numbers) might have been of some interest to Luftwaffe intelligence; but every 1914-16 issue would, along with local papers, have helped to piece together, for what it was worth, a fascinating picture of the way Kitchener's army was developing. But was it 'security' that led to there being so little in the magazine about the effects of bombing in Scotland in the spring of 1941, even when later obituaries and other items record ministerial casualties and shattered manses? *Life and Work* had surprisingly little to say about the home front, (too much to say sometimes about the horrors of gin-drinking on the Gold Coast or the sale of excisable liquor on church premises to soldiers billeted or stationed there).

But there was to be a 'phoney war' before the total war: it yielded a good deal about evacuees (who were helped by seventy church sisters) and the blackout, said to be restoring family life. There were mild and Christian words about not making war on the German people but on the philosophy which had been foisted on them. There was soon support for a Kirk appeal in aid of the Finns, when their Lutheran archbishop had appealed to the Christian world for help after their resistance to the demands that Hitler's partner Stalin was trying to foist on them. There was a welcome for the BBC talks inspired by Melville Dinwiddie which were to become 'Lift up your hearts' and later 'Thought for the Day'. But the good things were mingled with bizarre scraps like advice to congregations to fight unemployment among organ-builders— 'war casualties of which one reads nothing in the daily press'—by tackling necessary repairs at what the average congregational board must have thought a singularly inappropriate time.

For a time of course, there was war coverage, in the 1914-18 manner, of the Church Huts and Canteens in France. It had a distinctive flavour: some of those who went out to be the Huts managers and organisers in 1939-40 had been the customers just over twenty years before. Lewis Cameron, for example, who had been sorely wounded in the earlier war, went back to write in March 1940 of the things that were the same—the cafés full of singing troops, the grouses, the old soldiers' tall tales—and the things that were so different now that the French had rebuilt and reploughed the old ruins and battlefields.

But war was to pass that way again, devastating but with lightning speed, and a second Cameron piece which appeared in June, as the front was disintegrating, told of an ENSA entertainment with Will Fyfe when the troops still lacked the strained faces 'of men who have faced death across No-man's Land'. On the Belgian border he found that the Kirk had acquired a five-storey hotel and that the local leader, a young minister called Harry Whitley, was planning an annexe. Events intervened. Carstairs, still unable to raise a cheer for the appointment of Churchill as captain-general of Britain's courage, was claiming that there was new courage and calmness of spirit from the sense of being in God's hands.

The next month he wrote of the marvellous deliverance of Dunkirk— 'indeed as an escape out of the snare of the fowler'; but most of the magazine was about the General Assembly, though in a sense the coverage of it was not completed till August when a German refugee minister, Heinz Golzen, wrote about church and state in Germany, and warning that the church struggle was only a symptom of a wider conflict of national socialism and Christianity. He had meant to deliver the speech at the General Assembly but had been interned by the time it met, as had Bernhard Citron and probably most of the thirty German ministers that Golzen said were in Britain at the time.

SCOTLAND FOR EVER!

40. 'Gott strafe England' (see page 160)

Editor Carstairs wrote—like the people of the church and nation—of waiting undismayed for the launching of the threatened great attack, though even in this finest hour he couldn't apparently mention Churchill. But he did write of a historical parallel when once before 'England was left isolated in its island fortress'. Despite their preoccupation with defence and threatened invasion his readers had time to be indignant. The name of the island, they rushed to point out, was not England. It was a Scottish usage with honourable precedent; Robert Louis Stevenson, very much the Scot abroad, could write of himself with some emotion as an Englishman (in *An Inland Voyage*). So could David Livingstone. But the Kirk's readers reacted like the Scottish infantryman in one of the few really good *Punch* cartoons of the First World War. He has captured a battered village with '*Gott strafe England*' scrawled on the wall. In the interests of accuracy he deletes England and substitutes Britain. So too did *Life and Work* readers.

As the Battle of Britain—not of England only—reached its climax over the south coast in September, they had the satisfaction of having an abject editor admit that the blunder 'was inexcusable' and allow himself one of the rare excursions into humour during this time:

> It is not surprising that it should have led to a quite appreciable increase in the postal revenue for the month.

At some time, as that golden summer turned to autumn, the finest hour came and lingered and passed. And at the year's end the fashionable American theologian Reinhold Niebuhr wrote about the Christian defence of civilisation, by which he meant the war that Britain was fighting while his own country remained neutral (and, of course, the Soviet Union remained Hitler's ally).

It was a piece of some power and passion, perhaps of contemporary relevance in its sense of 'the sinfulness of all historical values' and its determination that 'we must act in history, even when we have a guilty conscience in our action'—even prophetic in its fashion in that at one point it wandered off the theme of resistance to Nazism to anxiety of expiation for the white man's sins of racial price and arrogance. But in 1940 we had to take the Americans as we found them: and it was an evident comfort that such a notable theologian (and one with such a Missouri German name) should commit himself so clearly to the cause which Britain had the honour to defend, an honour which the Americans had not yet had thrust upon them.

A few months later, when Britain was still alone save for the exiles who sought our shelter and joined our ranks, President Henry Coffin of the Union

Seminary in New York struck a less highfalutin note and realised how many people in Britain felt:

> We must have seemed apallingly slow to you. We beg you to recall our composite population, our remoteness from the scene of strife . . . the Churches have stressed international friendship to a degree which has made a large section of the clergy and vast numbers of their members, particularly their young people, pacifist.

But not everyone who read it may have been pleased to find that Britain was still bracketed with China and that President Coffin—perhaps anticipating only too well President Roosevelt's more secular attitude—wanted to guard against the pride we dislike in others. 'We must not seek God's blessing on an Anglo-Saxon ruled future.'

Yet the full horror of Nazi domination was not appreciated. The Jewish Mission speculated on the new situation that might arise for its aims in Poland now that the Jews had been concentrated round Lublin. What was to happen was too horrible for civilised men to conceive of till it was too late. And when the Hungarians temporarily got back much of Transylvania from Roumania the colporteur in Kolozsvar (as Cluj had become again) claimed record sales of the scriptures and the committee found it 'fortunate' that it was easier to supervise this work from Budapest. Miss Haining had 'so far found it possible to continue' there in charge of the girls' home. Soon she was to disappear, in 1944, into the company of the martyrs as well as the saints. It was not till about the end of 1942 that the full horror of Nazi intentions to the Jews became evident in *Life and Work*.

In war the editor seemed to lose some of his feel for international affairs. Carstairs, one presumes it was he, was at his best in prayers and meditations, which a later time might have called sermonettes. If he farmed out or passed round this work it maintained a high standard, as well as the unity of style which makes it look like his own work.

There were also new names and young men to give spiritual guidance. A minister in Leven called Hugh Douglas made skilful literary use of Pepys's account of the Great Fire of London to face up to the new fires and destruction which were to destroy the kirk building of the dying ex-editor Fleming. Another young minister called Tom Torrance, later to win a quite unacademic reputation with the Mediterranean Huts and Canteens, warned the common man that theology was for him too. The whole German nation was poisoned, he said, in its politics and society, even much of its church life, by the effects of a 'natural theology' that made people think too much of themselves, believing that men were divine in their nature and fundamentally good. 'Actually they deified their badness.' His point was not that all Germans were arrogant and anti-Christian—he insisted they were not—but that the idea of a God whom we made conform to the 'natural rights and aspirations of man' led to a totalitarian state. 'We must keep the Cross absolutely central, Jesus Christ died for us. That alone can keep us truly humble.' And Nevile Davidson, of Glasgow cathedral, wrote of finding one of the worst rascals in his army unit at the Lord's Table although, 'I suspect that he has never been confirmed'. He recorded a Confirmation service in which forty-five men of the battalion joined the church.

The tides of war flowed and swirled. The Soviet people faced the ordeal that Stalin's blunders had ensured for them and some silly things began to be said about their industrial efficiency (which was questionable), and their solidarity, which was eventually more or less preserved, not from love of Stalin or even the Soviet system but through the cruelty and hatred which accompanied the Nazi occupation. By 1943 there were signs of an exaggerated optimism about the future freedom of religion in the Soviet Union, and also of warmer feeling in the editorial bosom for Winston Churchill. There was also a 'lift of the heart' when the Beveridge report on social security appeared, though Lewis Cameron wrote a significantly constructive criticism of its mood. 'There is not and cannot be a single reference to spiritual security.' Are financial resources enough in dealing with the children deprived of parental care and guidance, or the loneliness of the old? He wanted to be ready to meet new and greater demands on church social work in a new age. This was the age of William Temple; of Christian socialism enthroned at Canterbury; of a search in the Scottish Kirk for God's will for church and nation 'in the present crisis'; of a perceptible move towards what the 1944 General Assembly called 'a greater measure of common control of the means of production', part of the mood which was to produce the rejection at the 1945 General Election of the country's war leader and the outstanding Englishman of the century.

But the church was thinking about internal evolution. In 1944 an overture seeking ordination of women to the eldership was sent down to presbyteries, a majority of whom favoured the change. In 1945 the presbyteries were asked to think about it again in consultation with kirk sessions and congregations. A dialogue in *Life and Work* at the war's end showed that there was a lot of life left in the argument, Professor G D Henderson wanting the church to indicate it was 'alive and awake' and finding himself up against Roy Sanderson, Glasgow Barony minister and a future Moderator. Dr Sanderson wasn't 'against women' but God had offered them motherhood as an even greater distinction than the eldership. To create a conflict between a vocation as a woman and the traditions of the eldership would 'threaten not only the sanctity of the home but the future of the race.' Admission of a few women to the eldership would segregate them from other women and other women's work. To his credit Carstairs had earlier noted that twenty-two churches in the World Presbyterian Alliance had moved ahead of Scotland, though he seemed to regard the argument that 'in none of these Churches have women been elected in large numbers' as an argument in favour of the overture. It was to take another twenty years for the change to be made.

By the time Roy Sanderson was fighting that vigorous rearguard action, however, Carstairs was on the point of retirement. The following month the new editor Jack Stevenson—who had already brought his zest and style to describing a General Assembly much closer to his own mood than to Carstairs'—said the expected but still heartfelt nice things about his predecessor, a lovable man 'full of good talk and endless jest' and the writer of light verse for the social functions of the church offices. He also revealed an Indian story of Carstairs disguised with local dress and speech to gain a point in an argument with a high military official. He complained gently that Carstairs might have censored himself overmuch and added, for the benefit perhaps of mildly grumbling readers:

> Turn back to your pre-war copies if you have them and look again at the wealth of material that used to be brought together before the axe descended—and you will add your own thank you.

Was it a more left-handed compliment than Stevenson realised? The mood and style of the Kirk has never been, and is not yet, given to errors on the side of undue brevity. Neither Carstairs nor his contributors mastered the art (as Stevenson was to do in the post-war years of austerity) of making the most of the limited paper supplies which the Kirk's Publications Committee argued about with bureaucracy. Moreover the Carstairs that emerges from his rather dignified pages is not exactly full of endless jest. He was, perhaps, an idealist rather than an optimist—a sound Christian position—but neither the mood of the later wartime years not the mood of his own years (he was over sixty) made it possible for him to be the effective guiding and at times restraining influence that the situation called for.

He died in 1948, and Jack Stevenson printed a sonnet he wrote towards the end of his life. It ended:

Old age, I find, is but a coming home
Dear scenes, dear loved ones cluster round,
And all the treasures gathered by the way.
Life's ardour cooled, I would no longer roam,
But dwell with these awhile, and then sleep sound.
And wake all fresh and eager to the Day.

41. Editor Stevenson

Chapter 12
The age of
Jack Stevenson

'The amazing thing about Jack Stevenson was how one so distinctive in character and so rich in personality contrived to be so utterly self-effacing as editor of *Life and Work*. He shaped and moulded the magazine without ever showing himself in its pages.'

(From a tribute by Andrew Herron, February 1974.)

Perhaps it is a piece of presumption by one editor about another to think of the post-war era in *Life and Work* as the age of Jack Stevenson.

It would be easier to call it the age of the crumbled alliance, or the cold war, or the Welfare State, or of full employment, or the partial revival of religion and the church that came as another generation of servicemen returned—in many cases to be ministers and in far more to be elders.

It was the aftermath of Hiroshima and Nagasaki; the time soon of the first of many stately lowerings of the Union Flag over cantonment and Government House.

But in the recording of the life of the Kirk, and to a large extent in moulding, shaping, and interpreting its life and work, it was the age of Jack Stevenson.

Was he the perfect editor? There is no such person, but his talent at that place and time probably made him as close to it as anyone could be. If he had faults they perhaps included that self-effacement, especially in the later and middle years of his twenty years' editorship. Sometimes he might have been better to have intruded his personality as well as his ideas.

The 'literary minister' has always been an obvious possibility as editor for *Life and Work*. Jack Stevenson was a journalist as well as a minister, but in the best sense of the term. He was one of nature's journalists as well as a master of professional skills. In other words he was concerned with the present; he had a sense of immediacy and the proper use of the printed word. All too often the communicators of a church which has rightly gloried in the spoken word of the sermon have in its written communication merely transcribed their pulpit techniques. And he had stronger political opinions, sometimes reflected in a left-centre emphasis and editorial selection, than the gentleness and grace of his personality suggested at first sight.

The end of the war, which brought such turbulent times in a changing world, in fact brought a period of progressive stability in the church in Scotland—indeed in Western Europe. It lasted perhaps twenty years, and so did Jack Stevenson as editor until his retirement in 1965.

In some ways it is a time too near our own to understand, interpret, and assess. Most of those who will read this probably lived through it or at least grew up into it. Moreover, it has inexorable themes rather than grand climaxes, save perhaps for the Suez crisis, which was to stir passions in the church and perhaps give Jack Stevenson his most troubled time. But for those agonising days, which coincided so tragically with the Hungarian national rising, there would hardly be a single climactic event to concentrate the minds of church and nation on the decline of British power and prestige, which for long enough was concealed by the relatively gentle change from Empire to Commonwealth and the special relationship with the United States. Yet Suez came nearly a decade after the two events which most clearly demonstrated the change in Britain's world position, perhaps showing it in its best and its worst light. These were the transfer of power in India, a success qualified by the communal conflict in the Punjab, and the abandonment of the untenable mandate in Palestine when it was clear that British withdrawal would mean a Jewish-Arab war.

At home the event which set the mood and pattern of the post-war years had already taken place before the mushrooms rose above the Japanese cities. The mood of the Beveridge report and its reception had been given political form by the return of a massive Labour majority and the installation of the acute, unspectacular Attlee as premier in place of the man of destiny. Britain sought a quieter destiny. Indeed for the twenty years after 1945 the Labour victory then settled the mood of British politics and the range of political possiblities, even though Conservative prime ministers were in Downing Street for thirteen years after 1951.

Perhaps the spirit of this post-war period was best caught in a non-political article (which in fact reflected a number of highly political and controversial assumptions) by Lesslie Newbigin, a Church of Scotland missionary in South India who had become bishop in Madura (and later Madras) in the united church there which made such an impact on the thinking and style of the ecumenical movement. Writing in 1948, in the issue after Stevenson had got a little-known lecturer called Dr William Barclay to help people to understand the Bible and start reading it, Newbigin began some reflections on furlough:

> The first thing I saw when I landed was a queue. Perhaps it will seem ridiculous to say that it brought a lump to my throat but I confess that it did.

Later he said that, 'no serious person in any political party' believed in the removal of all controls and 'the return to nineteenth century capitalism. Criticism of controls must surely be within the framework of a clear understanding of the kind of society we are trying to create . . .' This notable missionary was sounding like a social engineer. He was also assuming the dangerous pontifical privilege of defining who were 'serious persons'. Thirty years later he managed to mix the same view of market economics with his greetings to the Kirk as Moderator of the English union of Presbyterians and Congregationalists, the United Reformed Church.

The destiny of the new Britain might have been even more placid if the war had not resulted in the creation of a Russian imperial boundary in central Germany and the capture for communism of the Chinese Revolution that had begun long ago in 1910. But even the 'special relationship' no longer concealed the weakness and vulnerability of Britain in the nuclear age in which the Hiroshima bomb gave way to the H-bomb. In an age of power *blocs*, several of the countries with which the Church of Scotland had close historical and personal connections were not only cut off from western contact, especially in the last years of Stalin's reign, but reconstructed on new assumptions, one of which was that man had outgrown religion. The same assumption was to grow in the very different society of the West, though it did not have the machinery of the state at its disposal.

How was the place and the mood of the church in this divided and changing world reflected in *Life and Work*? It is harder than might be expected to answer the question by simplifying and summing-up, and not only because of the overlapping with the experience of so many survivors into the last quarter of the century. There are two other good reasons.

The first is a severely practical one. Wartime controls which lingered in the aftermath of war kept the size of the magazine at little more than what it was reduced to during the war. From 1947 to 1949 the magazine was not much bigger than in 1945, and well below the level of 1941. And even when paper supplies eased and Stevenson was no longer forced to cram everything into

42. William Barclay: communicator extraordinary

sixteen-page magazines the committee policy of keeping down the price, and the burst of inflation which accompanied the Korean War, prevented any return to the scale of the pre-war *Life and Work*.

The second reason is that the skills of journalistic compression and topicality with which Stevenson tackled his problems and reshaped the more compact magazine make life harder for the historian. Unlike all his ministerial predecessors he had a feel not just for literary but for topical journalism. The *Scots Observer* and his spell as the Kirk's 'press secretary' had developed his natural aptitudes for a style of journalism whose nearest secular equivalent was probably that of the *Bulletin*, the mid-market Outram daily which perished through atrophy in the 1950's after making some wild changes of course. It was a style which was at once popular and serious, brisk but never sensational, combining high thoughts and plain words. But the compression and the topicality sometimes make it harder to quote. The most purple passages of unconscious prophecy in the century often come from the discursive style which disappeared with Stevenson, though it had never been quite the same since Livingstone moved from the UF *Record* to take over the magazine of the reunited church.

Perhaps the most symbolic, as well as one of the most skilful, demonstration of this sense of topicality, comes in the 'Gist', a supplement to *Life and Work* which in the 1950's and into the 1960's presented a summary of the proceedings of the General Assembly—a far cry from the stately, and sometimes ornate sketches which described the Assembly for most of the century. Yet it was a format which could not match the immediacy of broadcast coverage with recorded extracts. There was also an enthusiasm for th 'Kirk Week' lay movement which offered a supplementary, if not exactly alternative, forum for the people of the church. It seemed at the time (in 1957, for example, when one thousand two hundred elders and other leaders gathered in Aberdeen) to be shaping a new Reformation.

But what would the historian of the next century pick out? In most of the vigorous 'record' that Stevenson provided for and of the church at home there is topicality that reflects gradual and constant change. For all its conservatism in its domestic affairs the Kirk has been a constantly changing church, mainly because of the vast scope for local initiative and not because of any radicalism in the General Assembly. Despite its reforming moods (as in 1978) the Assembly has often caught up with changes rather than pioneered them; and perhaps that is a better way to do things. But in home affairs the historian of the dim and distant future might pick out one encouragement of changes that didn't take place. Under Stevenson *Life and Work* often reflected the views of the Kirk's leadership rather than the hesitations of the grass-roots, even when the hesitations were probably justified. *Life and Work* went out of its way to give what Stevenson would have considered a fair hearing for the 'Bishops Report'—perhaps because so many people in the leadership thought it was getting a very unfair press, most notably from the *Scottish Daily Express*. Perhaps he was right. When the scheme foundered on the hostility of the Kirk's normally silent majority, and not because of the noisy polemics, no-one could say that the idea of bishops-in-presbytery had not got a fair hearing as well as a proper verdict. In July 1957, for example, Stevenson coupled praise of press coverage at the previous Assembly with complaints about the handling of the 'new bishops war'. He was at his best, a unique mixture of gentleness and forcefulness:

> But doesn't something need to be said frankly, and in a spirit of friendship, about a certain kind of reporting?
> It is this. The pitfalls in the reporting of religion are deeper and more treacherous than anywhere else. The temptation to highlight the wrong things is stronger.
> Sacrifice is demanded—a hard sacrifice when time presses and the front-page story is demanded—sacrifice of the slick judgment, the sensational headline, the chance to get a less-wise Churchman to publicise his indignation and resentment. But the gains to be won are enormous.

A 'newspaper man' (not one of the *Express* pacemakers) replied two months later claiming that the blame for any mishandling was the church's for failing 'to acquaint church members with the trend of thought which was developing', adding that any responsible churchman coming out with frank support for bishops-in-the-Kirk would 'have been sure of quite a bit of space in any Scottish newspaper'. There was also coverage for such defenders of presbyterian polity as the National Church Association, but without the signs of editorial encouragement that seemed to accompany the presentation of Dr Archie Craig's case for the report.

For all his gentleness Stevenson was no fence-sitter, though he was prepared even in 1957 to accept the possibility that 'it may be that the closer unity of the Church doesn't lie in that direction'. He spoke out strongly himself and he risked—and sometimes incurred—charges of bias by trying to let those whom he saw as leaders deploy their arguments and powers of leadership. In that same issue, for example, he carried most of the speech in which Craig tried to win a sympathetic hearing for the report, claiming that it sought full unity through an exchange of anglican and presbyterian insights, and by beginning 'to draw off the poison which history has infused into certain ecclesiastical terms'.

When the scheme foundered it was in spite of the way in which such men as Craig and Stevenson had backed it. The mood of the Kirk was perhaps closer to that of a future *Life and Work* claim that for the Anglicans to insist on officers called bishops in every part of a united church was as far-fetched as for the Salvation Army to insist on it having officers called brigadiers. It is even possible to say that the eventual decision was utterly right and yet that the Kirk desperately needed, and often lacked, that mood which Stevenson breathed into *Life and Work*: a joyful, confident readiness to seek God's will in a changing world.

He was indeed no fence-sitter, and perhaps not always a balance-keeper. That 1957 Assembly, for example, brought complaints about the way he had handled the Suez issue and, more generally, the issues of Christian involvement in the world and its politics. Probably the keynote of Stevenson's ministry was a conviction that there should be a Christian influence on the whole of life. The Suez crisis under Anthony Eden's premiership, however, had perhaps divided Britain more deeply than any other political confrontation since the General Strike to the present day, certainly not excluding the miner's strike and the first 1974 election which it provoked.

It certainly divided the members of the Kirk and the readers of *Life and Work*. The Commission of Assembly had been vague enough to be interpreted both ways but the World Council of Churches and British Council of Churches—not quite such predictable bodies then as now—had come out against Britain and France's action to 'separate the combatants' in the Egyptian-Israeli clash. In this clash there was alleged to be collusion with Israel (and there had certainly been consultation) and it was indisputable that the 'separation' involved an attack on Egypt, though it was mounted with such painful slowness that all chance of a decisive coup was lost.

Stevenson was an enthusiast for the United Nations and the *Life and Work* line was anti-Eden. It was also worried about the impact on world opinion and Christian opinion outside Britain. In January 1957, for example, when it was clear that there was much division and even ill-feeling in church as in nation at home, Bishop Lesslie Newbigin wrote from South India, not only writing of the 'deliberate repudiation of international morality' but worried about the impression that anti-Eden feeling in Britain had become a 'spent force'. Ironically, so had Eden himself.

This was the background to criticism which found voice at the General

Assembly, and which had the backing of such a formidable elder as Bernard Fergusson, the soldier and author who as Lord Ballantrae was later to be a Lord High Commissioner to the General Assembly. It was to draw a reply from Stevenson which, by a nice irony, gave great satisfaction to a later editor who had not dissimilar trouble, but from a very different point of the political compass.

Looking back on the Assembly criticism, Stevenson conceded that critics might legitimately complain that this or that article, especially in a section called 'To-day's Christian and To-day's News', might have been misconstrued as representing the voice of the church, or might 'appear as something more than a conversation on the great moral issues of the day', or might not have done justice to differing interpretations and judgments on events. He went on:

> The editor has no quarrel with that criticism. What he asked of the Assembly was that this criticism of certain individual articles should not be used as an argument for abolishing the whole endeavour. This would certainly be the result of insisting that nothing should appear editorially in these pages which might be 'at variance with much Christian opinion within the Church of Scotland.' . . . It is not enough for this magazine merely to throw a bundle of individual opinions at its readers. It must be prepared to attempt some assessment of the issues.
>
> We may be wrong in our interpretation—of course we may. But surely it is better sometimes to be wrong and to be corrected than to give up the attempt.

Perhaps the issue would not have been put so plainly but for the events of Suez and the mood that followed it. But in fact there was friction over a wider range of issues, as there must be if an editor with any convictions has any capacity to put them across, and to draw on the vast range of articulate opinions in the Kirk. Bernard Fergusson, for example, accepted the point about 'a bundle of individual opinions' but wanted assessments made from a standpoint 'near the middle of the see-saw of Church opinion.'

Perhaps the difficulty in such cases will always be defining where the middle ground lies. Fergusson clearly thought Stevenson was on the left and was not always ready to share his limited space to let the opposite Christian case be effectively put. At the time Stevenson probably seemed left of centre on Suez, on nuclear arms, on the Welfare State, on South Africa, and on Central African Federation, where the African opposition in what were then Nyasaland and Northern Rhodesia endured that the powerful missionary lobby in the Kirk would be at odds with the British Government while it supported the white-dominated and Rhodesia-based Federal Government in Africa. (Macmillan deserted it in about 1961.) Yet from today's standpoint he would certainly occupy the middle ground, probably even as defined by his old critic Bernard Fergusson, on African issues at least—for at that time white domination of South Africa was so secure that opposition to apartheid scarcely raised the dilemma posed for white Africans by revolutionary 'liberation movements'. In the two decades after the war it was assumed, even by liberals in the West and the most sympathetic friends of the emergent nations, that while it was necessary to co-exist with communist power, and to learn from the energy and dedication of communists, there was no possibility of any dialogue which conceded Marxist, far less Leninist, assumptions, about the nature and chief end of man.

In the pre-war period the rise and temporary triumph of Nazism in Central Europe gave *Life and Work* some of its most memorable writing (and some of the material it would like to forget). In the post-war period the triumphs of communism, apparently more lasting, produced some of the most moving and vivid writing.

In 1948, when the Communists, by a mixture of willpower and threats, took power in Czechoslovakia, Stevenson was writing that it was a judgment on us 'that the children of this world should know their job so much better', though his profounder warning was that 'we have assumed that we could separate our economic life and set it apart as a thing by itself, something governed by laws of its own—and then live our Christian lives privately. We have forgotten that the claim of the Gospel is to turn the world upside down.' At this range the emphasis he put on the youthful idealism of communism seems surprising, and the takeover in Prague seems to be explained in terms of the economics of the 1930's rather than the great power politics of the post-war era.

Later in the year Robert Smith, who had seen the twilight of Czech democracy before the war, was back again from Prague and reflecting at the General Assembly how daring in modern Europe was the assumption of speaker after speaker of an unquestioned right to judge all things by the Spirit of Christ. Every act proclaimed 'our belief in the Christian basis of society . . . and that is heresy today in much of Europe'. (It still is):

> . . . The State is assuming the right to judge the Church by its own standards of political reliability, and granting a meagre freedom of worship in terms which stifle and silence the Christian conscience.

173

Ironically (in the light of later trends and events) the Russian Orthodox Church was absent from the first assembly of the World Council of Churches in Amsterdam, which virtually filled the October 1948 *Life and Work*, protesting, no doubt under intense pressure, that the new WCC was 'involving itself in politics'. Indeed it is hard for us thirty years later—when the world has changed, when some enthusiasms and organisations have gone stale, when a new kind of confessional church, free and protesting, seems to be needed—to sense the dynamism that the post-war years had, or the sheer scale of the physical reconstruction and practical humanity that was needed. There was a sense of solidarity with the Christians of Europe which we have largely lost, partly because the concerns of Europe now seem dwarfed by the needs of the rest of the world, partly because the spiritual and physical reconstruction of the late 1940's gave Europe the stability which it has so largely used for secular, selfish, and even trivial purposes.

Perhaps the clearest evidence of this solidarity then is one which the historians now might understandably overlook: the enthusiastic identification with German Christians in what was not only a divided country but a shattered and at times even a despairing one. We have got used to the rich, efficient German whose problems seem to arise out of the discontents of affluence. A fair proportion of the readers of *Life and Work* in the late 1940's probably had to fight (being Christians) against an inclination to hate the Germans as a nation and even as people. Perhaps they wondered if the injunction to do good to those who hate you also applied to those whom you found it hard to forgive. But this was a case where, whatever their other failures, the British churches gave a strong lead and the Church of Scotland had an honourable place. It should also be recorded that in *Life and Work* (and elsewhere) the church in East Germany got full support and understanding in its long attempt to maintain its spiritual unity with the rest of the German church and, within East Germany itself, to render to God the things that are God's. In the one case it had to yield to pressure and circumstances, but not in the other.

Yet when the historian of the next century, or of Christian centuries beyond it, sifts through *Life and Work* it is probably not the coverage of the reconstruction of Europe, or even the Soviet partition of Europe, that will strike him as most significant. In the broad sweep of world history it may be the account of the last days of the western mission era in China.

There are other overseas reports, sometimes in very moving words, from missionaries who were caught up in conflict and of local Christians who did their best in harrowing situations, for example in the Calcutta communal riots of 1946 and the wave of hatred that broke over the partitioned Punjab, when India and Pakistan went their separate ways in independence. There was even a Moderator, Dr Matthew Stewart, who went on an official visit to Palestine, passed the wreckage of an ambushed Jewish convoy on the Jerusalem road, and watched in lace and breeches as an Arab raiding party attacked a 'hospital armoury': a phrase that does more than thousands of words to sum up the state of the country as the mandate reached it inglorious end.

Yet in China the courage of the missionaries, some of them survivors of wartime hardship, exile, and imprisonment, was set against a tragic and titanic movement of history which settled (who knows, save God, for how long) the course of the Chinese revolution and that encounter with the western world of which the missionary presence was itself a part. By the strangest irony of history the Chinese, often impressed and even more often influenced but not for the most part convinced, by the western presentation of Christianity, were to be overwhelmed, in the spirit as well as the flesh, by the western deviation from the Christian tradition shaped by the lapsed Jewish Protestant from Trier, Karl Marx.

In June 1948, for example, John Fleming was interviewed when he flew home to Scotland before returning to the Manchurian city of Mukden, then under communist siege. There were three strong congregations there at the time, one of them in 'a huge building always packed', and a new church had been opened in what had been the Japanese part of the city during the 'Manchukuo' period. It was already clear that the city might fall, and the missionaries had decided 'to stay with the Church', fairly confident that medical work at least would be able to continue in a city which had two hundred thousand refugees, many of them living in derelict factories.

They were to stay until forced out; and when in 1973 John Fleming (then of St Andrews University) described a brief return visit in *Life and Work* he had been to Shanghai and Peking but had been denied access to Mukden, which the Chinese call Shenyang.

By March 1949 it was clear that the communist victory in the north, which had overwhelmed Mukden, was being followed by a collapse of the central government. Chinese Christian leaders were writing of 'rethinking Christianity, dissociating the essential things of our faith from Western accretions' but missionaries were able to stay. In September the fall of Ichang, the old Church of Scotland mission on the Yangtse, was confirmed; but the news from Mukden was of hopes that 'present difficulties will pass', though there was a note of realistic scepticism about the assurances that there was to be 'freedom for and against religion'. John Fleming, cut off from Scotland for

175

six months, was eventually able to hear the opening of the General Assembly described on the BBC World Service and to write home about it.

For a time conditions seem to have been easier in Ichang than in Manchuria. In August 1950 the last of the Mukden missionaries, including John Fleming and his family, had to leave when the Chinese church had to agree that the point had been reached, during the Korean War, when their presence had become a hindrance rather than a help. Yet the railway station was 'thronged with a great crowd of Chinese Christians who dared the disapproval of the authorities'. In October Helen Maclean, who had been at Mukden, gave a vivid picture of revolutionary China, where 'the Communists have turned the world upside down', and there was no such thing as leisure while people struggled to 'learn the new way of life, a way of life at variance with all that Chinese loved in the past.'

In some ways the missionaries of the time may have been better judges than later Christian sinologists; perhaps some of the same people judged better then than later. As years went by Helen Maclean's prophecy seemed to have been fulfilled:

> The Communist régime in China will not be accepted or rejected because of its close adherence or otherwise to Marxist principles but by results. If it brings peace to this country so broken by wars, if it brings prosperity and food in plenty to this people so stricken by poverty and famine, then only, I believe, will it get the whole-hearted backing of this peace-loving and industrious, and long suffering people.

But writing in the mixture of relief and grief at their homecoming, in the freshness of the recently interrupted friendships with their Chinese colleagues, sometimes even in the vain hope that they might get back again quite soon, the returning missionaries testified not only to their love for China and the Chinese but to the cruelty of revolution. There was that hatred 'with a sameness about it all that palls', the mob law 'under which many have died' in the reign of terror, the zealotry for change and struggle. Helen Maclean summed up the difference between Christians and the 'best Communists' whose lives were marked by self-denial and self-sacrifice: the denial of God, the denial of Christian love, the denial of any rights to the individual, and the 'absence of any kind of freedom within the Communist way of life.'

It was May 1951, however, before publication of a letter from the Church of Christ in China marked the end of the missionary era which had already become a time of partnership. It had decided to cut itself off from western support. It was, of course, under pressure from 'the popular patriotic movement'. The terms of the letter made clear that it did not plan, whatever was to happen later, to cut itself off from the community of the world Church. 'We remember God's word to Ezekiel', said the Chinese, 'Stand upon thy feet and I will speak with thee.' The letter concluded:

> In Christ no thought or labour or prayer of love is ever lost. May the Grace of our Lord Jesus Christ be with you all.

There, for the time being, is the right place to leave the Chinese church. It would be possible to pick themes of almost as rich interest from coverage of other areas where the Church of Scotland was involved: South and Central Africa; Malaya (where John Fleming was soon working again with Chinese Christians); or Israel, where the barbed wire ran past St Andrew's and missionaries returned to Torrance's Tiberias and to Tabeetha School at Jaffa to find squatters in occupation. In 1951 when Dr Robert Mackie, a Kirk minister who was the WCC's director of the Inter-Church Aid and Refugee Department, went to Tiberias, there were rows and rows of huts to house Yemeni Jews. But in the Lebanon he 'was not prepared for the human tragedy' he encountered among the Arab refugees, 'whom no-one any longer wants and who are in danger of being forgotten except as pawns in Near East politics.'

A 'cruel century' Mackie called it, and noted only too prophetically that the Arab speeches 'ended in unforgiving bitterness and reckless promises of revenge'. But in Europe came the marvellous recovery that brought a new affluence, political stability for a long time (except in France, trapped first in Vietnamese and then Algerian war), and all the eventual troubles of full bellies and empty souls.

Stevenson was one of those who regretted the tendency of Britain to keep Western Europe at arms' length when it thought about unity as well as recovery. However it would be a mistake to sum up his remarkable tenure of *Life and Work* by making him seem so concerned with the worldwide church that he might have neglected its national and local presence. Far from it. He had a passion for the things of Scottish as well as church life, including literature and the arts. When space was short the poet George Bruce (and even the anti-clerical critic Maurice Lindsay) could be found writing about Scottish literature. Bruce could add his own enigmatic yet indisputably Christian contributions (as he did again in the 1970's) for example in an Easter poem for 1947 beginning:

> And Adam's curse is in us,
>   The Man upon the tree,

> The serpent mingles with the dust,
>> We fear the bonds that make us free.

There were times when Stevenson emphasised that the claim to be a 'national church' involved a rediscovery of the nation, meaning Scotland. The mood of the first post-war years, when the devolution movement had some of the drive and fire that later went into a more outright political nationalism found expression in *Life and Work*, as well as in Church and Nation Committee and General Assembly. But above all *Life and Work*, within its limitations of space, is a record of the church in Scotland: radio mission, industrial mission, social mission and the national mission of the 'Tell Scotland' mood.

It would also be a mistake to deduce from the controversy over the Bishops Report, mentioned near the beginning of this chapter, that the ecumenical mood was allowed to disparage the historic expression of Scotland's Christian faith in a distinctively reformed way. Most of Stevenson's work was done, of course, before the ecumenical explosion in the Roman Catholic Church and the new emphasis within it on the Bible. In a formal way the affirmation of Scotland's reformed Christianity accompanied most obviously the commemoration in 1960 of the fourth centenary of the Reformation. In some ways it was more evident a decade earlier when the Roman Catholic Church seemed to be erecting new barriers abainst biblically-based co-operation. 'Are we too afraid to offend minorities?', asked Stevenson in 1951—in an issue in which a much-respected Glasgow minister, Steven of Queen's Park, wrote of Rome's 'shameless mendacity' over mixed marriages.

The editorial comment warned 'that we are where we are as a Church because we cannot tolerate a certain bondage of the Roman system':

> If Rome sets herself to infiltrate into the councils of civic and educational affairs she must not be surprised if we meet her on the same ground. If she creates a new dogma of the bodily ascension of the Mother of our Lord she must tolerate our repudiation of it.

There is an assurance in those years about the essentially Christian (and protestant) character of Scotland which the Kirk of a quarter-century later has lost. Time will show if this is through realism or defeatism.

There is some gain, too, in the discovery that the Christian life and works which Stevenson (and even Fisher) found it easy to honour among Roman Catholics abroad could also be found at home. But the great change was probably on the Roman side as Christian experience found itself at odds with traditional and Tridentine dogma. Indeed a Roman Catholic cardinal, Gordon Gray, had written for *Life and Work* by 1972 along with a minister, D W D

Shaw, who had been an observer at the Vatican council (and was later Principal of New College). The cardinal's article—apparently inspired by a thought of Nevile Davidson, a former Moderator—was friendly rather than significant; and it was awkwardly timed in that it appeared just before a new editor took over in time to receive the complaints. But it affirmed in its way that no real damage to Christian unity can ever be done by any words of truth spoken in love, the standard by which the voice of the reformed church in Scotland has spoken for a century about the Roman church. Not the least of Stevenson's services to church and nation was to set that standard and make it easier for those coming after him to maintain it.

When Jack Stevenson took leave of the magazine in 1965 it was a first-rate expression of the Kirk for its time. It had drawn some criticism. For example, in a welcome to the next editor written by a journalist, it was claimed that 'the recent improvement in the appearance and content of *Life and Work* has not pleased everybody. Its approach to professional standards of production has roused our old Scottish suspicion of somebody being too clever by half.'

That was something between a half-truth and a left-handed compliment to the retiring editor, whose most remarkable professional achievement was probably not with the glossy paper of the early 1960's but in putting so much in sixteen pages in the austere post-war years. Even his undoubted achievement in providing so lively a magazine after twenty years probably counted for less than that.

There was, no doubt, some 'resentment of *Life and Work* having the temerity to start the yeast of controversy working in the Church'. In fact it was only after Jack Stevenson had gone that some of the difficulties of *Life and Work* were to be fully appreciated; and in the most acute phase of trouble the main problem was not controversy in the magazine's pages but controversy over its internal conduct and control.

That well-written but ill-informed welcome to the new editor also spoke of the increasing readiness of *Life and Work* to jump into the arena where social issues are being discussed.

Jack Stevenson himself was, as always, much better informed when in his farewell diary he answered a question about what was the greatest change in the church during his twenty years as editor. 'I should say', he replied, 'the growing conviction that Christians must claim for Christ the lordship over the life of the nation when strong pressure even in our own country is towards secular or neutral state.'

Stevenson retired to Dunblane, living in Leighton House where, in the shadow of the cathedral and close to Scottish Churches' House he hoped to see the development of an informal retreat and conference centre. From there he watched sadly and shrewdly as the magazine and his immediate successor ran into trouble.

He lived long enough to share his mellow wisdom with his successor once removed, and to approve the return to an editorial comment which he, too, thought gave character and coherence to a magazine. He was too broad in his sympathies to worry that the emphasis was sometimes not merely for another time but in another approach. And he was too kind to remind anyone of the point he himself made in his farewell that in trying to claim lordship for Christ over the nation and other nations, editors are in danger of blundering in 'some particular advocacy of the claim and opinionative rather than humbly seeking God's will.'

Shortly after a second long discussion at Dunblane with the present editor he died. He had been the Valiant for Truth of Scottish church journalism. He passed over, and all the trumpets sounded for him on the other side. Or rather, since our spiritual metaphors should reveal the aptness as well as assurance of the welcome among those many mansions, it might be better to say that as he surveyed the farther shore he found, to his surprise, that the newsboys of eternity were on the street with a special edition!

Chapter 13
The age of discord

To write this book so far has been undiluted pleasure. To tackle this chapter is a mixture of embarrassment, ordeal, and temptation.

It is embarrassing because in the late 1960's *Life and Work*, which had troubles enough in deciding its role and style, became caught up in a conflict between the church's Publicity and Publication Committee and the editor it had selected and, after five troubled years, tried to dispense with. But the editor, Leonard Bell, fought his case and won it as far as the supreme court of the church and the verdict of a committee of inquiry were concerned. However, sadly, he died before the General Assembly was able to receive the report of the committee of inquiry it had appointed.

It is an ordeal because some of those most deeply involved are still alive and may be hurt by whatever is written. Others, not all on the one side in the controversy, lived long enough for the present editor to know them well and work happily with them. Of the survivors several are friends of the present editor and have spoken very freely and frankly, and very honestly, about this appalling interlude in which people who did not know *Life and Work* came to think of it not as an auxiliary means of grace but as a symbol for feuding among Christians of the same room in the household of faith. Moreover, the honest accounts do not always coincide. They differ not only in their assessment of what went wrong and why, but in the factual details of what actually happened.

Therein lies the temptation. To explore the events of a minor tragedy on the fringe of church history is to understand how much greater disasters can be provoked and quarrels prolonged and embittered. To explore such a fierce quarrel among good Christian men is to discover the subtlety with which the Devil works. It is tempting to explore, to analyse, to pontificate. And it is impossible to write an honest history and avoid what happened; impossible, too, to follow the theme of all the earlier chapters—the view of church, nation, world, and eternity as seen through *Life and Work*—and not to make some comment, explicit or implicit, on the particular viewpoint of the magazine in

43. Editor Bell

those years, even if it is only to note that less of power and weight on church and nation seems to have appeared then than in other periods of the magazine's history.

But this is not a history of the internal organisation of local government in a suburb of the city of God. It is about the city itself and the view from its walls. The quarrel which involved much ill-feeling and a glare of newspaper publicity needs to be touched on, but not dwelt on. For one scarcely disputable fact is that whoever was right (or half-right or sometimes not entirely wrong), it was impossible in the atmosphere of acrimony, conflict, distrust, and lack of confidence to follow any rational and consistent course in planning the magazine's role and developing its personality. The wonder is that those directly involved and those unhappily caught up in the quarrel (especially the other staff of the magazine, the assistant editor Bill Black and the editorial assistant Betty Sinclair) managed to do much that was worthwhile in the years of discord.

Anyone who wants a fair and fairly detailed summary of what was involved in the quarrel should read the report of the special committee to the General Assembly of 1972, which after Bell's death found itself approving the terms on which a new editor was to be sought. The facts, in very brief outline, are that the Publicity and Publication Committee was dissatisfied with the way Bell ran the magazine. Complaints bred more complaints and a lack of confidence. Communications broke down. But the attempt to terminate the editor's appointment after a five year term and in line with a 'break clause' in his contract had gone awry. The appointment had been made by the General Assembly and the committee was apparently beyond its powers in itself trying to exercise the option. But the inquiry did not settle the matters which really lay behind the dispute though it seemed to imply that they had never been well defined and it certainly revealed that a system of consultation had been allowed to lapse. There had once been an editorial advisory committee (replacing the twenty-three gentlemen who had read the proofs in the Auld Kirk days). In the 1940's it became the main committee's executive, holding one annual meeting under another name. It was revived in 1966-67 and then lapsed again. One of the few good results of the miserable interlude was to put matters back on a rational and comprehensible footing for the editor after Bell, thanks largely to the clarity of the committee of inquiry's report.

Leonard Bell was appointed editor on Stevenson's retirement. He was a good writer, as he had shown in the *Scots Magazine* and was to demonstrate in *Life and Work*. A Glasgow graduate, he was a parish minister in Brechin who had previously been in Maxwelltown and he had an undoubted feel for the mood of kirk and community in the small towns and country areas. But why did the committee think he would make the best editor, better than five laymen and four other ministers who were in the field? That is not at all clear, and the water is muddied a bit by recollections in some quarters that this or that better-known name in the Kirk turned it down or perhaps wasn't pressed hard enough or didn't get to the point of putting in a formal application. It is not easy now to find those who thought then that Bell was the right man.

One thing that is certain is that the question whether, given the right backing, Bell could have made a more successful editor, is now unanswerable. The troubles of mutual lack of confidence, failure of communication, and later Bell's poor health and interrupted tenure make the question not only unanswerable but academic.

But perhaps this was an age of uncertainty and discord and not merely a clash of personalities. Before the row with Bell there had been a clash between the committee and its powerful, strong-willed minister-manager, Andrew McCosh. He left. There was a vast field for friction over the Kirk's gift horse, *The British Weekly*. Another spectacular clash there (or a closure) was probably averted only by the decision to let it go and seek its fortune elsewhere, and with it its editor Denis Duncan. There were also intermittent symptoms of friction in this decade with other Kirk committees.

That in itself is hardly remarkable. But the time was one of uncertainty. Church membership, which in 1951 had been almost as high as at the time of reunion, had begun to fall. *Life and Work* circulation, which a low price and widespread give-away distribution in many parishes had kept high, began to slip. It was two hundred and seventeen thousand when Audit Bureau of Circulation figures were first introduced in 1956, was still over two hundred and twelve thousand in 1965 but clearly beginning to slide, even before the coming of the great inflation. The twopenny magazine of wartime days was still only fourpence in the mid-1950's, though it is evident that throughout Jack Stevenson's reign it was starved of money even after the wartime and post-war problem of paper supplies had eased. In 1966 the price rose from 6d to 8d and in 1971 to 1s, in preparation for decimalisation at 5p.

In fact circulation trends compared not too badly with other religious publications and many other magazines. This was the age of TV and it was not, to put it mildly, an age of religious revival. But was the large circulation matched by real readership? Probably at all times in the century a proportion of *Life and Work* circulation has been out of loyalty rather than interest. No-one can really say how that proportion has varied from time to time, but the 1960's brought an uneasiness and uncertainty which would have made life difficult for an editor with more experience and diplomacy than Leonard Bell brought to the job. There were those who wanted a magazine that looked like *Reader's Digest*, others who still hankered after a weekly newspaper or at least a tabloid monthly, though their confidence must have been shaken by the poor showing of *The British Weekly* in Scotland during the period when the Kirk owned it (from 1957 to 1967). The circulation figures for the time it was under the Church of Scotland ownership look surprisingly good, but little of the increase was in Scotland.

Two important things need to be said to do justice to Bell. The first is that he set out to make the magazine more readable and more popular. The most serious trouble he ran into, outside the committee at least, was with those who thought that in trying to be readable and popular he sacrificed serious religious teaching and introduced chatty contributions which carried little in spiritual or intellectual weight. The second is that the job had become even more difficult; and the difficulty was increased because few people really realised it. The age of cheap publications was passing and inflation (not least in paper prices) lay ahead. The church was losing some of its hold, even in Scotland. The new challenges to faith and even the very different responses to them made it harder than ever to produce a consensus in keeping with *Life and Work*'s official status. To play safe and risk dullness was a formula which guaranteed criticism without offering much chance of doing something worthwhile or even stabilising circulation. But the Kirk, like the world Church and even the Roman Catholic Church, began to look like a coalition of very different styles of Christianity. A new radicalism aligned faith with social change and even social revolution. There was also a conservative, even fundamentalist revival suspicious of liberal, moderate traditions and inclined at times or in places to be a church within the church. There were charismatics, and there were very different schools of evangelical revival.

Bell, in addition to being a good writer, was a tenacious man if given encouragement and support (as his defence of his position showed after the attempt to get rid of him). But irrespective of his suitability for the job, his situation made him a weak editor. No editor who lacks the confidence of his management can be strong.

The result is that *Life and Work* faced the problems of the late 1960's, the most serious since the war for the whole Christian Church, harassed by both division and indecision. Even some apparently strong decisions, such as the redesigning of the magazine in 1968-69, the switch from letterpress to offset-litho, and the introduction of colour covers, concealed a great deal of indecision. They also, of course, aroused a good deal of criticism from readers—some of it ephemeral, some of it so well justified that some back-tracking had to be done. The easiest and least expensive bit of back-tracking would have been to abandon the ill-fated and unpopular notion of rendering the magazine's title as *Life+Work*. This fitted in with some fashions of the time but it never really caught on in the parishes, except with a few enthusiasts for change, some of whom actually called the magazine *Life plus Work* (which was never intended). By 1972 when a new editor arrived and proposed a reversion to the old style, no-one seemed to want the plus sign. But in the mid and late 1960's there was a concern with an up-to-date image and, perhaps, a failure to appreciate just how profoundly the church would find itself alienated from some of the trends of the time. Even the name *Life and Work* itself was not entirely safe. One school of thought sought a new title, though the only one of its thoughts to achieve immortality in the minutes was *Kirk News*. (When the present editor mentioned this informally to some fellow-elders they were still inclined that way. One, suggesting the work-ethic was out of date, suggested *Love and Joy*; another, adding the notion of radical politics, offered *Strike me Pink*).

The most important bit of back-tracking done—fairly quickly after the experiment had proved unpopular and unrewarding—was on the use of 'unjustified lines', or asymmetrical setting. To try to read this in the files is a jarring and bewildering experience. Readers at the time seem to have felt just as jarred and bewildered.

How, one may ask, did such a staid and traditional magazine tart itself up in such an odd manner? The 1960's was, perhaps, an age of illusion. In printing and publishing it was certainly an age of technical change and in the church it was an age when people still hoped that changes of style and presentation would create a new and more attractive image.

The *Life and Work* changes followed new thinking about the magazine and new ideas for its production. Some of the thinking and the planning which followed was sound, for example the establishment of a proper professionally run advertising department, with Frank Whitaker as a consultant and then David Carson as a skilful, realistic manager. The promotion of the magazine was also energetically undertaken by Bill Black (who succeeded to Glen Gibson's title of assistant editor and had to be acting editor during Bell's absences and after his death). The change from letterpress to off-set litho was also probably economically inevitable, despite the inevitable deterioration in appearance. A letterpress job on good quality paper looked better than good off-set litho printing on the kind of paper *Life and Work* could afford. Perhaps the mistake was to think in terms of improved design rather than merely

44. The Bishops' report was no laughing matter in the late 1950's. But 20 years later cartoonist Noël Watson had a new bishops-in- the-Kirk theme.

urging readers to be realistic. The minutes of the committee record an attempt to draw on the skills of some of Scotland's leading designers, and the new 'grid plan' was the work of one of them, though various teething troubles in the printing meant that he was far from pleased (like the readers) when the new design was introduced in January 1969.

Was it an improvement? Such judgments are highly subjective. But for what it is worth Bell's successor thinks that—as if there had not been enough troubles building up already—the editor of the late 1960's was landed with a scheme which made the magazine change for the worse in appearance. Perhaps a stronger editor would have said thank you to the designer and adjusted his plans to the realities of journalism. Again it is subjective judgment, but Bell's best-looking magazines came out before the great change and not when he was using a new design which was at first made much more inflexible than it needed to be. As originally applied it seemed designed to stifle all personality and originality; and Bell's one hope was to let both, together with his undoubted skill as a writer and his feeling for small-town and rural Scotland, shine through in the magazine.

However, this is not a history of committees or even editors, but a view of the world, most particularly of Scottish church and nation. What distinctive insight did *Life and Work* offer during the age of conflict?

There are forms of various sorts in which questions carry the admonition 'If none, write "none".' There are times in these years when it is tempting to write 'none', but that would be a sweeping, arrogant, and unfair judgment.

Perhaps if Bell had added a stronger evangelical or devotional dimension to his sense of the relation of the church to the Scottish community and to local communities things would have gone better. Many ministers and others (and even the 1969 General Assembly in a gently worded but important addendum to a committee deliverance) wanted more attention to the central doctrines of the faith. But there are times when what comes through the pages is a mild social gospel, without much passion for social change and no association with radical political notions.

The magazine itself was not in an obvious sense controversial, though in fact lively Kirk controversy broke through into its pages from time to time. In October 1969, for example, Bell had Andrew Herron (who was to be Moderator in 1971) writing a most powerful piece which was really the writing on the wall for the desultory direct conversations between the Kirk and the Episcopalians which had continued after the burial of the Bishops Report. But one detects both in the angry rejoinder from Professor J K S Reid, and from the storm this created in committee, that readers and committee were not really

45.   Lively Kirk controversy: Herron v Reid

attuned to the vigorous expression in *Life and Work* of what people really thought and said in private.

From an editorial point of view the substance of the dispute between Herron and Reid (whether it was worthwhile carrying on talks with the Anglicans) may have mattered less than the attitude of mind which Reid and many other excellent people in the Kirk found natural. After attacking Herron for his attitude to committee loyalty he complained about the editorial prominence given to what was, regardless of its argument, a newsworthy, well-written piece on a matter which, as the defeat of the bishops' lobby and their report had shown, was of much interest to many people in the Kirk. 'Print such a view of course. But in this select leading place?' Thus complained Reid, who alleged discourtesy, and disliked the idea of Herron taking the opportunity to state his view 'in public where his opinion cannot be immediately and equally contested'.

The point of Herron's piece, one of those which would have been a lot more readable in traditional 'justified' setting, was probably his question, after discussing Anglican notions of episcopacy linked to 'apostolic succession':

> Would it not be better for all of us to recognise the existence of this chasm—unbridged if not unbridgeable—and concentrate our efforts in seeking to effect large-scale union of those on the non-episcopal side of the great divide?

In fact by the time this piece appeared Bell's internal trouble with the committee was deepening. But the Herron-Reid exchange gives an insight into troubles that would have taxed the powers of even an editor of exceptional journalistic (as distinct from literary) skill, wide experience, and considerable tact; and these were probably not Bell's strongest suits. Fairness to him means recognition that he carried responsibility at what was almost certainly the most difficult time of the magazine's one hundred years' history. There is no time when it is less clear what the Kirk in general, and possibly the committee in particular, wanted from *Life and Work*. Perhaps they wanted a quiet life. It was one of the things the Kirk was not getting in the late 1960's and had no hope of recovering in the decade to follow.

But fairness to Bell also means looking at what the magazine was beginning to do, trying to do, or already doing well after it was clear that he had won his legal battle. Even where the ideas were not his (and he had allowed his assistant editor to take over 'content planning'), he was editor and took the responsibility and any fresh blame that was going.

The last issue published before his sudden death (aged fifty-nine) was

March 1972. To judge from later reader research its most popular article was almost certainly the one in which Professor William Barclay explained what the *Book of Acts* was about. One of the few happy results of all the wrangling and heart-searching about *Life and Work* in the previous years had been the decision to use Barclay's unique talent as a popular communicator for the regular exposition in *Life and Work* of the background to scripture. The readers responded.

There are signs of vigour too in the letters—though nothing like what was to develop later. There is also a new role for Andrew Herron. Here was a Moderator who (unlike most) had the knack of being a monthly columnist. He was given the chance.

The couthy, chatty, country matters have been much reduced and there is a reasonable flow of news, though it is oddly arranged and presented. Obituary notices, for example, seem to have been deliberately scattered through the news and the 'lead' (if the first item can be called that) is a puff for the Woman's Guild magazine.

There has also been a dramatic reduction in the material, from freelances and others, which is not obviously related to *Life and Work*'s role as a news service, teaching medium, and forum for the people of the church. In Bell's early years as editor he seems to have been dangerously susceptible to freelancers and even encouraged them; perhaps having been one in his spare time he had a kindly sympathy for them. He certainly was compassionate and kindly by nature. But by 1972 it would be unreasonable to suggest that there was anything wrong in the balance of material. Perhaps if Bell had been spared he would have had both an easier and more successful second five years.

The General Assembly's 'special committee anent *Life+Work*' (the wretched plus sign forced its way even into the official reports) recorded that 'there had been an undoubted improvement in the general atmosphere'. By now the main committee chairman was Ronald Falconer, retired from BBC religious broadcasting, and rich in professional, diplomatic, and spiritual gifts. Though a division into separate publicity and publications committees was to change his role, he remained for several vital years as chairman of the revived editorial consultative committee, proving a source of both help and inspiration for Bell's succesor.

Had Bell survived, the special committee would have recommended that he remain editor. But when its report was presented the problem was to define the terms and create the atmosphere for a new start.

The gist of this very notable report—far above the level of most Kirk and other reports in both power of thought and lucidity of expression—was that the editor of *Life and Work* should have the right to run the magazine in his own way, subject to proper consultation, and the right to be fired by the committee if that turned out not to be its way too. He would, indeed, have a right to petition the General Assembly, but the implication of this residual link with the old system has happily not yet been tested.

The editor must be independent, said the special committee, and he is 'inevitably in an isolated position', and one in which readers are bound to be critical of what is said and left unsaid about the church's attitude to current issues and in producing a magazine which is 'readable, informed, and balanced'.

He must pay heed to his critics and yet maintain freedom of initiative: 'Any attempt by members of any committee, however well intentioned, to control the content of the magazine is bound to undermine and even render intolerable the position of the editor.' It emphasised the importance of the consultative committee and the *Life and Work* sub-committee, whom any sensible editor obviously wants to treat as partners, and the damage done in other committees where the magazine's affairs had seemed to be discussed and settled behind the editor's back.

It was a good report, though it inevitably left very different opinions in different quarters about the original dispute. It also gave the committees and Bell's successor a set of fair and workable guidelines. Indeed whatever has been done since in *Life and Work*, for better or worse, has probably been on all important matters in line with both the spirit and the letter of the special report.

In that respect at least some good probably came out of what was certainly the least pleasant episode in the century of *Life and Work*'s service to the church, and possibly the time at which (largely because of the dispute) the magazine was least effective.

46. Ronald Falconer

47.   Editor Kernohan

Chapter 14
To be continued

In any history, whether of a parish or of the world, the chapter that carries the narrative up to the present day is frequently the worst. Contemporary history is probably no history at all. It lacks the knowledge and the perspective which can shape history out of the chronicles of another time and of the opinions which turned out to be wise or foolish. As this history has suggested, the wisdom and the foolishness lie pretty snugly together in *Life and Work*: and even if it were not written by a serving editor, with at least half his mind on the preparation of the next edition or the reception of the last one, it would be impossible to explain and assess the role of *Life and Work* in the last few years in the way that is historically reasonable and possible for the age of Charteris, Fisher, Livingstone, Stevenson or Bell.

As this is written the centenary of the magazine approaches. By the time it is read, God willing, it will have been reached and passed. The editor of the magazine at this time, if spared for the occasion, can be no sound judge on whether this particular century was put on to the scoreboard by a succession of swipes, mis-hits, and snicks through the slips or by elegant strokes of power and grace. In any event, this is a history of an uncompleted innings; and the cricket metaphor had better not be carried too far in case anyone thinks it is a prophecy that the next editor (being number eleven) will be the last man (or woman) to go in! Far from it. By God's grace, there will surely be editors to shape a new response to new needs as the second century of the magazine takes shape.

But to make the record as complete as possible a few changes of the 1970's need to be recorded. After Leonard Bell's death in 1972 the next editor was R D Kernohan, a journalist and church elder: the only layman apart from Livingstone to be appointed editor.

Some of the magazine's lines of development probably reveal a journalistic rather than a ministerial editorship. Others were intended to open it much more to different opinions within the church, though it can be difficult to draw the debatable frontier which separates constructive controversy from

195

acrimony. Both controversy and acrimony, of course, are highly newsworthy and have provided some (though by no means all) of the very generous coverage of the contents of *Life and Work* which both the Scottish and the London media have frequently provided in these years. Any historian in fifty or a hundred years will certainly find in its pages a wide range of those likely to be remembered in the history of church and state; and in more than some eras he will find a cross-section of lively, sometimes extraordinary, opinions from ordinary people. Somewhere among them are probably minor prophets whose importance today is only too easily missed.

Not all readers have always been pleased. A pressure group within the Kirk, and even some other nice people, have complained at times that the magazine is too conservative—by which they usually mean in political attitudes or assumptions though at times this has happened in theological matters too. On the other hand a member of the peerage, who happened also to be an elder, won it some useful publicity when he claimed it was so left wing that he would no longer have it in his stately home.

Moderators and others called to high office (who have had a very fair share of space) have on the whole been friendly and helpful. One of the nicest

48. An editor's accolade!

SCOTTISH
DAILY EXPRESS

No. 23,584   Friday April 23 1976   FOUNDED by LORD BEAVERBROOK   Price 6p

Amazing attack in Kirk's magazine

MIRACLE 'A THREAT TO UNITY'

By George Birrell

The Milton Street

Mr. Kennedy piles up furnitu

Riddle
Army

Moderators, however, found himself described in a noisy newspaper as 'slapping down' the editor for taking and expressing a protestant and reformed view of the 'canonisation' in 1975 of the seventeenth century Jesuit John Ogilvie. In fact such a comment was only possible, never mind expedient, because if represented a broadly based view in the Kirk, often more pithily expressed in private than in what was really a fairly restrained editorial comment. Had editor Fisher been around at the time to write his 'Events and Opinions' paragraph on the evidence linking Ogilvie to a 'miracle' in Easterhouse, the results would have been decidedly stimulating, and not at all to the taste of some ultra-ecumenists. But in fact the editorial comment, which some people thought was bold to the point of recklessness, had been judged in the light of what the editor knew both leaders and people of the Kirk to be thinking and saying, though sometimes not too loudly. Behind it lay fear that the event—quite uncharacteristic, incidentally, of the really significant thinking among Scottish Roman Catholics—might be given a national and ecumenical importance which it did not and could not possess. This was also one of the occasions on which the process of consultation with an informal committee worked very well. On other occasions, it is right to record, consultation with the advisers has meant that attractive ideas for outspoken comment have been quietly and sensibly set aside. Really significant comment and leadership of opinion is possible in *Life and Work*, but only if it finds and expresses a substantial consensus of opinion within the church.

No editor, of course, ought to hope to please all the Kirk all the time. Even some relatively mild comments on, for example, the World Council of Churches have from time to time displeased some of those in the Kirk most closely associated with it. And one of the sad things about trying to put life into the Kirk's magazine is that from time to time it is almost inevitable that one displeases people who, thanks to their personal qualities, one would much prefer to please. But to their credit it should be said that reactions against anything in the magazine have generally been evident in the magazine itself, and also that some of those who have said the harshest things about this or that editorial attitude have been the most vigorous contributors later of their own enthusiasm in print. There have been exceptions, brief threats of economic sanctions and occasional attempts to get committees to turn the screw this way or that, usually vigorously to the left. But when such criticism is developed with any real force or logic it is liable to make clear that the real target is not an editorial policy but the attitudes and assumptions of the people of the church whose beliefs and mood *Life and Work* tries to express or reflect as one of its primary functions.

What has probably mattered most, however, in the last few years has been the way these attitudes have found expression in print, even though the result has sometimes been to show the many minds and faces of the Kirk. But at a time when there are so many theological, sociological, intellectual and even political currents flowing through the Kirk, and when some of the different emphases within it are probably more important than some denominational frontiers, it would be difficult to carry conviction without accepting some of the consequences of this diversity. An editorial policy has to reflect the spirit and mood of the times as well as the unique, and in so many things the unchanging, claims of the Head of the Church. This is surely a time when there is a need for an emphasis on the fact that *Life and Work* belongs to the whole church and its people, not merely to the leading figures and powerful committees. Indeed the freedom of expression within the magazine and the widespread access to it for the people of the church probably give more force to the material which emphasises the 'official' line on, say, the financial crisis which inflation has inflicted on us.

How will the magazine develop? It would be easier to prophesy if we knew how the Kirk would develop. At the time of writing, for example, the outlook for such a modest ecumenical proposal as union with the Scottish Methodists (editorially supported in *Life and Work*) is not encouraging. The Methodists, despite the Kirk's unexpectedly warm response, appear to have closed the door. The pattern of future revival in an ageing Kirk is as hard to predict, for the younger revivalists belong to very different schools and styles. The future emphasis in the ministry and the role of elders may change. There are powerful radical currents in the Kirk but there is also a revival of conservative theology and even conservative attitudes, in some cases expressed as what a great theologian of our time, Tom Torrance, calls 'hyper-Calvinism'.

And in journalism all things change. A stagnant publication is a dying publication. It can be wise not to emphasise change too much—in 1968-69 *Life and Work* probably made that mistake—but it must go on. Titles are not sacred, though the Kirk would be foolish to change a century-old name on any passing whim. Formats change. Sooner or later, and probably from time to time, *Life and Work* will have to look at the advantages and problems of tabloid format. No doubt the old vision of a weekly newspaper will appeal to new enthusiasts. If enough potential readers would be present at the distribution point, the church door, every week it would be feasible. But is it wanted? Is it viable? *Life and Work* has over the years had the advantage of financial independence and the prestige of contributing from its profits, along with the other successful publishing activities, to the funds of the church. Some of the bolder ventures might need to draw on those funds; and to draw on those funds means that those with a share in allotting them will have their own ideas on what gives value for the money. Weekly publication would also surely demand too much of the thousands of volunteer distributors in the congregations on whom the magazine depends just as much as on staff and contributors.

It is also realistic to recognise that many of those for whom Christ died hardly read a newspaper never mind a religious magazine. Why should they when television and radio provide them with all they need in news and entertainment? Moreover, the material which Charteris and McMurtrie put into the Victorian *Life and Work* for working men and their womenfolk now seems complicated in style and syntax even for those in our time with above-average education and literacy. Many a graduate would need unwonted concentration to follow the 'talks with farm servants'. In a small and relatively unimportant way *Life and Work* encounters the problem of a reformed church which, if true to its living faith and past traditions, must call its people to the private reading of the scriptures, including the Epistles and the Prophets.

There has also been an important devolution in religious communication. One of the early roles of *Life and Work* was to encourage the printing of supplements, the ancestors to today's thriving tribe of parish and congregational magazines. And while printing costs might seen to price some types of local magazines out of the market, the duplicating revolution has made it possible for any congregation to run a readable and lively magazine. For example, one of the winners in the 1977 *Life and Work* parish magazine competition, singled out by the most professional of the judges for its liveliness, was from Muckairn, Taynuilt, in Argyll. It would not longer be worthwhile, even if practicable, to offer the printing service for congregational magazines which for much of the century was a major force in building up and maintaining the circulation of *Life and Work*, though there may well be a role for a link between the national and regional presbytery communication. Early in 1978 an experiment in this field was started with Inverness and Moray.

There is also an uncertainty about the future place of religion and the church in daily newspapers and broadcasting. BBC religious broadcasting seems to have retreated a bit from its alliance with the church and total commitment to supporting it; but the development of local radio has opened up an important new medium in which church news gets some of the help it has traditionally got from local newpapers. And as *Life and Work* must be the first to recognise, the daily newspapers, especially the Scottish ones, are probably the main medium through which national church news reaches church people. A church magazine, however vigorous, would not get such a regular total of column inches, even make occasional front-page leads and top leaders in important papers, if they did not still give a fair and at times a generous showing to religion, and not only to religious controversies.

But will this last? There are signs of uncertainty, quite apart from the natural and inevitable tendency to pick out the controversial story and the conflicts of ideas and personalities. There is enough uncertainty to make it important for the church to develop its own medium of periodical communication through the printed word. It has to match the development, so well handled in recent years in the Kirk, of other press and publicity services. It is realistic, however, to expect that the daily press will continue to provide a primary news service in print covering religious and church as well as other news. We should rejoice and be glad in that, as in the fact that there is a good representation of elders and other church members among Scotland's good journalists.

We who trust in God try to do his work and expect to be shown the way ahead as Charteris was shown the way. That great Victorian, and notable saint—one of a great army in Scotland before and since the Reformation—identified a need and met it so well that his successors had to adapt and adjust rather than start anew or even reconstruct. We cannot be sure whether we face an age of adaptation or of reconstruction, but God will surely make things clear. *Life and Work* remains a major part of a major (and successful) business in which bookshops meet a real need and lively demand, and in which The Saint Andrew Press shares in a remarkable period for Christian publishing. Indeed, in assessing the future role and pattern of *Life and Work*, one of the factors to be taken into account is the present and probable role of the paperback book, which finds an outlet not only in the bookshop but through the congregation.

Some of that publishing is for the whole English-speaking world. Barclay's success gave the Kirk's publishing a chance to meet Christian needs across the world, a missionary achievement which woud have been specially dear not only to Charteris but to his most missionary-minded successors, McMurtrie, Livingstone, and Carstairs. *Life and Work*, however, must primarily remain, in Charteris's words, 'a distinctively Scottish magazine'. But to be truly Scottish it must be alive to the needs and trends of the rest of the world. If it is vigorously presbyterian it must not be through remaining locked in a tradition. It must be because we see God's purpose and design in reformed doctrine and government which can order and comprehend both a constructive conservatism and a true liberalism. God's Word and Christ's love have time and time again broken through the barriers within which men have tried to confine them; sometimes through barriers erected in presbytery as well as through prelacy and papacy, or godless ideology. Let us hope that they also break through even any barriers which editors and their contributors might unwittingly erect.

Readers too can erect such barriers—occasionally by demanding too much, more often by expecting too little.

A few years ago the editor, due to speak at a luncheon, sat beside a minister who was to take the chair. As the coffee was brought in he asked the editor for some biographical information to introduce him. When he got it safely written down he looked up and asked, 'And why did you move from all that to a little thing like *Life and Work*?

May that minister read this book. May that minister find his answer in it, even if he has not found his answer in the magazine.

Appendix 1

The Editors of Life and Work 1879-1979

Archibald Hamilton Charteris (1835-1908): Editor 1879
Edinburgh graduate, also studied at Tübingen and Bonn. Minister, notably of the Park Church, Glasgow. Professor of Biblical Criticism at Edinburgh. DD. Moderator of the General Assembly 1892. Founder of the Woman's Guild and much else besides.

John McMurtrie (1831-1912): Editor 1880-98
Edinburgh graduate. Minister (notably at St Bernard's, Edinburgh). Convener of Foreign Missions. DD. Moderator of the General Assembly 1904.

Archibald Fleming (1863-1941): Editor 1898-1902
Edinburgh graduate, also studied in Germany. Minister. From Tron Kirk, Edinburgh, and *Life and Work* he went to St Columba's, Pont Street, London. DD. Pioneer religious broadcaster.

Robert Howie Fisher (1861-1934): Editor 1902-1925
Edinburgh graduate. Minister (notably at Morningside and St Cuthbert's, Edinburgh). In 'inner circle' of (presbyterian) Union Committee. DD.

Harry Smith (1865-1942): Editor 1924-30
Aberdeen graduate. Minister at Tibbermore, Old Kilpatrick, and Heriot. Convener of Publications Committee. For nineteen years editor of *Morning Rays*. DD.

William Pringle Livingstone (1865-1950): Editor 1929-34
Journalist. Editor Jamaica's *Daily Gleaner*. Became editor of United Free *Record* 1912. Author of many books. Set up Church Press Bureau. Reader of Church of Scotland.

George Carstairs (1880-1948): Editor 1935-45
> Glasgow graduate. Minister (originally of United Free Church). Missionary. Indian Army war service 1918. DD.

John Wright Stevenson (1903-73): Editor 1945-65
> Glasgow graduate who also studied at Edinburgh and St Andrews. Minister (notably at Culter). Edited *Scots Observer*. Church Press Secretary. Founder of Leighton House, Dunblane. DD.

Leonard John Armstrong Bell (1912-72): Editor 1965-72
> Glasgow graduate. Minister (at Maxwelltown and Brechin). Served in Mediterranean with Church Huts and Canteens. Died in service 1972.

Robert Deans Kernohan (b 1931): Editor 1972-
> Journalist. Glasgow graduate, also at Balliol College, Oxford. Served RAF. London editor *The Glasgow Herald*, and political executive. Elder.

Appendix 2

Editors of the Gaelic Supplement to *Life and Work*

The editor of the Gaelic Supplement since 1951, the Very Rev Dr T M Murchison (Moderator of the General Assembly in 1969), reports that as far as he has been able to ascertain he has had only three predecessors, or four counting Dr Malcolm Maclennan of St Columba's, Edinburgh, who had been the United Free Gaelic editor from 1908 and served as co-editor for a year or more after the union of 1929. He died in 1931.

The first Gaelic editor, the Rev Archibald Clerk of Kilmallie served from his appointment in 1879 till his death in 1887. The Rev John MacRury of Snizort in Skye was editor from then till 1907, when he died. The Rev Dr Donald Lamont, who may have done the work from 1905, was officially editor from 1907 till 1951, including the year as co-editor with Maclennan after the amalgamation in 1929 with the UF Gaelic Supplement.

Dr Murchison's own services were marked by a presentation in 1976 when he opened the church's bookshop extension in Glasgow and by editorial comment in the magazine which noted his contribution to Scottish Christian life and culture. It also added the thanks of readers of 'the English supplement'.

Fuller information from Dr Murchison, received while this book was in proof, appeared in the February 1979 *Life and Work* and is to be further amplified for the Gaelic Supplement's centenary in 1980.

Appendix 3

Notes on Books and other sources

Obviously the main source for this book has been *Life and Work* itself. Bound volumes for the whole century exist in the church offices, together with the bound volumes of the United Free *Record*. This succeeded the separate mission *Records* of the Free and United Presbyterian Churches, which united in 1900, though the Free Church's *Monthly Record* (still vigorously published) probably claims the apostolic succession.

Some early local supplements are in the editorial office, but the New College Library, Edinburgh, has the best collection.

The Mission Record of the Church of Scotland was also bound in annual volumes until absorbed in 1901 by *Life and Work*. The *Life and Work* volumes, however, were meant to be treated as books and not mere files, and were sold as such. This tradition continued strongly until the union of 1929. Thereafter changing tastes probably had weakened what the war almost wiped out. The scarcest *Life and Work* volumes, to the surprise of our helpful benefactors, are probably those since 1960, by which time they were being produced only for private record.

Other useful bound periodicals include *The Scottish Church*, a higher-brow defence against disestablishment launched in 1885, *Young Scotland*, and *Other Lands*, the UF missionary magazine which continued as a Church of Scotland publication and lasted (with changes of style and even title) till the 1960's. *Manse Mail*, founded by Jack Stevenson, continued under his successors till 1975, when the church decided it was uneconomic to run such a magazine for ministers, who had received it free.

At the time of writing no complete file of the Gaelic Supplement from 1880 has been traced but the centenary may provide this. Nor has the author seen a complete sequence of the Forces Supplement, which also almost covers the century except when its role was taken over by the distinctive *Scottish*

Forces Magazine edited for thirty-five years by Ronald Selby Wright, affectionately remembered as 'the Radio Padre'.

Christian Life and Work Committee and (later) Publications Committee reports will be found in the bound volumes of General Assembly reports. The report of the committee of inquiry into the events leading to the attempted dismissal of the editor, Leonard Bell, is in the 1972 *Blue Book*.

Minutes of the Church of Scotland and UF Publications Committees for some years before the Union, and for the post-1929 committee (whose name varied slightly) are in the church offices.

However, much of the information for the latter part of the book is inevitably based on private communications, formal and informal. The author has tried to thank those who survive to read the book, (and no doubt in places to disagree with it). Three important sources who died before they could be thanked were Jack Stevenson, Angus Nicolson, and Ronald Falconer.

Two historians who were generous with their help and advice on the early period of the book are Professor A C Cheyne and Dr James Bulloch, who very kindly allowed the author to read the later of the Drummond-Bulloch books mentioned below while it was still in proof.

Books

It is impossible to cite all the books which proved useful (and occasionally irritating because of omissions) because the scope of this book covers not merely the church but the history of the world in the last century. Special mention is probably due to Andrew Drummond and James Bulloch's *The Church in Victorian Scotland* and their subsequent *The Church in Late Victorian Scotland* (The Saint Andrew Press, 1976 and 1978 respectively).

J M Reid's *Kirk and Nation* (Skeffington) is a brilliant and under-rated summary strong on the Victorians and especially the Free and UP Churches. W H Marwick's *Economic Developments in Victorian Scotland* (Allen and Unwin) has supplied some of the background economic information. Professor Gordon Donaldson's *Scotland: Church and Nation through Sixteen Centuries* (SCM Press) is a fine book which has some useful insights for this period.

Among biography the outstanding source for this book's purpose was Arthur Gordon's *Life of Archibald Hamilton Charteris* (Hodder and Stoughton). Biographies of Gladstone, Rosebery, and Campbell-Bannerman are remarkable for what they don't say about disestablishment.

The Free Church's 1893 *Annals of the Disruption* is probably the best introduction, despite its forbidding appearance, to the other side of the national church's tradition from that expressed by Charteris, provided allowance is also made for the energy and enthusiasm of the UP element in the later UF Kirk.

Index